Super Simple Storytelling

SUPER SIMPLE STORYTELLING
A Can-Do Guide for Every Classroom, Every Day

Kendall Haven

2000
TEACHER IDEAS PRESS
A Division of
Libraries Unlimited, Inc.
Englewood, Colorado

This book is dedicated with special thanks to Jay O'Callahan and Waker vonBerg who were instrumental in shaping and developing my storytelling, and to Roni Berg, who lit the fires of possibility and of dreaming and who supported me in this wild fling into the unknown.

TEACHER IDEAS PRESS
A Division of
Libraries Unlimited, Inc.
P.O. Box 6633
Englewood, CO 80155-6633
1-800-237-6124
www.lu.com/tip

Library of Congress Cataloging-in-Publication Data

Haven, Kendall F.
    Super simple storytelling : a can-do guide for every classroom, every day / Kendall Haven.
        p. cm.
    Includes bibliographical references and index.
    ISBN 1-56308-681-6 (pbk.)
    1. Storytelling. I. Title.

LB1042 .H39 2000
808.5'43--dc21   99-088935

CONTENTS

LIST OF FIGURES

INTRODUCTION

I am often asked, "What do you do?" I reply, "I tell stories." They say, "No, I mean what do you do for *work*?" I smile. I've been through this conversation before. "I tell stories." Their faces fill with confusion, with consternation. "I mean for money, for *real*."

I then answer, "I *write* stories."

They nod in understanding. "Ah, a writer. Why didn't you say so in the first place?"

Why is it that, as a society, we refuse to acknowledge the legitimate worth and power of *telling* a story? (Even though most of us do it daily, and many of us depend on it for the successful completion of our jobs.) Maybe it's because there were no working (self-employed, independent contractor, tax-filing) storytellers in this country until the mid-1970s, and because still only a few hundred of us do it full-time. The reason may be that most adults never heard storytellers as children and teenagers and don't recognize the process of story-telling when they hear them now.

Or maybe the reason is that although there are beginning to be university degree programs in storytelling, there still are no "Departments of Storytelling," no Professors Emeritus of storytelling, no storytelling galleries and museums, and no newspaper columns written by famed and caustic storytelling critics. Perhaps the problem is that the word *story-telling* doesn't appear in six out of seven dictionaries I've checked. Maybe it's that storytelling isn't listed in the yellow pages. If you aren't in the dictionary or the yellow pages, how legitimate can you be?

Possibly the problem is that storytelling awakens our greatest fears. In every survey I have seen on the subject, death has never ranked higher than fourth on the list of what terrifies Americans. In *every one* of these surveys our number one fear is speaking in public.

In a 1992 survey of media attitudes taken by General Mills, the images most closely associated with storytelling were cardigan sweaters and rocking chairs. Mr. Rogers and grandparents rocking on the front porch: that's what our cultural collective psyche thinks of storytelling. While those are both valid storytelling images, they represent storytelling in the same way that 3 and 247 represent the entire number line. There exists an endless variety and richness of color in the world of storytelling that can never be expressed or even hinted at by two lonely numbers.

Even though we eagerly exchange stories and crave the experience of listening to a well-told story, it seems that the experience of storytelling has not been woven into our conscious cultural understanding. We do it. We enjoy it. But we don't consciously acknowledge it or understand what it is.

"Are you the storyteller?" Students ask this question all the time when I visit schools. Partly they just want to know if I am the one who will perform at the school assembly. But partly they mean by the question that a storyteller is somehow unique, that they think that they aren't one, and that I must be special if I am.

When I reverse the question and ask, "Do *you* tell stories?" two out of three students answer "No." By middle school, the number of "no's" is up to three out of four. If I ask, "Are you a *storyteller*?" the answer is "no" at least nine times out of ten regardless of grade level.

A more meaningful question to ask might be, "Is it possible for a human being who has to interact with other human beings *not* to tell stories?" Language research would suggest that the answer is "no." The general form and structure of story are so interwoven into our human psyche and into the way we understand, learn, and process language that it is not possible to converse for long without using stories.

Try it. Watch any friendly conversation that lasts for three minutes or more. I'll bet one or both people in that conversation drift into what everyone present will agree was a story. When I tell that to students (or to teachers) the typical answer is, "Okay, I tell stories. But they aren't *really* stories, and I don't tell them like a *real* storyteller."

Without discussion, without critical debate, without even conscious thought, virtually every person I talk to has created a two-tier hierarchy in his or her mind. There are the stories we tell to each other every day, and then there are real stories. There are those of us who muddle through our tellings, and then there are *real* storytellers.

Yet no one has ever been able to articulate for me the exact difference between these two levels of story and of storytelling. No one can define the boundary where one is left behind and the other begins, or even what criteria would define that distinction.

We all know that the difference is there. We recognize it when we hear it and see it. We just don't know what makes the levels different.

I contend that this difference to which everyone alludes does exist. However, I do not believe it is a difference of ability—it is neither the oral ability of storytellers nor their ability to structure material into story form. It is not a difference of talent. It is only a difference in understanding.

If you really understood what makes a story so powerful, you would automatically organize your tellings along those structural lines and others would say that you were wonderful at creating stories. If you really understood what an audience needs from a storyteller, you would naturally slant your storytellings in those directions and be called a *storyteller* by others. This is not a question of ability. It is a question of understanding.

This book is the culmination of a decade of personal research, observation, experimentation, and working with over a hundred teachers to find out what really works in the classroom environment. I have written it to share a more practical, efficient, do-able, and I think better, approach to organizing, learning, and telling stories. I am assuming that storytelling is not your primary goal, but rather that you want to use storytelling as part of some other effort: teaching, ministry, business, therapy, the law, coaching, etc. Hundreds of in-class trials of my system prove that it will meet your needs.

Telling stories is like singing, like sports, like dancing, like music. Some people are naturally more talented than others. The activity comes more easily, more gracefully to some. Still, every human is capable of competently performing each of these activities, *if* he or she is shown the skills, techniques, and tricks that form the foundation for the activity.

Telling stories and effectively using storytelling are no different. Every adult can adequately communicate his or her unique stories. Each one of us is capable of weaving together the tapestry of an engrossing tale. So is every child. We all just need someone to teach us storytelling's fundamental skills.

There will always be someone who is better at telling stories than you are, maybe many someones. So what? The one and only relevant point is that you are fully capable of engaging, engrossing, and fascinating your audience and successfully driving vivid, delicious images of your story into their minds and hearts. That success is what storytelling is all about, and it is easily within every person's grasp.

I graduated from the Military Academy at West Point, pursued an advanced degree in science (oceanography) after leaving the Army, and spent a decade conducting scientific research for the U.S. Department of Energy at one of its National Research Laboratories. At age 36 I jumped ship and became a full-time storyteller and story-writer.

That shift was mandated by a realization of how powerful stories are. I'd take my nephew to the park, planning to wear him out on the climbing structures and train. Eventually, exhausted myself, I'd give up and flop into the sprawling sandpit to make up stories for him. It turned out that's what he really wanted all along.

Those made-up stories in the park drew crowds. Kids still use their natural sensors, capable of detecting the vibrational patterns of a story, able to home in on the thick electrical fields of storytelling, always sifting the air for the vibrational power and rhythm of a story. I'd begin a story and kids would materialize from all over the park. Some would boldly plop down right in front and ask me to start over. They had missed the beginning. Others would cautiously pretend to play with a nearby leaf to have an excuse for lingering within easy ear shot.

Then the adults who brought those kids to the park would scurry over to see what was going on in the sandbox. Others would wander by to see what the crowd was all about. And time after time they stayed to listen. No one ever scoffed, "Oh, just a story," and left. Everybody stayed and listened.

I began to see how powerfully attractive stories and storytelling are, how hungry for stories most humans are. I also began to realize that most humans haven't had enough stories told to them and are suffering from story deficit, *needing* to soak up the majesty, wisdom, and joy of told stories.

Then I found out I could actually get paid to tell stories and joined the burgeoning ranks of professional storytellers. But I kept my scientific orientation and passion to tear things apart and see what makes them work. I focused this analytical drive on stories and storytelling. Why does one story move and enthrall an audience while another leaves them restless and bored? Why does one telling of a story enchant an audience while another telling of the same story seems lifeless and uninteresting? What aspects and elements of a story are an audience most hungry for? Why do the images and information in a story enter so deeply into the listener's psyche? Why are they recalled so readily?

These questions cannot be answered by writers sitting alone in their offices. They are answered by a performer who delivers the material to a live audience and receives line-by-line, unmistakable, instantaneous feedback. They are answered by someone who watches live storytellings and tellers.

I have presented over 5,000 storytelling performances and have closely watched another thousand by other storytellers. I also write all my own stories. So I have been able to control, adjust, and manipulate my stories as a direct function of the audience reactions I have observed. My understanding of the structure and form of a story and of the process of storytelling have come from these long-term observations and from an analysis of what the story and performer did to create those reactions.

I now work with teachers and students all across the country and have conducted literally thousands of workshops with students and hundreds more with teachers. Each of these workshops addressed the same general questions: What is a story, what is storytelling, and what elements are at their cores? Time and time again I have seen the lightbulbs click on as students and teachers begin to understand that there are specific, dependable building blocks to story organization and storytelling that they can master. Once they understand what really constitutes a story and what a listener needs from their story, they realize they are capable of storytelling. They can do this! The pathway toward that proficiency is what *Super Simple Storytelling* is all about.

I have written this book as a guide for two groups: first for teachers, ministers, business people, therapists, and others who would tell stories as part of their work if it were easier for them to do, and, second, for classroom teachers, school librarians, reading specialists, and parents who share the task of teaching effective use and application of language to students. The exercises and approaches in this book have all been tested in school classrooms across the nation and have proven themselves to be valuable in helping students learn more effective oral communication. I often say "you" meaning the teachers. But the exercises, techniques, and concepts presented here are equally valid for all professions.

One grammatical note: In this text I routinely refer to individual student storytellers in the third person. In correct usage, pronouns for the third person singular are he, she, him, her, his, hers, himself, herself. When the gender of a person is unspecified, to avoid sexism the forms usually used are "he or she," "him or her," "he/she," or "him/her."

I find this awkward, repugnant, and disruptive. "Each student tells his or her own story," reads worse to me than "Each student tells their own story." "After the student teller completes this process, he or she . . . " is more disruptive to my ear than is "After the student teller completes this process, they . . . " You have already encountered examples of the pronoun gender problem in this introduction. Didn't they disrupt your concentration and momentarily pull you out of the flow of the material? Because this book deals primarily with the oral use of language, I have used the pronoun forms that are more commonly used in speech—they, them, and their—to refer to the unspecified singular student as well as to the plural. While this is technically incorrect, I have seen it successfully used in a number of other books, and I think the text reads more smoothly and clearly this way. To avoid using a pronoun altogether, I have sometimes used the passive voice. I admit that this pulls energy from the text. But it does sneak around many of these awkward pronoun problems. The only problem I couldn't circumnavigate was reflexive pronouns. Following the logic above, himself or herself should become . . . themself? "Themself" certainly isn't right, but "themselves" definitely—and incorrectly—implies plural, so I have used "himself" and "herself."

Specific sources of information referred to throughout the book are listed in detail in the "References" section at the end of the book. Descriptions of various educators' use of storytelling in the classroom and surveys they did are based on my personal knowledge.

I owe a great debt of thanks to the 100-plus teachers who have let me use their classes as guinea pigs to test these exercises and to the 300-plus teachers who have tried these concepts on their own and provided feedback on how well they worked. This material works in large part because of their effort. I also owe a great debt to two talented women: Roni Berg, the light of my life, and Donna Clark, a good friend and talented writer, who both reviewed and critiqued this manuscript and vastly improved it in the process.

Enjoy this book. Explore and grapple with its exercises and concepts. Make it work for you; make it make sense for your storytelling. After all, your success is the only one that really counts.

*W*ho Is *Super Simple Storytelling* For?

KEY TOPICS IN THIS SECTION

> ❭ The difference between "professional storytellers" and "professionals who use storytelling"
> ❭ How to decide if *Super Simple Storytelling* is for you

There are dozens of books on storytelling. I have ten on my own bookshelves. So why write another? What hasn't already been said? Wrong question. The question isn't *what* hasn't been said, but *whose* needs haven't been addressed? I wanted to write a book for professionals who recognize the value of storytelling in their work but who aren't at all sure they have the natural talent to tell a story and make it work. That is, this is not a book for professional storytellers (who already know they are good tellers and want to get better) but for professionals who might want to use storytelling *if* it were easy enough for them to master.

It's fine if many of you have to drag yourselves, kicking and screaming, to storytelling because you recognize its value but view the act as an embarrassing, horrific burden. It's fine if you only anticipate telling a few stories a year and will only do that if the process of learning and prepping a story isn't too much of an anxiety-producing pain.

For professional storytellers, storytelling *is* the end product, the sole point of their preparation, the culminating activity. For professionals, it's well worth it to pour time and energy into every nuance of every aspect of every story. That's their job. For most people, storytelling is one tool, one means (albeit a most powerful and effective means) to accomplish their real work. For these tellers storytelling has to stand in line along with a dozen other demands on time and energy. These tellers need a system of storytelling that's easy, time-saving, and fun. They need *Super Simple Storytelling*.

Who are professional tellers? Certainly those who tell for pay. But more generally, professional storytellers tell for the sake of the telling. They will tell each story they learn many times and so can justify spending great amounts of time and energy on the learning. Professionals often take months to develop a story, telling it repeatedly to test or practice audiences before they tell it at a real performance. Because the point of their activity is the telling, itself, they must be concerned with every nuance of performance and character development. They must be prepared to face a variety of settings and types of audiences and so must explore the range and variations of each story. Storytelling is their activity, so there is nothing else for them to prepare.

Does that sound like you? Is that what you want to do with your storytelling? Probably not.

The great majority of people want to *use* storytelling as a powerful tool to assist them in some other mission, be it education, therapy, ministry, healing, motivation, business, administration, management, or anything else. For these people, storytelling is not the end product, but merely a means to a greater end. Storytelling is only one part of their focus, their preparation, their planning, their activity. These are storytellers who will use and tell stories as part of their work but for whom storytelling will never *be* their work.

These are the storytellers for whom *Super Simple Storytelling* was written. Super Simple tellers have tightly limited amounts of time to devote to story preparation. They rarely tell a single story repeatedly and often tell it once a year or even once only. Super Simple tellers need to reap the powerful benefits of storytelling while minimizing the costs of time, anxiety, trauma, and emotional turmoil that can be associated with the process of storytelling.

Teachers often assume that the theatrical, dramatic, highly polished style used by professional touring storytellers is the only correct way to effectively communicate a story to their class. Nothing could be farther from the truth. In a classroom setting, the natural, familiar oral style of a teacher will be more effective and will sound more real than some artificially adopted theatrical storytelling facade.

Teachers have precious little time to devote to story prep and must get the greatest bang for their temporal buck. Professional tellers must go for the "biggest bang" regardless of the required time investment.

Teachers know their audience (their class), and that audience knows them and their natural talking style and will expect stories to be delivered in that established, natural style. Teachers have established a rapport and routine with their class.

None of these facts is true for a touring storyteller, who must create the illusion of intimate rapport while performing before total strangers.

Super Simple storytellers need a different approach than professionals, one that requires less rehearsal, gets quickly to the real meat and power of a story, and lets them successfully incorporate more storytelling into their ongoing job without having to devote all their free time to storytelling rehearsal.

Storytelling is emerging as a prime teaching tool and curriculum enhancement strategy. It is a powerful addition to a teacher's arsenal, one which can be successfully mastered by any classroom teacher. However, surveys show that few teachers feel either adequately skilled or trained to effectively use storytelling. Most believe effective storytelling is a "gift" possessed by a relative few, rather than a basic oral communications skill well within the grasp of every teacher. These storytellers need *Super Simple Storytelling* to guide them past that misconception and into the full use of their natural storytelling potential.

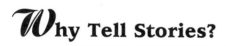hy Tell Stories?

KEY TOPICS IN THIS SECTION

> The value of storytelling to language arts teaching

> The value of storytelling in all subject areas as a cross-curriculum teaching tool

> The value of storytelling for student motivation and self-esteem

> The cost-effectiveness of storytelling

David Dawson, a high school biology teacher, decided to test storytelling's effectiveness on his general "Introduction to Biology" class. He reorganized his material on four scientists (including Darwin and the Austrian monk, Gregor Mendel) into story form. He even borrowed appropriate costuming from the Drama Department. He also restructed quizzes, chapter tests, and mid-term and final exams to isolate questions relating to material he delivered in story form.

After two years of testing (four one-semester courses) he found that his students retained and recalled information far better when he delivered it in story form. On "story days" he was able to impart less curriculum information than on regular lecture days because part of the period was consumed with *story* information rather than with biology information. Still, in both a relative and an absolute sense, his students absorbed and retained more on story days and scored better on subsequent tests. More impressive (to him), they were significantly better able to apply information and concepts in new applications and situations when they were presented through a story.

A graduate student in the upper Midwest recently conducted a test on four fourth-grade classrooms. He presented the same story to each class. In one class he handed a copy of the story to the students and had them read it. He read the story to a second class, showed a video of the story to a third, and *told* the story to the fourth.

A month later he interviewed students from each classroom to see how the images they held of the story varied as a function of the mode of delivery. Students from the classes who had read the story and had seen the video needed prompting to remember the story at all. Consistently, the students with the most detailed, vivid, and expansive images of the story, and the students that were most excited by the story and their memory of it, were those in the class that was told the story. The message is clear. Telling a story creates more vivid, powerful, and memorable images in a listener's mind than does any other means of delivery of the same material.

Still, the question, "Why bother to tell stories?" needs to be addressed. Why is it worth your while to destroy the rejuvenating tranquillity of much of your free time struggling to master stories when the prospect of storytelling ties you up in stomach-churning knots? Why fight to be able to include storytelling in your classroom curriculum?

The answer is simple: Because storytelling works. Because storytelling is one of the most powerful and effective tools in your arsenal of teaching and motivational techniques. Because storytelling requires no capital cost and has no equipment or supply cost. Yet it delivers more educational power than most hi-tech, hi-cost learning systems.

Most of the available research has focused on the more general topic of "story," or on storytelling's cousin, story reading, rather than directly on the benefits of storytelling. However, a slim (but growing) body of rigorous research and a vast body of anecdotal study and classroom observation both support the conclusions that can be extrapolated from the available body of whole language, reading, and general language arts research. This research consistently identifies 10 benefits of storytelling as an educational tool:

1. Storytelling is a powerful and effective element in an effort to improve and develop all four primary language arts skills (reading, writing, listening, and speaking).

2. Information (both concepts and facts) is remembered better and longer when presented in story form.

3. Storytelling is a powerful and effective interdisciplinary, cross-curriculum teaching tool.

4. Storytelling positively motivates students to learn. Told stories focus student attention and learning and excite students to pursue related studies.

5. Storytelling effectively builds student self-confidence and self-esteem.

6. Storytelling effectively engages and develops the skills of imagination and creativity better than any other single classroom activity.

7. Storytelling engages and entertains.

8. Storytelling creates empathy and a sense of connectedness.

9. Storytelling improves analytical and problem-solving skills.

10. Storytelling creates valuable links to community and heritage.

Several of these conclusions, such as number 6 (that storytelling develops creativity and imagination) and number 7 (that storytelling entertains), represent the commonplace expectations of all teachers. Others require some explanation.

1. **Storytelling and language arts.** Studies confirm that storytelling is the single most effective activity to engage and develop oral language skill (speaking and reading). Surveys by *Harpers, The New York Times,* and others have shown that 93–94 percent of working Americans claim that successful execution of their job depends more on their ability to communicate orally than on their ability to communicate in writing. A 1992 study conducted at Harvard concluded that the best common denominator of successful people is a large vocabulary. Storytelling not only provides the best modeling of effective oral communication and not only stands as the best single activity to develop oral language skills, but it also actively exercises and develops *all* of the major language arts skills.

Studies have consistently shown a strong positive correlation between storytelling and the development of the four basic language arts skills (reading, writing, listening, and speaking). This correlation between storytelling and language arts improvement seems to hold true even when a teacher simply tells stories to students for entertainment. Various language studies conducted in New Zealand, the United States, and Europe have shown that language-related skills are linked so that development of one language skill crosses over to affect the other three. A diet of story listening, as well as one of storytelling, improves oral *and* written language skills.

Further, storytelling is unique among language-related activity in that it directly engages all four language skills. The process of telling a story virtually requires the teller to read, write, listen, and speak. No other single language arts activity so effectively addresses all four skills.

In national surveys in taken in 1989 and 1991, almost half of the adult respondents said that they never read books. The last year in this country in which library checkouts exceeded checkouts from video stories was 1988. I have heard that the ratio is now over 20 to 1 in favor of video store checkouts. Worse, library checkouts include videos checked out from libraries. In an increasingly visually based world, storytelling is an effective bridge from visual media back to the library-based world of narrative literature. The visual way in which told stories are received and interpreted by a listener makes this especially true for students who struggle to master written language.

2. **Story information is remembered better.** To me the true measure of the value of storytelling is that studies show stories (and the information they contain) are remembered longer than are other narrative forms. The two informal studies by David Dawson and the graduate student from the upper Midwest, mentioned previously (see pp. xvi–xvii), point to this powerful conclusion. The sparse smatterings of available academic research and the extensive class-room experience of thousands of teachers verify that storytelling is an efficient teaching tool. Factual and conceptual information is retained longer, recalled more readily, and applied in new situations more successfully when the information is received as part of a story.

    As a fledgling storyteller, I was invited to return to a school—this an Orange County, California, school—about a year after I first performed there. As I entered the building, a second-grade girl passed me in the hall and said, "I remember you. You told us stories last year."

    Then that seven-year-old girl proceeded to tell me both of the stories I had told to her a year before. She had only heard them once. (I had written both stories.) At that time her only instructions had been to march single file into the multi-purpose room, sit cross-legged on the floor, and be quiet. Still, a year later, the complete stories bubbled vividly and accurately into her mind with no prompting. Told stories get remembered.

    Recently the eighth graders at a Catholic school in Las Vegas, Nevada, strolled into the room I was using for writing workshops. Several recognized me as someone who had performed there before. Within a minute the group was eagerly recalling and retelling a story I had told them three and one-half years before on my previous visit. They recalled the story accurately, in detail, with no prompting, 42 months after the one and only time they had heard it.

    Stories and story-related information lodge deeply in each listener's brain during an effective storytelling, so curriculum information woven into the stories is more quickly recalled than if the information were presented in some other way. I annually receive dozens of letters from teachers who first try telling stories and are amazed at the results they achieve.

    Recent neurological research has shown that memory depends on specific sensory details. The greater the number of specific sensory details filed away into memory surrounding an event or idea, the easier and more likely it is that a person will recall that event or idea.

    The process of storytelling creates vivid, multi-sensory details. Details create memory.

    Many linguistic researchers focusing on early language development believe, in effect, that the form and concept of story is hardwired into human brains, that story forms the very foundation of how we understand and conceptualize language. Maybe, then, we respond so positively and powerfully to stories because we are genetically predisposed to favor the form.

3. **Storytelling is a powerful cross-curriculum teaching tool.** Stories also create context and relevance. Information delivered as part of a story does not hang as an unassociated frag-ment in the brain. Rather it is grounded into an entire web of details and relationships that provide context for that bit of information. My tenth-grade nephew wrote in a letter to me on why he thought storytelling was important:

    > Last year we studied revolutions, including the Bolshevik Revolution. Instead of having us memorize dates, battles, and the names of generals (unassociated fragments), our teacher asked us questions like: Who were these people? What

were their motives? What were their feelings and opinions about what was going on? (story questions) In answering these questions, he helped us build stories about the Russian people (context). Through caring about these people, the entire revolution and its complex forces became fascinating and I still remember it very well.

Because storytelling is such an efficient means of transferring information, and because the act of storytelling, itself, is an effective part of language arts development, storytelling has emerged as an important vehicle for cross-curriculum teaching. Studies show that storytelling engages higher learning and thinking skills and that effective storytelling engages students through any and all of the seven intelligences.

I realize I am making storytelling sound like the wonder cure-all potions barked from horsedrawn wagons by late nineteenth-century medicine men across the burgeoning towns of the dusty West. In fact, storytelling *is* akin to a wonder food. For too long we have thought of storytelling as dessert—sweet and satisfying, something to finish off the day in a pleasant way. So in our minds we relegate storytelling to the classroom ice cream parlor and drag it out for "special treats." Just as we gaze longingly on double chocolate fudge decadence ice cream, so we look on storytelling as a luxury, definitely not something you should have every day, and certainly not a significant part of a healthy diet.

Oh, how wrong we have been. For storytelling is truly a wonder food. Sure, it's sugary sweet, smooth, and delicious—just like a hot fudge sundae. But storytelling is also packed with all the teaching protein, vitamins, and minerals of the best meat-and-potatoes main course. Maybe it is because the arguments in favor of these benefits are so pervasive and persuasive that 38 states specifically include storytelling as a valuable and important element in their "Language Arts Framework." Ten states mandate storytelling as a language arts classroom activity within that framework.

4. **Storytelling motivates students to learn.** I have talked to many teachers who believe that the greatest value of storytelling is its ability to motivate students for classroom studies. I have received dozens of letters from teachers at schools after the students heard one of my stories, "The Commissioner of Balloons." In every case students were willing and eager to both undertake and plan a study of helium and other noble gasses. (In the story a child flies with a handful of helium balloons.) The eagerness stemmed from their attachment to the story and their desire to find out if the story could actually happen. Hearing the story created the energy, enthusiasm, and motivation to study and explore.

Dan Fossler, a California high school music teacher, took a storytelling course and created a story about Vivaldi to tell as his final exercise. The story was a rousing hit. So he told it to his orchestra the next fall before assigning them a Vivaldi piece. He was amazed at how much more quickly this orchestra mastered the difficult piece than had previous groups of students.

Dan scanned the students' home practice logs (each of his students is required to log every practice session into a notebook) and found that this group was practicing an average of 20 percent more on this piece than had his previous "average" orchestras and significantly more than this orchestra had on previous pieces. When he asked them why, they weren't even aware that they were practicing more, but generally felt that Vivaldi was "cool" and said they liked him and his music. Ten students had gone to the library on their own time to check out additional reading material on Vivaldi.

The teacher told me that this had never happened before. His Vivaldi story surrounded the difficult music of this composer with human context and relevance. It made Vivaldi seem real, important, and interesting. It motivated the students to practice more and to voluntarily pursue exploration of this Italian musician.

5. **Storytelling builds student self-confidence.** Examples abound from classrooms across the country of how the telling of relevant stories has fired students' motivations and passions to study and learn. But the fires of storytelling also burn hot and beneficial when students, themselves, become the storytellers.

   As the second of her fourth-grade students finished her story in front of a sell-out crowd at a local storytelling festival, California teacher Peggy Buzanski beamed, "Storytelling—both mine and theirs—is one of the best things that ever happened to my classroom." She was amazed at the confidence-building power of student storytelling as well as the language arts benefits that induced her to include a unit on storytelling in the first place.

   Teresa Tobin, a Eugene, Oregon, middle schooler, had the opportunity to perform stories at local elementary schools. She wrote of that experience, "The opportunity to tell stories has left me more mature and confident. If I can stand up and tell stories to strangers, I can't imagine there will ever be anything I can't do."

   Danny McLaren, a Waterford, California, middle schooler, had a similar experience. He wrote, "What I like best about storytelling is that I can take someone anywhere with vivid description. Telling stories is the first time I have really known that people were listening to every word I said. I can make people laugh, sit quietly, or even cry, just with words. It makes me feel like I can accomplish or become anything!"

   These are powerful but not isolated examples. Thousands of students across the country have similarly proclaimed the empowering, self-esteem-building benefits of telling stories. Storytelling is an exciting, positive project to actively involve students in learning while building self-esteem and self-confidence, all while rocketing oral language skills toward the top of the class.

6. **Storytelling creates empathy.** Certainly performing storytellers rely heavily on this characteristic of the process of storytelling to establish the requisite connection with an audience. However, there is real value here for education.

   Dr. Nelson Kellogg, a professor in the California State University system, complained that he couldn't get college freshmen and sophomores to relate to, appreciate, and empathize with the struggles and accomplishments of seventeenth-, eighteenth-, and nineteenth-century scientists. Students derisively dismissed them as ignorant buffoons because they lacked modern technological sophistication. So he began to tell stories to his students and found that, through stories that made those historical scientists seem real, interesting, and compelling, he could create that sense of empathy and connectedness that opened his students to the grandeur and importance of early scientific development.

7. **Storytelling improves problem-solving and analytical skills.** Several small studies, especially Donald Davis's study of North Carolina fourth graders in 1993, done for his school district, have pointed strongly toward this curious side effect of storytelling. Certainly, more study is needed before a solid correlation can be established. However, it seems that every story is really a problem to solve. Information arrives at the listener, who must create a mental hierarchical framework to organize and correlate—and then re-correlate—the information until, finally, they understand the story. Told stories carry enough intrigue and power to induce even struggling students to complete this complex mental exercise.

The ability to sift through incoming information and hierarchically prioritize that information is a valuable skill, which lies at the heart of problem solving. A steady diet of listening to storytelling has, in several studies (see Donald Davis's 1993 study and Peggy Buzanski's 1995 study, p. xxi), been shown to increase problem solving and analytical skills enough for the effect to be detectable in improved math and science grades.

8. **Storytelling links to community and heritage.** Finally, stories and storytelling offer a unique link to the structure, traditions, people, and heritage of family and community. Stories, both those written and those preserved only in oral form, are our prime link with our own past and with the history of how we came to be who we are. These stories create a sense of belonging and continuity and create a sense of empathy with distant characters and periods. They establish a feeling of involvement, a sense of permanence.

I have a collection of letters from over 500 teachers documenting and substantiating these benefits of storytelling. Other storytellers have collected their own sets. Storytelling is an effective, cost-free, efficient and powerful teaching tool which fascinates, enthralls and motivates students—and which just happens to be incredibly entertaining. That's its value.

*W*hat *Is* Storytelling?

KEY TOPICS IN THIS SECTION

> ❯ The *what* and the *how* of storytelling
> ❯ The things we never think of that control how we tell a story
> ❯ Are the different kinds of storytelling really different?
> ❯ Storytelling and acting

There is an old adage that has stalked the halls of writing conferences for years and that applies equally well to storytelling. The storytelling version begins, "There are only three rules to great storytelling . . . " At this point the room quiets. All eyes and ears expectantly turn toward the speaker, who, after a suitable pause, concludes, " . . . Unfortunately, nobody knows what any of them are."

The crowd groans. That saying survives because it seems to contain a sizable grain of truth. Name any aspect of storytelling organization and performance that would seem suitable for a "rule" and you will find successful, respected storytellers who consistently and successfully violate the rule and advocate for the opposite point of view. Should you use gestures when you tell? Should you move or stand still—or sit? Should you use vocal characterizations? Physical characterizations? Should stories be told in the third person? In the first? Should stories be presented in chronological order? Should you avoid costumes and props? Or use costumes and props?

It seems that there is no agreement on how to tell a story and that, in reality, there are no rules. If it works, it works. Period.

But there *are* rules—actually, more like natural laws—which, like a lighthouse beacon, can serve to guide every teller around the shoals and jagged reefs of storytelling disaster and trauma. I call them natural laws because, like the law of gravity, they do not tell you what you should do (as a speed limit law does), but rather they describe the way the process naturally works. From these natural laws we derive insights and understandings which, like effective rules, guide us to more consistently successful storytelling.

The first and most important of these natural storytelling laws is found in the answer to the question, "What is storytelling?"

Most dictionaries don't even list the word *storytelling*. Both of those that I have found that do include it offer the same lame definition for my profession: "the telling of a story." True, but there's no real information there.

What is storytelling?

At first glance it seems simple. The dictionary is right. It is just the telling of a story. But what a professional teller does on stage under a hundred spotlights in front of a packed house at Carnegie Hall seems to be entirely different than someone sitting at the kitchen table telling his family about how he got stuck in traffic that day. And don't both of these types of storytelling feel different than what you'll do when you learn and tell a story to your class? Don't different rules apply to each of these three very-different events?

The short answer is "yes . . . and no."

The National Storytelling Association (NSA) struggled for almost two years to construct a comprehensive definition and description of storytelling. Their final statement is listed in the appendix.

There are two key passages in this extended NSA definition. The first is their overall definition of storytelling. "The art of using language, vocalization, and/or physical movement and gesture to reveal the elements and images of a story to a specific, live audience."

That's what we all do every time we share a story with a friend, weave a story into a lecture, or try to entertain 60 sugar-crazed kids during a school camping trip to the nature center. It says *what* we do, but not *how* to do it.

The second passage is their description of the role of the storyteller: "The teller's role is to prepare and present the necessary language, vocalization, and physicality to effectively and efficiently communicate the images of a story. In addition, it is the duty of the teller to ensure that their stories, and the story characters, will be relevant for, accessible to, and appropriate for, each specific audience, and that their material is in appropriate story form."

For *Super Simple Storytelling* we can be more precise and focus on a clearer description of how professionals using storytelling to accomplish their part of the cooperative dance that is a storytelling.

Before reading the *Super Simple Storytelling* definition, try to create your own. What language would you use to define what a storyteller has to do to make it work? You probably have found that you aren't sure of what sorts of elements to talk about in this definition, let alone the specific wording to use. That's because we don't consciously think about *how* we tell our day-to-day stories.

Following is the *Super Simple Storytelling* definition of storytelling, which describes what you need to do to make your storytelling effective and successful.

> **Storytelling is the conscious, intentional integration of two independent aspects of a story: *what* you say and *how* you say it, so that the resultant telling sounds real, genuine, and compelling.**

That one, simple sentence contains the heart of successfully telling a story. There are two parts—the story, and the way it is told—and they are not automatically linked. Develop one and you haven't necessarily developed the other.

Are both aspects—*how* and *what*—of equal importance to a successful storytelling? Isn't it most important to communicate the story, *what* you say?

Think of it this way. When there is a discrepancy between *what* someone says to you and the *way* they say it, which do you believe? The words "Don't you look nice today," form a compliment. However, if they are uttered with a sneer, an exaggerated roll of the eyes, and a sarcastic, sing-song whine, no one would interpret the words as such. The listener's interpretation of how the statement was said *always* overpowers the specific meaning of the words alone.

How something is said is more important than what is said. **HOW** is more powerful than **WHAT**.

You're likely thinking, "That can't be true. I never think about or plan *how* I tell stories about the events in my day to friends and family. I just think about *what* I am going to say and it comes out just fine."

It is also probably true that, if you already tell stories from books to your class, you don't plan *how* you are going to tell those stories either (vocal patterns, emotional expression, pauses, character voices, etc.). And those stories typically *don't* work well. That's why you are reading this book: to find a more successful way to tell stories.

The truth is that you *do* plan how you will tell your personal day-to-day stories. You just don't do it consciously. You have a natural, subconscious storytelling style and system that you have developed over a lifetime that works very well indeed. The problem is that when you get stories from books you don't use that natural system and don't replace it with another. *How* you are going to tell a story from a book is typically *not* planned, and that is the biggest reason for teachers' lack of success with those stories.

You might say, "Then give me a new system that works for stories I get from books. Isn't that what this book is about?"

No. That would be acting. Acting is where you try to change *you* to say and do things in ways that are not natural for you to fit with some printed material. That takes concentration and work. Storytelling is supposed to be natural and fun. Telling stories is something we spontaneously burst into when we are having fun with friends, family, or co-workers.

Storytelling is not acting. In *Super Simple Storytelling* you want to use the natural storytelling style and system you already successfully use for *all stories* regardless of the source—because that is what already works for you. Don't adjust *you* to fit the story, adjust (or select) stories to fit you.

I know, stories that happen to us feel different than those that come from a book. We naturally think that different rules should apply. After all, you have to *learn* a story from a book.

No. Same rules apply. You have to learn stories that happen to you, too. The process of filing them away into memory (learning) is all handled automatically, subconsciously. You may not be consciously aware of it, but it still happens.

The real problem is that we typically try to apply different strategies for learning and telling stories that come form other sources than we do for stories that happen to us. Enter *Super Simple Storytelling*, a system for making the natural system you already use for your own stories work for all stories. *That* is what this book is about.

*W*hat Is Super Simple Storytelling? A Quick Overview

KEY TOPICS IN THIS SECTION

> Natural storytelling versus formal storytelling
> What's the same, what's different; what should be the same, what should be different
> The three supporting pillars of *Super Simple Storytelling*

Let's compare the telling of two stories by a typical teacher. We'll call her "you."

First story: While on vacation you hike up a windswept, craggy mountain, one of a chain of saw-toothed granite peaks. Wispy fingers of cloud swirl past, masking the radiant blue of the sky here above timberline. You fear that they will condense into blinding fog or deadly snow. Powder-fine dirt billows around your boots on each step as if it were barely subject to the laws of gravity. You realize there is a rugged, almost desert-like quality to the delicate life clinging to this pinnacle of earth high above the thick pine forest 2,000 feet below. You are struck by a mystical, powerful feeling as if you were an intruder in an alien world.

Later you decide to tell your class the story of this moment. You feel you don't need to learn or practice the story because it happened to you. You were *there* and you figure you already know the story. Your telling is halting. You often pause to remember some detail or to search for the right word. You are sure you aren't using the most descriptive or powerful phrasing. But you are awash in the remembered emotion of the moment and concentrating on individual words is difficult. You backtrack and repeat several parts. But your class hangs mesmerized on every word. As if they, too, were climbing that mountain, they seem to "get" the point of your telling even if you're sure you're not telling it as well as you should. The story and the telling work.

Second story: You *read* a story about a woman who climbed a high peak alone in the swirling fog. You are struck by the beauty of the author's words and the power of the scene as this lone woman realizes she is an alien in this pristine world. You decide to tell the story to your class and to give them the same experience the words gave to you.

You spend three nights memorizing the words, practicing them over and over again, mumbling them in the shower each morning, silently repeating them to yourself before you drift off to sleep each night. Before you tell the story to your class, your heart pounds and your throat feels dry. You find you don't trust your voice to flow with its normal power and conviction. You take a deep breath and focus on the words, believing that they are the important part, picturing them on each page of the story.

You begin and then realize that your class grows quickly fidgety. Two boys secretly toss spit wads at each other. Several girls gaze out the window. Your underarms grow clammy. You stumble over several of the words and gulp a deep breath, struggling to remember the exact string of verbiage that moved you so and that you carefully memorized. Your class is no longer listening, bored by the whole affair. The telling is a disaster and you conclude that you can't tell stories.

What's the difference between these two tellings? Both are the same story, same setting, and same audience. The only difference is the way you learned and told the two stories.

You reply, "Of course they're different. One happened to me and one I got from a book."

No. Both stories had to be filed away into your mental memory circuitry. Both had to be recalled by your conscious mind. Both had to be reformed from mental images into words. *They* were the same. *You* chose to treat them differently.

For the first story, you:

➤ Relied on your natural storytelling style and strengths.

➤ Learned sensory details and feelings instead of words.

➤ Told the story in your own words, concentrating on details and emotions.

For the second story, you:

➤ Memorized a string of words.

➤ Tried to make someone else's words sound natural and real (which rarely works).

➤ Put all your energy into remembering and repeating a string of words instead of into *how* you said those words.

➤ Tried to tell the story from words instead of from remembered sensory details and feelings.

➤ Ignored your natural style, rhythms, and oral strengths.

➤ Ignored what your audience really needed from your storytelling.

In the first story you naturally delivered what your audience needed from your storytelling. In the second you did not. In the first you learned the story in the natural way you learn all stories. In the second you tried to artificially memorize a string of words.

The first telling was pleasurable for you. The second was not. Storytelling is supposed to be FUN—fun for the listeners and fun for the teller. And it will be—when you see every story in your mind as if it had happened to you and tell it the way you would something that happened to you.

Unfortunately, our automatic habit is to learn and tell stories we get from sources other than our own experience in the worst possible way—worst because it makes the telling more stressful and less successful. But the way you think you should learn and tell a story you get from a book is just a habit—a bad habit. You can replace this habit with one that is more successful. That's the *Super Simple Storytelling* system. It is not a process of developing new talents. It is merely a system for changing the way you approach telling stories.

It's just that easy.

There are three pillars (concepts) that support *Super Simple Storytelling* and will make it work for you:

1. You have a natural style of oral presentation (talking) and certain oral strengths. Your storytelling should be based on the successful aspects of that natural style.

2. Not all parts of a story are of equal value. Concentrate on those story aspects that have the greatest impact on listeners and don't sweat the rest.

3. Stories happen inside a listener's head. Be aware of what a listener really needs from your telling and don't sweat aspects of a story the listener doesn't absolutely need.

It's as easy as 1-2-3. Each of these pillars is described in detail in the Parts I and II. The actual, step-by-step, Super Simple process for using that information to direct the way you learn and tell a story is presented in Part III.

PART I

NATURAL STORYTELLING
100% Natural You—With
No Artificial Additives

$\mathscr{T}$he Right Question Gathers the Right Answer

KEY TOPICS IN THIS SECTION

> ❯ The stories we naturally tell
> ❯ We all tell; we all tell well—just not often
> ❯ The real question we need to answer

I often begin faculty in-service workshops by asking how many currently tell stories in the classroom. Typically one-third raise their hands. If I ask, "How many *don't* tell stories?" the hands of another one-quarter to one-third go up. If I pause and ask, "How many aren't sure?" many, if not most, change their vote to this less committal option. Participants at storytelling workshops often nervously ask each other, "Do you tell stories?" "Are you a storyteller?"

However, the question is as meaningless as asking, "Do you breathe air." We *all* tell stories—personal day-to-day stories—every day. You've told stories virtually every day since you were three years-old. That's what humans do. Our daily stories aren't the elegant affairs that get published in books. Our informal tellings don't mimic the theatrical performances of polished professionals. But so what? The dictionary still says that they are stories and we are still telling them to a live audience.

Actually, the question, "Do you tell stories?" is worse than meaningless because asking it implies that someone could plausibly answer "no." It implies that it is possible *not* to tell stories and that some people don't.

We all tell little stories of our experiences and personal dramas to friends, family, and acquaintances. Yet many aren't sure if these tellings count as "storytelling." Somehow our natural, unrehearsed stories don't feel official.

Certainly, professional tellers are much more consistent and effective in their telling; their stories seem more memorable and engaging. It appears that there is a huge gulf between their polished and perfected presentation and our halting, improvisational storytelling efforts. However, that gap isn't nearly as wide as it appears to be.

After quick reflection, many think that a better question to ask is, "Do you tell your stories *well?*" Sometimes we've all done a lousy job of telling our stories so that they fell flat and didn't work. We've all been cornered at office parties, family functions, and reunions by someone who droned on through endless and painfully boring stories: Uncle Philbert's trip to the Little League Hall of Fame, Aunt Penny's mortification at being 30¢ short at the checkout, a classmate's intriguing life as the third assistant vice-president of marketing.

Those experiences are certainly not what we want to create as tellers. So you might think that it would be relevant to ask someone if they are capable of telling a good story before you settle in to listen.

Again, this is a meaningless question. I guarantee that every reader of this book at *some* time, in *some* place has told at least *one* delightfully mesmerizing, enchanting, totally effective story. Maybe it was only to three of your best friends or two co-workers over the water cooler. Maybe it was only to your own family. The subject of the story doesn't really matter. It could have been your laugh-filled account of getting stuck in an elevator, or the peace and serenity of lying in a flower-strewn meadow on a sunny afternoon, or the flash of terror when you momentarily lost a child at the fair. It might be a scornful account of how one co-worker elbowed his way past others on his march up the corporate ladder.

Maybe it has only happened a few times in your life that you felt really "on" and your audience seemed to hang eagerly on every word. But the point is, I guarantee it has happened. That is, at least once each of you has told a story well. Audiences do not respond well unless the story is told well.

Thus, "Do you tell your stories well?" is also a meaningless question. Of course you do, or at least, you have—which means that, yes, *you can.*

The problem, then, is not innate ability. The question is, can you plan to tell a story well, or do you have to simply hope that it comes out well all on its own? In other words: *"Do you know what you do when you tell your stories well?"*

That is the right question to ask.

For virtually every person in this country the honest answer to that question is, "No. I don't have a clue." Our personal, day-to-day storytelling has become an automatic, or subconscious, process. We throw our stories out there and, with a prayerful shrug, trust to luck.

Natural storytelling, then, is like many other automatic things we do. We do it. We just don't know how we do it. Tying shoelaces is a good example. You do it every day, and yet I will gladly bet that you cannot write down on a piece of paper what you do in exact temporal sequential order with each finger and thumb when you tie your shoelaces.

I am willing to bet that you know neither how many fingers and thumbs you use, nor in what order, when you button a button. You do it repeatedly every day. Yet without slowly mimicking the motion, you consciously have only the vaguest idea of how you do it.

If you knew what you did when you told your stories well—that is, if you knew your natural storytelling style—you could plan *any* story around that style and become much more consistent in the quality and effectiveness of your telling. The next section describes what someone's "style" consists of and will lead you through the process of becoming aware of your own.

Storytelling is not acting. It is not about mimicking the performances of others. or about dramatic theatrics (unless they are natural and comfortable for you). You don't worry about such things when telling your daily-event stories to friends and family members. So don't try to force yourself to worry about them for other stories.

Remember that you have nothing to learn to be able to deliver consistently good (effective) stories. You already know how to do it and have done it (just not consciously). That knowledge is one of the three pillars of good storytelling, and you already know it. You just have to become consciously aware of what you already know. That awareness begins with an investigation of your natural storytelling style.

our Natural Style

KEY TOPICS IN THIS SECTION

- ❯ Learning the first pillar of *Super Simple Storytelling*
- ❯ Your natural style: the good and the bad
- ❯ Learning to use your own natural style
- ❯ Comfort is the key to natural storytelling

Everyone wants to jump straight to the "how do you do it?" part with the step-by-step directions. But before learning something new, it is important to take stock of what you already know. What you "know" is your natural style of storytelling. It is a powerful and effective pillar upon which your *Super Simple Storytelling* will depend.

How do you naturally tell stories? That is, how do you decide what information you will say and in what order you will say it when telling of some past experience? How do you decide how loudly to speak at each moment of the story? How do you decide what gestures to use? When to pause? What facial expressions to adopt? When to change the pitch, volume, and tone of your voice? How do you choose and order the specific details and images you include or exclude? How do you decide whether to, and how to, mimic the voice and mannerisms of some person (story character) you are telling about?

How do you learn and remember stories that happened to you? How do you recall them to your conscious memory?

Most would have to honestly answer these questions with a firm, "I don't know. It all just happens." Of course, we know that, somehow, we must be controlling our own storytelling. We just don't do it consciously. So often these unplanned, impromptu tellings work better than the ones we plan and practice. To improve our formal, stand-up telling, a good place to start is with a thoughtful assessment of our casual, everyday telling style.

There are three aspects to your natural storytelling style that you need to explore.

➤ First is the general pattern of presentation you naturally use when things are going well and when you're excited about your story and feel comfortable with the telling. We'll call this your *natural storytelling style*.

➤ Second is to become aware of when and why this natural effective style operates—and when it doesn't.

➤ The third aspect is to identify that set of habits and tendencies that you fall into when you no longer feel comfortable with your telling, when things aren't going well and you wish you were someplace else.

1. **What is your natural style?** This first aspect is the backbone of your storytelling. As a Super Simple storyteller you won't change this natural style of presentation; you'll use it. You will not try to act like some other teller, or even like the story characters. You will act like *you* by using your natural, effective storytelling style when telling about those story characters.

What is a natural storytelling style? It is the set of habits, tendencies, and mannerisms that you have settled upon over the course of your life to use when you speak effectively. Your natural style is that set of things that you do when you tell a good story that, collectively, make it a good story.

Try to become aware of those moments when you feel good and smooth when talking to your class, friends, co-workers, or family and especially of those moments when those listening to you are paying rapt attention. Those are moments when you are using your natural, effective storytelling style. The more aware of it you become—what you do, how you talk, and what it feels like—the easier it will be to mold stories to that style so that your storytelling becomes more consistently comfortable and successful.

Keep a log of this "style information" as you gather it. Figure 1.1, "The Elements of Your Storytelling Style," is a form you can use to help build a profile of your natural storytelling style.

It is often easier to notice *how* you say something (your style) and what you focus on while you speak during exercises than during daily conversations and interactions. I have included several exercises for this purpose. Exercise 1.1, *The Wave Game* (page 119) demonstrates both our natural focus on content instead of delivery and our lack of conscious awareness of how we and others say things. *The Wave Game* also demonstrates each participant's general style tendencies. Were you bold or halting when you mimicked the previous person? What kind of gesture and vocal pattern did you invent to use? Your tendencies in this exercise are representative of your "natural style."

Exercise 1.2, *What'd You Have for Dinner?* (page 121) is another excellent vehicle for uncovering your natural storytelling tendencies, habits, and style. The assigned story situations are just silly enough to allow the tellers to experience both their natural storytelling style and the nervous habits they tend to drift into. This is an excellent exercise to repeat with a different content topic after each participant has completed an assessment of their personal style to see if they really tell the way they thought they did.

Oral styles can be flamboyant and theatrical, straightforward and factual, embellishing, quiet and reserved, or emotional and passionate. You may tend to draw stories out or cut quickly to the punchline. No one style is any better than any other. Some stories are tailor made for your style while others must be edited to blend effectively with your style. (Tall tales, for example, work best with a straightforward, unembellished, informative style but don't work as well with a theatrical style. Many oriental and Native American stories work best with a quiet, simple style while others benefit from the raucous exaggeration of a flamboyant, theatrical style.)

You can use the chart in Figure 1.2 (page 6), "Your Personal Style Profile," to help you decide what sort of style you have. Remember that the categories listed on that chart are generalized aggregates. You may or may not fit neatly into any one category.

Figure 1.1. The Elements of Your Storytelling Style.

There is no *correct* natural style for storytelling. Each style has advantages and disadvantages. To effectively use your own natural storytelling style, you must first understand what that style is. The first step is to become aware of the elements that define a storytelling style.

1. **GENERAL** (Natural enjoyment of the process facilitates all styles)
   Do you enjoy telling everyday stories to friends and family?
   Do you create opportunities to tell daily events and happenings?
   Do you consciously recognize events as potential sources of stories?

2. **VOICE** (The most important element of all)
   Do you vary pace, volume, and inflections when you speak?
   Does your voice carry energy?
   Does your voice effectively convey the emotion of the stories you tell?
   Do you vocally mimic the people you talk about?

3. **GESTURES AND BODY** (A powerful and effective element of successful storytelling)
   Do you naturally use directional gestures? emphasis gestures?
   Do your hands mimic what you talk about?
   Do you physically mimic the people you talk about?
   Do you move (pace) or sit/stand still when you tell a story?
   Do you smile a lot while you tell?
   Do you tend to lean toward your listeners?

4. **ORGANIZATION OF MATERIAL** (Do you tend to make things into stories,or just factual reports?)
   Is it easy for you to remember the events of a story?
   Can you readily "see" them in your mind when you tell?
   Do you tend to stretch material and add new details?
   Do you tend to quote the people in your stories or just tell what happened?

Figure 1.2. Your Personal Style Profile.

Base your answers on your own daily, informal stories with friends, family, and co-workers.

Score each question from 1 to 5, where 5 means "Yes, a lot" and 1 means "No or rarely"

WAYS YOU PRESENT STORY CONTENT

1. Do you embellish your stories? _____
2. Do you build stories to a dramatic climax? _____
3. Do you describe character reactions? _____
4. Do you add extra details? _____
5. Do you "just give the facts" (1 pt) or interpret those facts (5 pts)? _____
6. Do you portray character emotions and feelings? _____
7. Do you "get carried away with yourself" while telling? _____
8. Do you show your own emotional reactions to story events? _____
9. Does it take you longer than others to tell a story? _____

PHYSICAL STYLE ELEMENTS (hands, body, face)

10. Do you physically act out your stories as you tell? _____
11. Do you physically mimic (act like) the characters you tell about? _____
12. Do you move very much when you tell? _____
13. Do you use many gestures? _____

VOCAL STYLE ELEMENTS (pace, tone, volume, pitch, variations)

14. Does your voice show the character's emotions while you tell? _____
15. Do you tend to vocally mimic the characters you tell about? _____
16. Do you use lots of pauses? _____
17. Do your pace and volume change a lot while you tell? _____

Ratings—Add up your score from numbers:
- 1, 2, 3, 4, 5 & 9. Divide by 6 for an **Embellishment Rating** _____.
- 3, 6, 7, 8 plus 10 &14. Divide by 6 for an **Emotional Rating** _____.
- 6, 11,15. Divide by 3 for a **Characterization Rating** _____.
- 1, 2, 3, 4, 5, 7, 9, 10, 11, 12, 13, 14, 15, 16, 17. Divide by 15 for a **Theatrical Rating** _____.

Interpretation: _____ **If Your Rating Is:**

CATEGORY	1.0—2.5 Your Style Tends Toward: ▼	3.5—5.0 Your Style Tends Toward: ▼
THEATRICAL	Quiet, reserved	Flamboyant, theatrical
EMOTIONAL	Informative	Emotional
EMBELLISHMENT	Straightforward	Embellishing
CHARACTERIZATION	Factual	Characterizations

If you fall between 2.6 and 3.4, your style includes elements of both.

Is one style better than another? No. *Better* is the wrong word. Theatrical, energetic, flamboyant styles are more flexible and so work well over a wider range of stories—but not for all stories. It is easier with these styles to cover up shortcomings and mistakes. Quieter, more reserved styles work equally well when the story material is organized and planned for that style of presentation. Tellers with quieter styles typically need to plan a story more thoroughly.

As a Super Simple Storyteller, you will not try to change your basic storytelling style; after all, you already use it every day. Rather, you will try to become consciously aware of it and its strengths and to use that information to select appropriate stories for you to tell and to adjust stories to fit the way you can comfortably tell them. Over time you will become more aware of which kinds of stories you can work with and which kinds are easy for you to tell.

2. **When does it work?** You don't use your natural, effective storytelling style *every* time you tell little day-to-day stories. Sometimes the story works and your natural storytelling style flows powerfully, positively, and unimpeded. Sometimes everything comes out wrong and the story is a disaster. Sometimes you're on. Sometimes you're not.

When does that automatic, subconscious, natural system work? It seems to work admirably whenever two conditions are met:

1. The story must have happened to you.

2. You must be comfortable in the setting and activity of the telling.

When we violate either of those two conditions our automatic, natural storytelling style seems to falter, if not completely disintegrate. We automatically rush into whatever nervous, self-destructive habits we have as defensive mechanisms to minimize the embarrassment of such moments.

Typically you stop feeling comfortable and natural when you don't know what to say and have to grope for words, when you feel rushed, when you feel that your listeners don't like your story, when you feel that you are being critically judged, or when outside distractions disrupt your concentration. You begin to feel anxious, embarrassed, nervous. You stop thinking about the story and begin to think about you and your situation. This is a perfect setup for a storytelling disaster.

If one goal of *Super Simple Storytelling* is to become aware of and use your natural storytelling style, another goal must be to become aware of what you need to feel comfortable enough to use that style. Remember, storytelling is supposed to be FUN. Fun means being comfortable with the process—and yes, you can do it! The Super Simple system is all about learning what you need to remain comfortable while you tell—tell a variety of stories in your own classroom in your own natural storytelling style.

3. **What do you do when you become nervous?** What happens when you *don't* feel comfortable while telling a story? Everyone who has tried to tell stories as part of a formal presentation, or in a presentation to peers, or to large groups of students, has become nervous and uncomfortable at regular intervals while storytelling. But these feelings also arise during more informal telling of day-to-day events to neighbors and even family. You forget what comes next. You sense that your listeners are losing interest. The story and your telling of it seem to disintegrate. Those things happen to everybody.

What do you do at those moments? Your natural tendencies, your nervous habits at those moments, are probably self-destructive. Becoming aware of them and learning to sidestep them will do wonders for your telling and keep you feeling much more comfortable when you tell.

So, what do *you* do when you become nervous and uncomfortable while telling a story? Watch your use of hands and voice at those moments. Do you make everything bigger and louder (as if to ram the story down the audience's throats until they pleadingly surrender and listen)? I found that that was what I naturally did. Do you blush and stop the story with a shrug and a lame, "I guess you had to be there . . . ?" Do you "ummm," and stutter? Do you use more "like's" and "you know's?"

Do you speed up to get to the end or to a part you are more comfortable with? Do you grow quiet, allowing your voice to shrink to an inaudible whisper, as if to disappear and leave the story alone in front of the audience? Do your hands try to hide in your pockets or behind your back? Do your feet pace needlessly across the floor? Does your body rock and sway? Does your mind take a mini-vacation, pretending to be somewhere else? Does your face go blank and your voice become as monotonous as a computer generated voice? Do you find that your storytelling becomes flat and lackluster, as if you had pulled the plug and drained away all your energy and emotional expression, when you become uncomfortable? Do you omit detail and visual imagery from the story and provide only the essential plot points when you are nervous?

Certainly these tendencies are more apparent when they happen during a formal storytelling. There you are, stuck in the story, and you can't simply stop when it doesn't seem to be working. But you can also spot these tendencies during friendly, day-to-day stories. They still happen.

Each of these counterproductive tendencies starts a vicious cycle when telling in a classroom environment. First, you do what you naturally do to signal that you are a bit uncomfortable. However, listeners don't interpret any of these sets of actions as saying that you "like your story just fine, but are in a rough spot that makes you momentarily uncomfortable and nervous." They interpret them as meaning that you, the teller, are bored with the story and with the act of telling it. *That* is what those nervous habits all look like. Listeners figure that, if you're bored, there's no reason for them to listen, so they grow bored and fidgety. Sensing this audience reaction makes you more nervous. So you accentuate your nervous tendencies even more, which reinforces the audience's interpretation that you don't like this story and wish you were elsewhere (and by now, you do). So they reinforce their bored attitude, which makes you all the more nervous, etc. etc. . . . Crash!

The way out of this downward spiral is to learn to recognize what you feel like when you get nervous and begin to employ your particular nervous habits. It is especially difficult, however, to become coolly, rationally aware of your physical, facial, and vocal patterns when you are already nervous and stressed. It is far easier to begin the process of unraveling the core of our destructive oral tendencies during exercises that isolate those behaviors during some game-like activity.

Six exercises in this book can be effective in helping identify these nefarious nervous habits: Exercise 1.2, *What'd You Have for Dinner?* (page 121), Exercise 1.3, *Your Favorite Story* (page 123), Exercise 3.3, *Describe the Scene* (page 144), Exercise 3.11, *A Better Excuse* (page 163), Exercise 4.7, *The Retell Game* (page 186), and Exercise 5.1, *The 30-Second Story* (page 192). Of these, *What'd You Have for Dinner?*, *A Better Excuse*, and *The 30-Second Story* are the strongest and surest for this purpose.

Make a game out of it. Have one of the goals of playing each of these exercises be to identify destructive nervous habits. Offer rewards to those who help you identify yours.

Once these dastardly brutes are unmasked, how do you fix them? First, don't bother to "fix" them. Breaking lifelong habits is too much work and starts to sound too much like acting. When nervous tension strikes, you can break the cycle of escalating nervous habits. *That* is easy to do. At those moments, pause in your story, suck in a deep breath, and intentionally **do the exact opposite of your natural nervous tendency**.

First become aware; then learn to do the opposite. If your nervous tendency is to speed up and talk softly, pause, breathe, and boom out the next few sentences with over-exaggerated slowness. It does wonders to shake both you and your listeners out of your nervous and growingly detached stupor. Suddenly you're back into the story and that wave of nervous panic passes.

Your natural storytelling system already works. But we are all a little like Dumbo the elephant. He always could fly but didn't believe he could. Then a smart mouse handed him a worthless "magic" feather as a way to show Dumbo what he already knew. The more you become aware of what you already know—that is, of the effectiveness of your own natural storytelling—the more you realize how much you already know and the readier you are to successfully take on stories that come from books. The Super Simple system will guide you into comfortably and successfully telling those stories.

Your personal day-to-day stories always work for you because they're *your* stories and because you learned them the natural way. Pick stories from books that work for your style and learn them in that same natural way that makes you more comfortable when you tell, and you're ready for anything. The rest of Part I covers what your listeners really need from your story and your telling. (Knowing that will help make you feel comfortable.) Part II discusses the true anatomy of a story. (Mastering the key elements of a story will also help make you feel comfortable.) Part III presents the step-by-step Super Simple Storytelling system for learning a story (which will definitely help you feel comfortable when you tell).

$\mathcal{T}$he Golden List: The Audience Speaks

KEY TOPICS IN THIS SECTION

> ❯ Learning the second pillar of *Super Simple Storytelling*
> ❯ What listeners really need (and don't need) from storytelling
> ❯ What The Golden List means for tellers

Have you ever thought about what your listeners need—I mean *really* need—from you when you tell a story? Have you organized your story learning and preparation around these listener needs? Are you sure that the things you do and say when you learn and tell a story match what your audience really wants?

Interestingly, most storytellers would have to admit that, consciously, no, they haven't and don't. But isn't that really the whole point of storytelling: to give an audience what it needs to be able to conjure vivid, intriguing images in their minds?

Some might argue that second guessing what each individual listener needs is mind-bogglingly impossible. But stop and think of what makes you, as a story listener, like one teller and not another, or one story and not another.

The truth is that this seemingly mysterious maze of listener wants and demands is extremely predictable and simplifies into a short, straightforward list of key characteristics of a story and of a telling that effectively sway *every* listener, *every* time. This short list is important enough to earn the name, The Golden List.

I have included three exercises in *Super Simple Storytelling* designed to illuminate the desires, preferences, and needs of story listeners. These are *Your Favorite Story* (Exercise 1.3, page 123), *What Makes It Real?* (Exercise 1.4, page 125), and *What Makes It Fun to Listen To?* (Exercise 1.6, page 129). These exercises cannot be done by an individual. They are activities for groups. Because your class will be your primary audience, they are the perfect group for these exercises. From them you will learn exactly what your listeners will need from your storytelling.

The lists a class creates for *Your Favorite Story* and *What Makes It Real?* are surprisingly simple and similar. The elements that make a story seem real also make it attractive to listeners. It doesn't matter if I conduct these exercises with second graders, middle schoolers, college seniors, or teachers. Every group votes for the same reasons. Almost always these few reasons to vote for one story over another are mentioned in the same order.

Following is the list of reasons to vote for one story over another, which I have culled from conducting these exercises nearly 1,000 times. In general the first items listed are more frequently mentioned. Compare them with the lists your specific class generates.

The Golden List

1. What Listeners Say They Need from the Story:

   - Arresting details
   - Relevant, interesting characters
   - Intriguing story problem, tension, and suspense (often mentioned under the catch-all term "excitement")
   - Humor
   - Information and conciseness
   - Believability

2. What Listeners Say They Need from the Telling, Itself:

   - Confidence
   - Emotional expression
   - Enthusiasm
   - Energy
   - Humor

That is The Golden List. Short and simple, isn't it?

Notice one item that is not on this list. No one has ever voted for a story because the teller got all the words right. Listeners will never know, nor will they care, if the teller successfully memorizes and spews out every word in order.

Now what do those two parts of The Golden List mean?

1. **From the story**: Details are always the first item mentioned. Appropriate details make a story seem real. Details allow listeners to create rich, vivid, complete images of the story in their minds. Without a steady flow of relevant details a story is always boring.

   In a larger sense, all of the items in this part of the list are different ways of saying that the listeners needs to be quickly convinced that this story will be worth their time to listen. **They need to believe that this story will be worth their time and mental energy.**

   Story details help create that belief. Humor helps create it because humor is always worthwhile. Interesting characters help create it. Above all, that belief is created by providing the key information that defines a story. That is what the "how to" Part II of this book is about.

2. **From the telling**: Look at the five items listed in the second half of The Golden List. They all refer to listeners' perception of the style and presentation of the teller. The listed items refer not directly to what the teller did (use of gestures, facial expression, vocal pacing, etc.), but rather to the listeners' interpretation of what the teller did. Really, they are all different expressions of a central need of every listener. **Each listener needs to believe that the teller likes their own story.** If they believe that the teller believes in the story, then they, too, will believe.

   How do listeners decide if they think that a teller likes and is excited by their own story? By the *way* they say it. Mostly at a subconscious level listeners decide if the teller appears confident and comfortable. They check to see if the teller appears to be enjoying their own story, if the teller appears to be enthused by their story. Storytelling is supposed to be fun.

   I have included one additional exercise to spotlight how we naturally hear and connect with stories. Exercise 1.5, *What Do You Remember?* (page 127), is designed to help participants identify those aspects of a story and of a storytelling that actually drive vivid imagery into their minds. As you review the images each participant remembers of the story snippets told during this exercise, you will be able to demonstrate that there is an excellent correlation between The Golden List of audience needs and the memories they hold. That is, when the teller provides the key elements of The Golden List, listeners remember the story. Where there are large gaps in student memory, there were gaps in what and how the teller delivered story material.

The Lemon List

KEY TOPICS IN THIS SECTION

> ❯ How natural tendencies lead us astray
> ❯ What derails a storytelling
> ❯ The difference between the words of a story and the story

Of course everyone knows that storytelling isn't that simplistic. The problem is that what we *think* we should do when we are the teller and find a story to tell in a book is very different from what our listeners really need (The Golden List) and also very different from what we naturally do when we tell personal day-to-day stories. We abandon our natural, successful storytelling style and disregard The Golden List. No wonder storytelling seems difficult, if not impossible!

If you were going to tell the story of Little Red Riding Hood tomorrow, what would you do tonight to prepare? Read and reread the story in a desperate effort to memorize each word? Focus on simply remembering the characters' names? Plan and rehearse specific gestures and body movements to amplify key parts of the story? Try to at least memorize the plot? Do you believe that if you can just get through a telling without forgetting any words and the order of story events, disaster will be averted?

Those are all common thoughts of beginning tellers. But compare them with The Golden List. Are any of the areas listed above on the list of listener needs? No. Compare them with the way you naturally tell personal stories to friends. Do you worry about getting all the words right? Do you worry about placing each event in temporal sequential order, or are you willing to jump around as parts of the story pop into your mind? Do you plan and rehearse specific gestures and movements?

If the list of audience needs is The Golden List, let's call the list of what we naturally think we should do when we prepare to tell a story The Lemon List. Lemon because it sours the telling and is nearly worthless. Actually, The Lemon List is worse than worthless. It is counterproductive. It leads tellers into activities that make it *harder* to successfully tell and that waste their time.

What are the most common elements in The Lemon List? Make your own list and compare it to the list I have compiled from talking to many teacher-tellers.

The four items that repeatedly bubble to the top of most people's responses are:

The wording (get the words right)

The plot line (get the sequence of events right)

The facts (get what happens right)

Specific cute or humorous repeated lines

On first read this list sounds perfectly reasonable. However, each of these story elements is *plot* related. Once a teller focuses on plot (it's true for story writers as well) they seem to ignore the elements that really make a story work and that listeners really need. Yes, there will always be a plot. Something will always happen in a story. But plot is not what drives a story and excites listeners (see Part II).

Compare The Lemon List to The Golden List. They are almost mutually exclusive. What we tend to think we should learn and deliver as tellers is close to the opposite of what our audience really wants and needs from our telling.

Exercise 1.6, *What Makes It Fun to Listen To?* (page 129), offers a chance for your class to explore what they think they want and need as story listeners. You will find that the language they use when they describe what they want (action, murders, scary story, etc.) often lean closer to The Lemon List than The Golden List. It is another example of how we focus on plot and miss the real core of a story.

After using Exercise 1.6 to open a general discussion, try Exercise 2.2, *Is It a Story Yet?* (page 133) with your class. Here you will find that the elements of story your students need to vote "yes" during *Is It a Story Yet?* are significantly different from the list they create during *What Makes It Fun?* and closely match The Golden List.

We have now uncovered the general concepts that form the foundation pillars upon which *Super Simple Storytelling* is built. It's as simple as 1-2-3:

1. Become aware of and use your own natural storytelling style and tendencies. Select and mold stories to fit with your style of oral communication. As part of your natural style, learn to recognize and avoid your personal nervous habits and tendencies. We all have them and we all drift quickly into them the moment we perceive that our storytelling isn't well-received.

2. Be aware of what an audience really needs and use that list as a guide to leaning and preparing a story rather than your own instinctive ideas about what you should learn and prepare.

3. Make sure that you have a strong, effective story to tell.

These pillars are the keys to unlocking successful *Super Simple Storytelling*. They describe what we need to accomplish as tellers and provide the logic behind the Super Simple approach to learning and telling stories. Now for the easy part: We can discover exactly what makes a story work and exactly what to learn and how to learn it so that the storytelling will be smooth, efficient, successful, comfortable, . . . and FUN!

PART **II**
ANATOMY OF A STORY
The Power Behind the Words

*W*hat *Is* a Story?

KEY TOPICS IN THIS SECTION

> ❯ Learn the third pillar of *Super Simple Storytelling*
> ❯ What a story *is*, and what it *isn't*
> ❯ Finding the elements that drive every story
> ❯ If not plot, then what defines the structure of a story?

If you are going to *tell* stories (instead of write them) you might be tempted to say, "I don't need to worry about what a story is. When I find a story in a book, there it is. Period. That's all I need to know."

There are three reasons why it's worth your time and effort to learn about what makes stories tick:

1. Some aspects of a story are much more important than others. That means that there are some elements of a story you don't need to focus on when you learn or tell a story and the story will still come across to your listeners just fine. Knowing the anatomy of stories saves you time.

2. The more you understand the core elements of a story, the easier it is to learn a story and the more comfortable you will feel telling it. Understanding stories lets your natural style shine through better.

3. The basic story you tell will be the same as the story in the book, but the words you say will be different than those in the book and the *way* you will say what you say (emphasis, pacing, tone, emotion, etc.) is not included in the printed story at all. Not understanding a story can get you into stressful trouble when you tell.

It would seem obvious to say, "Make sure you have a good story to tell before beginning the process of learning and telling." Without a powerful story to deliver, the burden on *how* you say it is greatly increased. It becomes highly probable that you will experience those stressful, self-destructive, nervous moments that *Super Simple Storytelling* is designed to help you avoid.

However, no teller can be sure they have selected, adapted, or created a good story until they understand what a story really is. The discussion I include here is a condensed version of the presentation on "story" I published in *Write Right!* (Libraries Unlimited, 1999), the companion to this book, which focuses on a breakthrough system for teaching creative writing using storytelling techniques.

What is *a story?* A story is a unique and specific narrative structure with a specific set of necessary characteristics and which includes a sense of completeness. This unique structure creates the incredible power and allure stories possess. Stories pass on wisdom, experience, information, and facts. Stories shape beliefs and values. Stories are the building blocks of knowledge, the foundation of memory and learning. Stories model effective use of words (language). Stories create empathy and connect us to our humanness. Stories link past, present, and future by teaching us to anticipate the possible consequences of our actions (cause and effect).

But these are only descriptive characteristics of a story. What *is* a story?

I have asked thousands of students and teachers for their definition of a story. Virtually all the answers I hear revolve around plot. *A story is when you tell about something that happened. . . . A story is something you make up about something and write down. . . . A story is when you tell about a series of events. . . .* And the most frequently offered answer of all, *A story is something with a beginning, a middle, and an end.* True, but so what? What *doesn't* have a beginning, a middle, an end? A magazine article does. The phone book does. So do a sewer pipe and a peanut butter sandwich.

My favorite definition came from a fifth-grade boy in western Pennsylvania. My asking the question, "What is a story?" seemed to trigger one of those rare life epiphanies. For one brief moment my question brought the universe into clear, brilliant focus for this kid. His face glowed with the glory of true insight. He raised his hand so hard it lifted him out of his seat. His legs snapped straight, shooting his chair back to clang against the radiator. He cried out, "I know what a story is. It's when you have a subject and a verb!"

I didn't have the heart to tell him he was wrong. I had to say that yes, that was the definition of a short story—a *very* short story—but that I was looking for the definition of a *longer* story. He was satisfied. The class wasn't too misled.

All of these definitions are *plot-based* definitions. Sound familiar? The Lemon List is plot based. The Golden List is character based. Plot-based stories fail to engage listeners just as plot-based story learning and telling fail to excite them.

The problem with plot-based definitions is that they miss the elements that make a story enjoyable, powerful, memorable, and effective. That is, plot is not what draws listeners into a story. Plot is not what allows them to understand and internalize a story. Plot is not what listeners crave and require from a story. Plot is not what uniquely separates story from other narrative communication.

Plot is the servant of character. "Fiction is Folks." More generally, stories are characters. If any storyteller doubts the truth of that statement, consider this. Every year Americans consume over eight *billion* person-hours watching soap operas. Nothing ever happens on the soaps. You can be gone for months, only to come back and find the same telephone conversations still in progress. The soaps are character studies. That's why we stay glued to our TVs every day. We know every secret flaw, goal, and twisted motive of every character, and that makes them irresistible. Stories are about characters.

But *what is* a story?

When does something stop being something else and start being a story? What differentiates a story from an article or an essay? What gives a story its amazing power and allure?

Try Exercise 2.1, *What Is a Story?* (page 131) with your class. Let them struggle to identify the elements that make a story. It is appropriate for you to question and re-question their answers. Most likely they will *describe* a story rather than identify those aspects of a story that set it apart from the rest of the narrative world.

Exercise 2.2, *Is It a Story Yet?* (page 133), is designed to identify the moment when the last critical bit of information is stirred into the mix and a series of paragraphs is transformed into a story. Try it with your class. It is best to use *Is It a Story Yet?* while their definition of a story from *What Is a Story?* is still fresh in their minds. You will want to compare the results of these two exercises.

Is It a Story Yet? is a very telling and important exercise. It clearly identifies character and conflict (or struggle) as being the core focus of every story. It identifies character, problems, and struggle as three of the key, character-based elements that draw a listener into a story.

While it identifies the fundamental concepts from which to form a definition, the exercise itself still doesn't define a story.

So, what *is* a story?

The *Super Simple Storytelling* definition centers on four letters that flow straight from the concepts uncovered in *Is It a Story Yet?*

A story is:
a narrative account organized around four central character elements:

C, C, S & G.

Those four letters, I am sure, were on the tip of your tongue. Math majors may call it C^2SG. Chem majors may say, C_2SG. Brits may say, "Double-C, S & G." The letters stand for:

Characters
Conflicts
Struggles
Goals

Characters are the central element of any story. The **Goals** of these characters are what the story is about. The **Conflicts** block those characters from their goals, and their **Struggles** to reach those goals are the engine that drives every story.

These are the elements that draw us to a story. They create purpose and structure for a story and allow us to understand it. They are the elements we demand to learn from a story. These four elements form the defining core of a story. Note that these core elements all relate to the main story characters and not to the plot. The following sections describe exactly what each of these terms means and what you need to know about them to effectively, comfortably tell a story.

Stories are about characters. All elements of a successful story flow from the characters and their goals, conflicts, and struggles. All other elements of a story are dependent upon the characters. Plot derives from character and struggle. Setting is defined by the needs of the characters. The beginning, the middle, and the end are written to serve the needs of the characters.

And yet, in our culture, we tend to think first of plot when we think of story. Even though as listeners it is information about the characters we crave (see Exercise 2.2, *Is It a Story Yet?*), even though successful stories are character-based creations, still we have drilled it into our heads to think plot. We even assign plot-based stories to our students. "Write a story about *what* you did over summer vacation" is a plot-based assignment. The returning stories are invariably boring, because they are plot based, not because those kids can't write.

Try it with your class. Have your students make up a story, quickly, spontaneously, with no time for planning. They will think first of an event, an action, a plot line, and will then struggle to identify what the story is about, how it will end, or where it is going.

Now use Exercise 2.3, *The Big Three* (page 137), to have the class try a different approach to creating stories. If they begin by creating character, goal, and obstacles, they will simultaneously define all parts of the story, including the plot, the ending, the climax, and the theme.

An example: Once there was a young ant named Carlile (character) who wanted to find food to save his family (goal). But the terrible rains had turned the valley into a giant, rampaging river and the rock Carlile's family had crawled onto was surrounded by miles of muddy, swirling water (conflict number 1). Besides, ant-eating birds circled overhead. If Carlile stepped out of the protective crevice where the family hid, he would be eaten (conflict number 2). Of course, if he didn't venture out, the family would starve.

How will the story end? Carlile finds food. What will be the climax? Carlile will have to face the birds or some other (and yet unidentified) foe that stands between him and food. What's the theme of this story? Placing the good of the group over personal comfort and safety. It is the hero's journey Carlile will march out upon.

Some readers may be thinking, "Hold on here. I'm just going to tell stories, not create or write them."

Making up, or creating, stories was an easy demonstration only. The point is that these same four elements are what makes a story work for listeners when you tell it. These four elements should be foremost in your mind whether you are going to write the story or tell the story, if you want that story to captivate those you give it (tell it) to. If you get these four elements right when you tell a story, listeners will allow you a multitude of other errors and transgressions and will still love the story. The next sections show you exactly what these elements look like and how to find them in your story.

$\mathcal{F}$iction Is Folks

KEY TOPICS IN THIS SECTION

> The importance of the five layers of the character onion

> How to make listeners care about a character

A searing summer sun blazed down its wilting heat during a long summer drought as a worm crawled across the cracked and parched earth. At best, that's mildly interesting. Add character and goal—It was a young worm named Wilby who has to cross that cracked and withered landscape with a vial of medicine tied around his neck with a red ribbon which is the only way to save his dying grandfather—and listeners want to know how it comes out. Add more risk and danger—a flock of fierce, starving crows circle hungrily overhead, casting black, fearsome shadows across the dirt.

Now we're hooked. It is the characters, their goals, conflicts, and struggles that hook us every time and make us care about what is going to happen in a story. Plot is the servant of character. Understand the characters and the events of their story make sense.

How does a storyteller make sure that they understand, and will effectively present to their listeners, interesting, compelling characters? The answer isn't luck. It is a specific set of information that every teller can find in a story—or create (for those elements not overtly stated in the story).

I was well into my third year of analyzing stories and struggling to find the keys that made them work before I found this first and greatest key: Forget plot and focus on characters. I was at a national storytelling conference in Jonesborough, Tennessee. The audience for an evening concert were all practitioners of the art, adult professional storytellers. Five tellers performed. One was a man with a wonderful reputation as a master teller. He told a simplistic children's story. The entire plot can be summarized as: Two children fall into a book, land on a cookie, meet some raisins and their king, fall out of the book, and go home. There is precious little I have omitted.

As he began I thought, "Oh, this poor, misguided man. We're a sophisticated audience and he's telling us a mindless children's tale. Everyone will hate it."

Everyone loved it, myself included. I sat up long into the night analyzing the storyline and plot structure of that story. Over and over again I came to the same conclusion. Nothing of significance happened in that story. How could we be so satisfied by a story where nothing happens?

Then it hit me. We didn't love the story. We loved the characters. We loved the raisins and the kids. If an audience likes the characters, they will like the story. Period. If they don't like the characters, they won't like the story. There is no way plot and action alone will pull listeners back into the ranks of the satisfied.

Yes, that teller passed up a golden opportunity for a magnificent story by not creating something significant for those delightful characters to do. But with characters alone, that story was the hit of the night.

What information makes up, or creates, an interesting story character? Humans aren't transparent, single-purpose organisms. They are complex. They are often contradictory. They are surprising. They are multi-faceted. They act differently in different situations. Characters, like humans, are built on concentric layers of history, belief, experience, and interpretation. Layers stacked upon layers—like the layers of an onion—make up a character. It is the sum total of all these layers, rather than any one individual layer, that makes a compact, sturdy, interesting whole.

All of the information you can discover about a character can be divided into five groups, or character layers:

➤ Core character information—central driving forces and motives of the character

➤ Personality—how the character relates to, and acts within, the world

> ➤ History—what has happened to the character and what the character has done in the past

> ➤ Activity—what the character does

> ➤ Sensory information—information your sensory organs could directly record

These five layers, and the basic character information they create, are shown on Figure 2.1, "The Layers of a Character," and are described in the following two sections.

Figure 2.1. The Layers of a Character.

- **SENSORY IMAGE**
  Information available directly to the senses.
- **PERSONALITY**
  How the character relates to and interacts with the world.
- **ACTIVITY**
  What the character does.
- **HISTORY**
  What the character has done in the past.

These are four of the five character layers a writer must address.

*T*he Core of a Character

KEY TOPICS IN THIS SECTION

> ❯ How the core of a character defines a story and forces listeners to care
> ❯ How to find and use the four elements of the character core
> ❯ How to uncover hidden core elements
> ❯ The value of the core

The place to start understanding a story character is from the core out. Remember that the form of story is defined by these character core elements. There is no information more important to understand than the core of the story's main character.

What do core elements for a story character look like?

> *Sixteen-year-old Caroline wanted more than anything to learn to read. But in Colonial America in 1768 women did not read. Caroline's parents forbade her to even talk about it. "Society would ridicule any female," they said, "who wasted her time in idle reading." They were a poor family and needed every able-bodied member to work in the family candle shop. Through the small window where Caroline dipped tapers into liquid tallow, she watched the sons of rich merchants carrying books back and forth, discussing various passages. And she burned with envy and resentment. When one young man left a book on a nearby bench, Caroline rushed out of the shop, snatched that book, and clutched it to her chest. Silently she swore that, no matter what the consequences, with this very book, she would learn to read!*

That passage contains the core character elements. What are they? See if you can identify all four as each is introduced and discussed below. Figure 2.2 (page 22), "The Core of a Character," illustrates these core character elements.

1. **Character first impression.** A story character is built of interweaving layers of information: core information, personality, history, sensory data, quirks, habits, schemes, hopes, dreams, routines, fears, etc. Where does a teller start to build this mountain of detail? What does the teller present first? The answer is to start with a first impression, a quick, thumbnail sketch just to identify the character for listeners. First impressions are like introductions.

   The first impression does not create a complete character. But it identifies enough to give listeners a sense of who this character is and what they are about in the story. Remember that listeners need good first impressions more than readers do because readers can always scan back over earlier pages to help remember who a character is. Listeners cannot. If listeners get confused they will probably never recover.

   Listen to other storytellers (live or on audiotape) and see how they first introduce characters and what they say to ensure that the characters will not be forgotten. If your story doesn't come with strong first impressions, try to create your own by looking for the information about the main characters that is most important to you.

Figure 2.2.   **The Core of a Character.**

There are six bits of information that are commonly used to build these valuable first impressions of a character. They represent a quick sampling of each of the layers of character information:

1. Species. What is the main character? A tree, a snail, a human, or a shoelace? Start by identifying *what* the character is.

2. Age and gender. Age need not be in exact years. Old, baby, young, fully grown, or teenager-ish create a sufficiently accurate mental picture of the character.

3. Name. Names are important. We all have many names: formal names, nick-names, what friends call us, what family call us, names used when others tease us, names we call ourselves. Some of those names we like; some we can't stand. Which names are used to describe a character, and how the character feels about those names, tells the listener a lot about the way this character views himself or herself and the way others view them.

4. Appearance. Create one or two highlights, or prominent aspects, of the character's physical being.

5. Vocation. Identify one aspect of the character's activity. It can be their job, their role in society, or a favorite avocation.

6. Personality. Find a one-word, snap impression of the dominant trait of this character's personality. Are they pushy, meek, friendly, quiet, hardworking, lazy, etc.?

Some examples of character first impressions follow:

➤ Piney, a sad, aging fir tree whose branches had grown bent, withered, and scraggly

➤ A young, cocky frog named Shirley with an extra-long tongue that could clip a fly out of the air at four feet. Her friends called her "Sure shot." Other frogs called her "Surely Stuck-Up."

➤ Born Samantha Vanderslice III, she was now a 28-year-old, frazzled housewife with four kids. Everyone called her "mom," or "Mrs. Frank Frudgel." She hadn't heard anyone use her own, real name, the name she had cherished all her life, for five years.

These are first impressions: quick snapshots of a character for listeners to log in and remember. First impressions can be quick and simple or can grow fairly elaborate. But even a short first impression creates interest in the character.

A final example: *A cowboy rode into town*. No one would care about or remember a character with a first impression like that. Let's add more.

An aging cowboy in a trim gray shirt sat straight and tall in the saddle as he rode into town. Silver bullets glistened in his gun belt. A black mask hid his eyes. His badge proclaimed that he was no cowpoke but a Texas Ranger—a ranger who rode alone.

Now we can remember who we're taking about.

2. **Goal.** Character goals are the hidden key that unlocks the structure of a story. If a character has no goals, no wants in the story, there is no need for them to struggle or to face the conflicts before them. No need for them to risk; no need to face danger. Conflict, risk, danger, and struggle must be undertaken for a reason. That reason is a character's goal.

    We are each stuffed with more wants and goals than can be fulfilled in a lifetime. Some of our desires are noble, almost saintly, and deserve to be announced from the pulpit. Some we keep tucked away in the deepest, darkest recesses of our souls and don't share with anyone.

    We want peace on Earth, a clean environment, a new car, better rose bushes than the neighbors, a better job, more pay, more time off, a feeling of self-worth, to lose ten pounds, to eat whatever we want, smaller taxes, more government services. We want the rain to come so the grass will grow. We also want to never have to mow the lawn. We want to get involved in community projects and we want to sit home like slugs and relax in front of the TV. We want reliable justice for all and we want to personally get away with our own convenient transgressions. Human wants don't have to make sense. We could want to sky dive even though we are terrified of heights.

    If listeners are going to appreciate story characters, they have to know what those characters want in this story. If a storyteller is going to make those characters seem real and vibrant, that teller needs to clearly see what the characters want and how they are going to make that goal clear to their listeners.

    What characters want to do or get in the story and their motives for wanting it are their *story goal*. If the story is going to work, this story goal must be relevant to the intended audience. This sounds simple and obvious. Of course the main story character has a goal. "Once there was a young frog named Fernly who wanted a raspberry fudge ice cream cone." Character and goal.

    The goal tells us where to end the story. *"And so the sheriff rewarded Fernly with a double-scoop cone of raspberry fudge ice cream and little Fernly was the happiest frog in the county. The End."* Stories end either when the character reaches the goal or when they realize they will never reach the goal. Period. Those are the only two story endings there are. Goal creates ending.

    The main character's goal tells us what the story is about. "This story is about a frog who wanted an ice cream cone." The goal defines whether or not each event is relevant to this story and thereby establishes the structure of the story. It tells us how to interpret every story event. The goal gives those events meaning. The listener will interpret everything that happens as either helping or hindering Fernly from getting his ice cream cone. There is no more important information for a teller to give to listeners.

    But in many stories goals are anything but obvious. Goals are often buried and inferred. In many folk and fairy tales, character goals have been altered and/or lost over the ages so that only plot elements remain. The teller will have to infer from story events and character reactions what the main character is after.

    "Goldilocks and the Three Bears" is a good example. In the opening paragraph Goldi commits felony breaking and entering. Why does she do it? Why does she risk five to ten in the slammer or death by bear claw? Stop and ponder this delinquent girl for a moment. The story never overtly says what she wants. Ask your class to analyze Goldi's goal and see if their answers hold up.

    The three most common goals ascribed to poor Goldi are curiosity, hunger, and being tired. None makes any sense. Do you know any kids who would break *into* a house at great personal risk for a bowl of oatmeal? Most of the kids I know would break out of the house to get away from oatmeal. She can't be *that* hungry. Besides, there is no indication that she smells porridge before she busts in. Finally, if she were really hungry, wouldn't she search the cupboards for something better? And why, if she's so hungry, does she eat only the *smallest* of the three available bowls?

Curiosity makes no real sense either. Goldi doesn't act curious either inside or out. The story never says that she curiously rummages through closets, drawers, and medicine cabinet after she's inside. Besides, curiosity is an exceedingly mild emotion to spark a major vandalism and destruction spree—unless poor Goldi is uncontrollably, obsessively driven by a curiosity compulsion. The adrenaline-rush of committing ultra-dangerous crime is not a mild emotion. If she is a normal kid, the emotional charge of breaking and entering would overpower curiosity long before Goldi crossed the threshold.

Finally, put yourself in Goldi's place. You've broken into the *bears'* house. You've eaten their food. You've hung around long enough for any of the neighbors to call 911. You've smashed most of the livingroom furniture. One swipe from any paw of any resident and you're dead. Can you honestly say that at such a moment you would consider wandering upstairs to take a nap? She would have to be one cool customer to be able to sleep at a time like that!

I honestly have no idea why Goldilocks broke into that house. Was she bored and searching for mischief? Lonely and desperately reaching out for a friend? A juvenile delinquent just out for the kicks? A thoughtless girl who wandered willy-nilly anywhere without ever heeding her mother's advice or commonsense cautions?

If you want to tell the story, *you* will have to figure out why you think she broke in there. What is she after and why is she after it? Once you do, you will make that simple story instantly more powerful and engrossing. You will have allowed listeners to glimpse the main character's goal. Listeners no longer simply watch things happen. They now understand the significance of each event and become more involved in the outcome.

That's as close to magic as story planning gets. If a storyteller makes the main character and their goal seem real, relevant, and topically important to listeners, then that audience will be hooked on the story. That relevancy criterion, by the way, is why parents and teachers get away with curiosity as Goldi's goal for a kindergarten class. Five- and six-year-olds *are* curious, and they're not yet able to anticipate the consequences of their curiosity. So curiosity seems plausible and relevant to them.

No, you cannot say that Goldilocks has no goal. If Goldi goes into the bears' house, she *had* to have some reason for that action. It is the storyteller's job to uncover those reasons and motives—whether or not they are overtly stated in the story. That knowledge of the character's inner self will automatically affect the way the story will be told and make it more successful.

As a final example of the power of a goal to direct the listener's understanding, let's see what a goal might do for the Lone Ranger. Consider how differently you would view this character and the subsequent story events if, as he rides into town, he were pondering these three different goals:

1. His goal is fairness, safety, and justice for all in Texas.

2. As his hair begins to gray and thin, the Lone Ranger has been thinking a lot about how he has no 401k, no rollover IRA, and no retirement package. Now he is thinking that a bank job or two of his own would be just the nest egg to set up his golden years of putting on the golf course.

3. Just one more success. Just one more important arrest. His eyes were going bad. Arthritis was acting up in more joints than he could count. He had missed his last eight shotswith his trusty six-shooter and bungled his last two arrests. The townsfolk were beginning to talk and sadly shake their heads. He just hoped he had enough left in him to solve one more important case before he had to hang up his guns for good.

Goal defines what a story will be about. The sooner you make goal clear to listeners the better off you both will be.

3. **Conflict.** Story conflict is the composite result of several related story elements:

1. Obstacles—Flaws and Problems. The main character can't have reached their goal yet or there wouldn't be a story. A man wanted a thousand dollars. He had a thousand dollars. There's no story there. It only becomes a story if the character hasn't yet reached their goal. That means something must be keeping them from attaining that goal.

Those somethings are called obstacles and they are the springboards to launch a story. There are only two kinds of possible obstacles: those that originate from outside a character (problems) and those that originate from inside a character (flaws). If the bears come home, Goldilocks has a problem. If the cops show up and arrest her, that's a problem. Whatever drove her into the bears' house in the first place is a flaw.

A flaw is any internal drive, feeling, or motive that prevents a character from obtaining a goal. Flaws can be, but do not have to be, negative. Certainly there are enough negative flaws to fill a thousand years' worth of stories: the seven deadly sins; the flaws warned against in the ten commandments; countless possible vices: fear, hate, revenge, superstition, anger, laziness, cowardice, prejudice, lack of self-esteem, bad self-image, etc. The list seems endless.

But flaws can also be neutral (ignorance, misunderstanding, misinformation, etc.) or even positive (self-sacrifice, nobility, etc.). Putting one's family or nation ahead of one's self can be an obstacle to obtaining a personal goal as easily as fear or self-doubt. They are all flaws in the eyes of a story.

Most often, flaws and problems come coupled. That is, the onset of a problem forces a character to confront a dreaded flaw. A wise storyteller should, as the second step of learning a story, list and study all problems and flaws that beset their main character to ensure that they are relevant to the intended audience and sufficient to carry the story.

A knight of old must rescue the fair princess from an evil wizard and his henchmen dragons. But the wizard lives in the top of a twisting turret high atop a jagged mountain cliff. Our hero has a dreadful fear of heights and is allergic to dragon breath. Still, he *really* wants to save the princess . . .

Flaws and problems: They exacerbate each other and are far more formidable in tandem than either would be alone.

Finally, it is important to realize that not all problems and flaws are created equal. The bigger the problem, the deeper the flaw, the better listeners like it, and the more engrossing is the story. But how does a storyteller decide which of the obstacles in a story is "bigger?" How does a teller decide which problems they will emphasize in their telling of the story?

2. Risk and danger. It really isn't the obstacles themselves we care about. The bears Goldilocks waits for could be koala bears—declawed koala bears—tame circus-performing declawed koala bears. Takes the punch out of the story, doesn't it? The evil wizard mentioned above could be a bumbling weakling who hasn't cast a spell correctly in 20 years and is afraid of his own shadow. His dragons could be friends of Puff the Magic Dragon. The knight's fear of heights might only be activated after he eats spicy food.

    No, it isn't the actual flaws and problems we care about. It is the *risk and danger* they represent for the main character that grabs our attention. Danger is a measure of the severity of the consequences of failure (what *could* happen). Risk is a measure of the probability of failure (the *likelihood* that the danger will be realized). Increase the danger or increase the risk and the listener is more strongly captivated by the story—as long as the risk and danger are relevant to that audience.

    It is possible to have a story with little or no risk and danger. It would almost certainly be a *boring* story, but it would still be a story. I prefer to include risk and danger as core elements of a story because no one sets out to tell a boring story, and, without risk and danger, they will almost surely reach that disappointing outcome.

    Risk and danger—relevant, unavoidable risk and danger—are what grab listeners and won't let them go. Search for ways to increase the flaws and problems that beset the main character. Search for ways to increase and emphasize the physical and emotional risk and danger associated with each obstacle.

Typically, storytellers think of, and work with, flaws, problems, and their associated risk and danger as a single, connected whole. The term *jeopardy* is often used to describe this powerful foursome. Jeopardy creates conflict. At its heart, then, every story centers on a character and the jeopardy they must face.

The bigger you can make the story jeopardy seem when you tell a story, the more listeners will care about the character and the better they will like the story. Search every story for obstacles and try to locate and envision as much risk and danger as possible for each.

An example will be helpful. We'll use the third of the possible goals listed earlier for the Lone Ranger to represent what he is thinking and feeling . . . *as he wearily sits on the edge of a creaking rented bed in the town hotel, scrapes mud off his boots, and rubs the small of his back where his sciatica is acting up. He polishes his bullets, hobbles downstairs for an early dinner, and chats with Miss Lilly outside in a rocking chair as the sun sets.*

We're all eagerly waiting for something to happen. In truth, *plenty* has happened. Everything mentioned in the previous paragraph is an event, a plot element. We feel that nothing has happened because there is no conflict to launch a story.

> *Dudly Dust, bank night clerk, races down the street screaming that there is a bank robbery.*

Now *there's* a problem and some possible conflict. Our hopes rise.

> *L. Ranger dashes around the corner and smacks into Old Milton Milktoast, toothless, 84 years old, senile, and blind, who has just made off with $8.13 from the bank. L. Ranger tucks him under one arm and hustles him to jail. The case is closed.*

Not satisfying, eh? We had a problem but no accompanying risk and danger. Let's add some and see the difference.

> *Dudly Dust, bank night clerk, races down the street screaming that there is a bank robbery in which the life savings of every person in town is being stolen. If the robbers succeed the town is doomed. He also waves a note that says that Milton Milktoast and his gang of 12, blood-thirsty, heavily armed, vicious brutes have planted 1,000,000 pounds of dynamite under the town that will incinerate every living person in 15 minutes and that they have also tied up the sheriff in barbed wire and laid him on the railroad tracks where an express train is due to rumble through in six minutes.*
>
> *The Lone Ranger hears this news and is racked by waves of self-doubt. Can he stop the bank robbery, save the sheriff, and find the dynamite, all in time? Worse, he doesn't have time to climb back upstairs to fetch his guns. He'll have to do the job with what he has on him—one silver bullet and a pocket comb.*
>
> *Miss Lilly cries, "You're our hero. . . . And you better get it right this time!"*

Now we're hooked. We *need* to find out what happens. Will he do it? Can he do it? *How* will he do it? That is the effect of combining character, goal, and serious jeopardy (problems, flaws, and the associated risk and danger).

As you read a story you want to tell, write down the main character's goal and list all jeopardy items you can find in, or infer from, the text. Learning these will go a long way toward making the story work when you tell it.

4. **Struggles—action, reaction.** Sir Isaac Newton first presented this concept as one of his universal laws of motion. For every action there is a reaction. It is a basic law of nature and of characters.

Story characters must do both to seem real. They must act and they must react. Struggles are the actions a character takes to overcome conflict. No action, no story.

The character must *do* something. It is during these struggles that risk and danger are confronted and realized and that excitement and tension build. Now that the story is understood in terms of the main character's core elements, the plot is both easier to learn and remember, and makes more sense to an audience.

Listeners want to, and need to, know what this character is willing to do and risk to reach a goal. This is the final glue that binds us to characters and their stories. We judge characters by their actions. We relate to characters in large measure through what they are willing to do.

The actions, or struggles, of a character will almost certainly be well documented in any written story. Struggles are not inferred as often as are goals and some elements of jeopardy. There will be no need to search for the actions of a character.

Reactions are a special subset of actions. Reactions are those unconscious, automatic movements (gestures, facial expressions, and utterances) made at the moment something happens, or at least within the first few seconds after it happens.

When anything happens we automatically react. Your basketball team scores a basket. You react. You never plan to do it. You never consciously think about it. You simply do it. You react.

The other team scores. You react again, differently. Someone trips and sprawls on the floor in front of you. You react. You laugh, stoop to help, flush with embarrassment, or snub your nose and turn away. A car crashes through your livingroom wall, you win the lottery, you get caught for speeding. You react. In whatever way fits your personality, you react.

There are three reasons I mention reactions:

1. There is nothing listeners crave to see more than how characters react to emotionally charged and stressful moments. Watch a live storytelling event and you will see that the moments when the audience howls with laughter or sighs with poignant sorrow will be moments when they have seen a character react.

2. Character reactions are a primary guide to understanding the personality of a character. If listeners see how a character typically reacts, they feel that they know that character better and will care about a character's story more.

3. Reactions are far easier to *do* while you tell a story (and are far more successful) than they are to *write* when you write a story. Character reactions will often be mentioned in the printed versions of stories. But they are supremely powerful moments if you emphasize them during live storytellings.

Reactions don't tell a character's feeling (She was sad). They show what she says and does. (Does her lip quiver? Does she clench her fists and tighten her shoulders? Does she laugh to cover the deep hurt? Do her eyes cloud over or blaze with passion?) Those are reactions.

My advice? See if you can figure out how your main character typically reacts. In your mind, try to *see* them reacting to various situations. If it is consistent with your natural style, if it is comfortable for you, include their reactions to situations whether or not they are written in the text of the story you are going to tell.

These are the elements of the critical core character layer. They define a story and make listeners care about the story and the character. This is the most important character layer. But there are four others to help you create an interesting and compelling story character.

*L*ayers of the Onion

KEY TOPICS IN THIS SECTION

> How the other four layers make a character seem real and interesting

> Using character information to help you learn (and remember) a story

> Finding, recognizing, and using character information

A character's core layer is critically important to the story, to the character, and to your listeners. I believe that studying the core layer of the main character is the surest, easiest, and fastest road to learning a story.

But that one layer does not build a complete, interesting character. The other four layers of character information (sensory information, personality, history, and activity) flesh out the character and make them real and complete.

Your goal in absorbing information from the other four layers is to make sure you can see the main characters of your story in your mind—see their face, see them move, hear them talk. There is no checklist of exactly what you need to know from these other four layers. What you need varies dramatically from story to story and from teller to teller. However, the more you know about the characters, the easier it will be for you to learn, remember, and tell their story.

There is a trade-off: more time spent envisioning (creating) details about the character while you learn the story produces a payoff of easier and more comfortable telling later. The better you can see the characters in your mind, the better listeners will construct those characters in their minds, which, after all, is the point of telling the story. As you gain storytelling experience, you will gain a better feeling for how well you need to see your central characters.

My recommendation: Be sure as you read a story that you can vividly see the main characters in your mind. If aspects of these characters are fuzzy to you then start to infer or create information to fill in the gaps. If character motives are unclear, create enough of a history to understand why they do what they do. If you struggle to picture the character, pretend they are there with you and describe what you would see, hear, and smell. If there seem to be great gaps in what they do, invent whatever is missing. Part III includes several exercises to assist in this process.

There is no fixed amount of character detail for these layers of information you *need* to know to tell a story. The question is: Knowing your individual style and personality, how comfortable and assured do you have to be to be willing to tell the story? The answer is different for every teller. If while practicing a story you feel overly tentative and unsure, study the characters more. Invent more detailed information for the five character layers. Most teacher-tellers find that this makes it much easier for them to tell.

It is true that you won't actually say very many of the details you have created about your characters when you tell their story. But character information is never wasted. Strong images of the characters in your mind affect the tone of voice, body movement, gestures, and facial expression you automatically use, which all help to communicate a sense of the characters to listeners.

Beginning with the outside layer of this character onion and working our way in, the other four character layers are:

1. **Sensory elements.** Sensory elements include any information you could learn directly through your own sensory organs: what something looks like, sounds like, smells like, feels like, and tastes like.

   Sensory information creates the physical reality of a character. It includes how they dress, their grooming habits, prominent features, expressions, how they laugh, how they keep and structure their environment, how they walk, sit, and talk. It includes the sound of their voice, the words they use, and the way they structure sentences. It includes what they eat, how much they eat, and how they eat. It includes scars, bumps, twitches, habits (nervous or otherwise), and whether others would notice them if they walked into a crowded room. It includes their physical strength as well as the strength of their jaw, whether they maintain eye contact as well as the color and shape of their eyes.

Most of this information will *not* be reported in the text of a story you plan to tell. You will have to infer the detail you see in your mind based on the information that *is* included. You will probably tell the details that were included in the text plus a few you add on to make the character clear to your listeners. The rest of the details you create help direct the *way* you talk about the characters (vocal tone, facial expressions, body postures, physical characterizations, etc.) and make it easier for you to remember the story.

2. **Personality.** A character's personality is a description of how they interact with the world. It is how characters deal with other characters. Are they honest, trustworthy, sullen, cruel, kind, glib, shy, quiet, boisterous, introverted, extroverted, foolhardy, or timid? Are they secretive, sensitive, hard-nosed, apologetic, or quick to blame? Those and hundreds of others are personality traits. Combined they create a personality profile.

    The personality layer includes more than just those one-word labels. Personality includes what excites a character, what bores them, their passions, their self-image, their sense of humor (or lack thereof). It includes what they are afraid of, what they long for, their loves, their hates, their doubts, and their beliefs. These personality elements are important motives for a character's actions and reactions.

    Personality is often implied by the events, dialog, and actions of a story rather than being overtly stated. Listeners need more explicit information than do readers (they can't stop a telling to ponder what they have heard). Tellers should absorb the story information, draw their own personality-related conclusions, and decide how to make those conclusions clear to their listeners.

3. **Activity.** The activity layer is really a subset of history. It is, in effect, present history. It is an accounting of the present pattern of activity in the character's life. It is a listing of what they do. Activity includes the character's job, hobbies, chores, habits, and games. It also can include such information as their possessions and how often they wash their hands and brush their teeth.

    You shouldn't need to add to the activity information presented in a story unless you find yourself wondering about what else a character does. When you do, invent an answer to your own question. It is far better for a teller to create an answer than to still have a question about a main character when they tell the story.

4. **History.** Writers often call a character's history their "back story," or what happened to the character before this story starts to make them the character they are today. Why should a storyteller care about a character's history? What has happened to a character in the past, and how they interpret those events, is a (if not *the*) major determinant of their present beliefs, attitudes, goals, fears, hopes, and personality affectations. A character's history tells us why they are as they are and why they do what they do. Who you are today is determined by your thoughts about and reactions to what has happened to you in the past.

    Sometimes elements of a character's history are included in the text of a story—and are usually powerful and meaningful bits of information. I suggest that you additionally consider a character's history only when you find yourself wondering about that character's motives. "Why did they say that, or do that, or think that?"

    You are free to infer a character's past events to explain current feelings, beliefs, and motives. You're the one doing the telling. That makes it *your* story. Usual targets in defining a back story include traumatic moments, major life events, the character's origins and family structure, how they have been treated by others, the history of their relationships and friendships, how they feel they have performed at work, chores, and studies, and significant moments from their past.

*E*valuating a Story

KEY TOPICS IN THIS SECTION

❯ Don't tell what won't work

❯ Questions to evaluate the potential of every story

❯ Picking stories that you will tell well

You read the gripping story of two parents so desperate for food and so at the end of their rope that they plan to abandon their own children in the forest to wander on their own as orphans. You say, "Wow, great story!" Then a nagging voice in the back of your mind adds, "But even in a story I could never act like Hansel's and Gretel's mother and be that cruel. . . . And I hate having old haggard crones for witches. I could never portray her that way. But what would I make her look like and act like? . . . And Hansel and Gretel sort of mush together in my mind. I don't see two distinct characters."

Those doubts are warning signs that Hansel and Grettel may not be a good story for you to tell, that the answer to the first of the two great questions for evaluating whether or not to tell a story (**Will *I* be able to tell this story well?**) might be "no." It's not that you couldn't figure out how to reinvent the characters and restructure the story to make the characters and events fit with your style and be comfortable for you. Sure you could. But that takes time and effort. Do you want to take the time to dig into these characters ito make the story work for you or do you want to set it aside and find one that is already well-suited for you to tell and whose characters you instantly understand?

How do you decide if you will be able to tell this story well?

➤ Do you like the story and would you like to learn it well enough to tell?

➤ Can you vividly see the characters in your mind when you read the story?

➤ Do you understand the characters and would you be comfortable portraying them?

➤ With your particular style of natural telling will you be able to present these characters and their struggles to your listeners effectively? (If, for example, it is a raucous farce full of physical comedy and you are a quiet teller, the answer is probably "no.")

If you answer yes to these four questions, this is a story for you! If you answer yes to three, glare skeptically at the story and decide if the effort to bring the fourth question to a yes answer will be worth it. Often it is, but not always.

Second, **is this a good story for my particular listeners to hear**? It is critically important that a story be relevant to and appropriate for its audience. How do you know if this is an appropriate story for your class?

➤ Will the characters be relevant and interesting for my students?

➤ Will their goals, obstacles, and risks and dangers be relevant, appropriate, and interesting for my students?

➤ Are the story's actions and events appropriate for my students?

If the answer to all three is "yes," this story will work well. If the answer to one question is "no," or is a qualified yes, decide if you can shift the emphasis of the story (emphasize some aspects and events and de-emphasize others) and shift the way you tell it to make it relevant and appropriate.

My "Mud Puddle" story serves as a good example. The story is about a girl playing outside who is jumped on by a mud puddle. She runs back inside and gets in trouble with her mother for getting muddy. She takes a bath and heads back outside for round two. For primary age students the mud puddle and the jeopardy it represents are real, so I emphasize the outside part of the story and tell it as if I believed it were gospel truth.

However, I have also told this story to fifth-grade audiences. The mud puddle is silly farce to them and only mildly interesting. When I tell it for this age group, I de-emphasize the outdoors part of the story and tell it as if I didn't really believe that a mud puddle jumped on her either. It is the indoors part of the story that is real and relevant to fifth graders. A child does something wrong, gets in trouble, and makes up a wild excuse to talk her way out of it. That scenario is very familiar to fifth graders. They bump into it all the time.

PART III

LEARNING AND TELLING MADE EASY

The Step-by-Step
Super Simple System

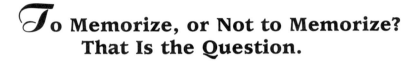

*T*o Memorize, or Not to Memorize? That Is the Question.

KEY TOPICS IN THIS SECTION

> ❯ What happens when you memorize a story
> ❯ Six reasons to change your mind and your natural habit

Be honest. If you had to tell "The Three Little Pigs" tomorrow and held a copy of the story in your hands today, what would you do? Would you analyze the characters to understand core character information and motive as well as character personality and physical and vocal characteristics? Would you think about how to merge this story with your natural storytelling style? Would you search for the information you need to decide *how* you will tell the story?

Probably not.

What *would* you do? Probably you would try to memorize the words of the story, muttering "Not by the hairs on my chinny-chin-chin" as you drift off to sleep and hope that you'll remember them long enough to blurt them back out the next day. Isn't that what you'd really want to do? (And you'd fall victim to the lure of The Lemon List.)

In truth, doesn't memorizing an author's words sound like an appropriate thing to do? After all, the words in the book were what drew you to the story. They were enough to make you like the story. Why won't they work on your class? Besides, *shouldn't* you present the author's words to your class? Who are you to rewrite the story?

35

However, your class isn't going to read a story as you did. They are going to *listen* to the story. You aren't going to present a manuscript to them, you are going to *tell* the story. You have changed media from printed narrative to oral storytelling. And that change radically changes the expectations and demands of those receiving the story.

We don't expect to see the gestures and facial expressions of the author when we read a book. We don't expect to hear and use the author's tonal, pitch, pace, and other vocal variations to interpret the story's words. We expect to rely exclusively on the words, themselves, when we read.

When you speak, listeners *expect* to receive a visual and auditory banquet of information to amplify the words of the story. They *expect* to receive much of the information of the story through channels outside the specific words. If you want to deliver only the words, have your students read the story for themselves. When you tell a story, *how* you say it is a critical element that cannot be ignored. It represents most of The Golden List of listener needs.

Still, the urge to memorize a string of words and rely on them to carry the storytelling is strong in most people. We are terrified of not knowing what to say and don't know any other way of preparing than to memorize. However, memorizing undercuts your storytelling in six important ways that almost guarantee you will not successfully, effectively tell the story:

1. **Memorizing is hard to do and it's time consuming.** Try it. See how long it takes you to memorize the words on this page. One page is only a small part of a complete story. Memorizing every word in a story is a frightfully slow and labor-intensive process. It is a still longer process to *convince* yourself that you have memorized the story and can actually remember the words—*all* of the words—in order, on command, when you perform the story.

2. **The words of a memorized story don't last.** Once you have memorized this one page, see how well you remember it tomorrow. Can you still recite it in two days? In four? Even if you can, I bet you're having to concentrate so hard on remembering the words that you don't sound natural and enthusiastic when you say them.

   Memorized words fade from the conscious brain almost faster than they can be learned and must be re-learned and re-memorized at regular intervals. Memorizing is mentally exhaustive and inefficient. The idea, theme, and main events of the story may stick in your head. But that is a far cry from correctly remembering every word you need to say to repeat the complete story.

3. **Memorizing a story makes it extremely difficult to tell it with any energy, enthusiasm, and expression—key elements of The Golden List.** The first two problems waste your time. This one undermines your ability to tell the story. If all of your energy is diverted into the effort to recall a delicate, mile-long string of words, little or none is left over to put into the telling of those words. Memorized stories tend to be delivered in listless, boring monotones.

   Try Exercise 3.1, *The Memorization Blues* (page 140), to prove this phenomenon to yourself. Concentrating on just the words quickly detaches a teller from a story. If a teller's focus is on remembering words instead of on the emotions, characters, scenes, and events of a story, it is almost impossible to match the *way* the story is being told to the emotions of the characters in the story. It will never sound real and compelling.

4. **The specific words a teller says are not the most important source of information for listeners.** In most moments of a story, there are a wide variety of wordings that will effectively communicate the story as long as the *way* those words are said effectively matches the emotion of the story characters and carries the enthusiasm of the teller. An audience listens more to *how* you say it than to *what* you say. When you place all your focus on *what* you say, you no longer serve listeners' needs.

5. **Memorizing a string of words prevents you from using your natural storytelling style.** This is the most damning objection of all to memorizing. No one memorizes the words for the stories that have happened to them. You probably have never written down or tried to learn the words for a personal story. Words are not what you naturally recall, focus on, and use as the prompts for telling your own stories. Memorizing words blocks you from using the natural style and system you have developed and perfected over a lifetime of telling experience.

6. **You will never fully convince yourself that you have successfully memorized a story until you have told it a number of times, something you may never do.** During the first few tellings of a memorized story a nasty little voice will whine at you from inside your head, "You're gonna forget it. Get ready to blow it. You won't remember this next part." That voice creates enough stress to virtually guarantee that you *will* forget.

   Don't memorize a story. It is destructive, hard to do, and counterproductive. However, if you *don't* memorize, you will change the author's words. Is that okay? Can you get into trouble if you change them? The author was the one who wrote the story. Don't they know the best way to say it?

   No, they don't. Hopefully they discovered the best way to *write* it. If it is that very wording you want to share with your class and if you feel that the author's words are too perfect and precious to change, then read it. Don't tell it.

   If you are going to tell it, you are changing the medium of delivery and must adjust the wording accordingly. When you tell a story, you must make that story sound real and natural coming out of your mouth. Formal, narrative English will not sound real and natural. If you are gong to tell it, put it in your own words. Otherwise, you are acting, forcing yourself to try to make someone else's words sound natural coming out of you. That's not storytelling. The question of the ethics and legality of telling a copyrighted story we will address later. Here we are still focused on the mechanics of getting the story told.

   There is a better, easier, less stressful way than memorizing—unless memorization is your natural storytelling style. Would you normally say to friends and family as you burst in the front door with a juicy experience to share, "The greatest thing just happened to me. I can't wait to tell you about it. But first I'm going to go into my room, write it down and memorize the words. Then I'll come back and tell you?"

   If you normally, naturally do that, feel free to ignore the Super Simple system and memorize your stories. For everyone else, it's time to see how a Super Simple storyteller approaches learning a story.

*W*hat Super Simple Tellers Learn

KEY TOPICS IN THIS SECTION

> ❯ What you really need to learn from a story
> ❯ The elements that make a storytelling work
> ❯ How to learn the things that make it easy

In the Super Simple Storytelling system you will still use your natural oral communication style and will not try to adapt it or you to fit a story. The Super Simple system will allow you to extend the range of this natural system into stories you obtain from books (that didn't happen to you) and to survive—even thrive on— moments of discomfort during a storytelling without drifting into nervous, destructive habits. That is, Super Simple Storytelling will allow you to violate one or both of the rigid conditions (listed earlier) under which your natural storytelling system flourishes and still have that system efficiently control your storytelling and deliver an effective performance:

1.   Make sure you have an appropriate, relevant story to tell. It will better engage your listeners and make you more comfortable in the telling.

2.   Learn the story in such a way that you coax your natural system to disengage its safety protocols and function even though the story didn't happen to you and even though you expect to feel regularly uncomfortable during the telling.

3.   Learn to identify and recognize your natural nervous, destructive habits so that, when you *do* become nervous and your natural system threatens to shut down, you can break the lifelong pattern and re-engage your natural system's drivers.

How do you learn a story, then, if you don't memorize it? What should you learn? How should you learn it?

Did you ever wonder why a story that happened to you 30 years ago pops back into your mind at the blink of an eye with no rehearsal, study, outlining, or note cards, while a story you spent the entire weekend trying to learn disappears from your mind by the time you're halfway to school on Monday? It is because you learned the two types of stories differently.

I know. You're thinking, "Of course I learned them differently. One happened to me and one didn't. I *experienced* the one that happened to me."

My answer is, "So what?" You still had to learn it. That is, you had to file specific information in your brain to be able to store the memory of the event and to recall that memory. You still had to recall specific images and information out of memory into your conscious mind when you told that story. That's exactly what you do with a story you find in a book. You file specific information in your memory banks and try to recall it into your conscious mind when you tell. The only difference is *what* you choose to file away and later recall for those two stories.

Let's begin by looking at what happens when you memorize a story and try to tell it. I have drawn a simple diagram of the process (see Figure 3.1). Yes, I know. Figure 3.1 is a system diagram or flow chart. I offer this solution for those who tremble at the sight of this frightful enemy: Don't think of them as flow charts. They are just picture outlines. We all like pictures. We're all accustomed to outlines. Flow charts are simple picture outlines, an organized visual way to walk through a series of steps in a specific order.

Figure 3.1. Memorize and Tell.

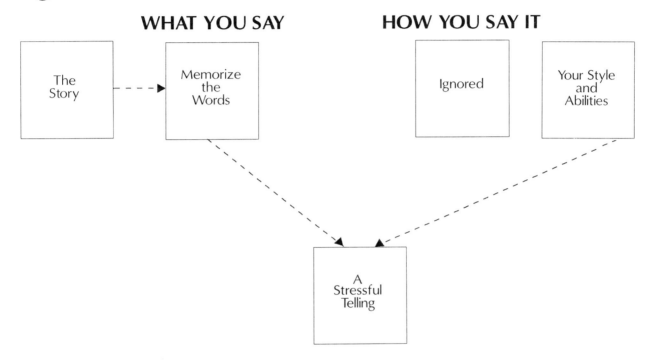

Now to see what Figure 3.1 shows us. First, there are always two parts to a story: *what* you say and *how* you say it. We learned that from the definition of storytelling. The teller must plan for both, either subconsciously (as with personal stories) or consciously (as with stories from books).

However, when a teller memorizes a string of words, they never account for *how* they will make those words sound real within the limits of their natural storytelling style. They never think about *how* they will make the telling of this story comfortable for them. They never think about *how* they can use the strengths of their natural storytelling style to make the story come alive and be vibrant and effective. In short, they never plan for the merger of *what* they say and *how* they will say it. However, whether or not the teller has planned *how* they will say the story, they still say it. Their voice, face, body, and hands will have to stand in front of listeners and do something.

Without having provided the necessary information to allow that natural style to function, the teller's hands, face, voice, and body don't know what to do to emotionally match what is being said. The result almost certainly will be that the teller's natural, successful style shuts down (the two conditions for its operation have been violated), and the teller drifts quickly into their self-destructive nervous habits. The telling is stressful for the teller, boring for listeners, and generally a total flop.

Try Exercise 3.2, *Stand and Watch* (page 142), with your class to create an inkling of what the stress feels like that is produced by this type of inadequately planned telling. The stress students feel while having to simply stand and do nothing provides a taste of what it is like to face an audience without knowing what to do. It is most unnerving and worth avoiding.

Now let's see what happens when you approach the process of learning a story a better way.

As a Super Simple teller, you will learn those aspects of a story that let you provide the elements of The Golden List for your listeners. You will acknowledge and adhere to the definition of storytelling. Both of these statements mean that you must find a way to use your natural storytelling style even though you will apparently violate one, if not both, of the criteria for its operation.

How do you do that? Actually, it's simple.

What do you learn for your *own* stories that allows your natural storytelling style to function admirably? Not sure? Try it. Remember a story (or incident) that happened to you when you were a child. Quickly tell it to someone, anyone.

What did you remember about the events of that story? I bet it wasn't words. No, you remembered *sensory details*, sensory images (sights, sounds, smells, etc.). As those images popped into your mind you described them one by one, verbally bridging between images to create a smooth story line. Remember, research has shown that sensory details trigger memory. Sensory details are what you are used to storing in your memory. Details are what allow memory recall to happen. Details are what support your telling. Those same sensory details also happen to be the number one item on The Golden List.

Use Exercise 3.3, *Describe the Scene* (page 144), to demonstrate the effect of being able to see vivid sensory details on how a story is told (and especially on the gestures used during the telling). When a teller intimately knows what they are describing, when they can see it in detail in their minds, they appear more confident and comfortable. Their gestures are definite and provide more information. They look like they are telling the truth. The story sounds real. Compare those characteristics with The Golden List.

Figure 3.2, "A Better Way," is a picture outline of a better way to approach the process of telling a story—the Super Simple way.

1. **Stories are all about characters and their associated core information.** The Super Simple teller finds and learns the character information lying at the heart of every story.

2. **Natural storytelling is based on vivid multi-sensory details.** These details are what Super Simple tellers learn from each scene and event of a story and file into memory.

3. **But a Super Simple teller goes farther than just learning the characters and details of the story (what they are going to say) by asking two key questions of themselves.** These questions are designed to help the teller decide *how* they will present the body of character information and detail that they have extracted from the story.

    ➤ Based on my comfortable and natural oral style, what can/will I do to bring the *story characters* to vivid, powerful life for my listeners?

    ➤ Knowing the strengths and limits of my own natural style, how can I effectively convey the *emotional flow and energy* of the scenes of this story to my listeners?

Figure 3.2. A Better Way.

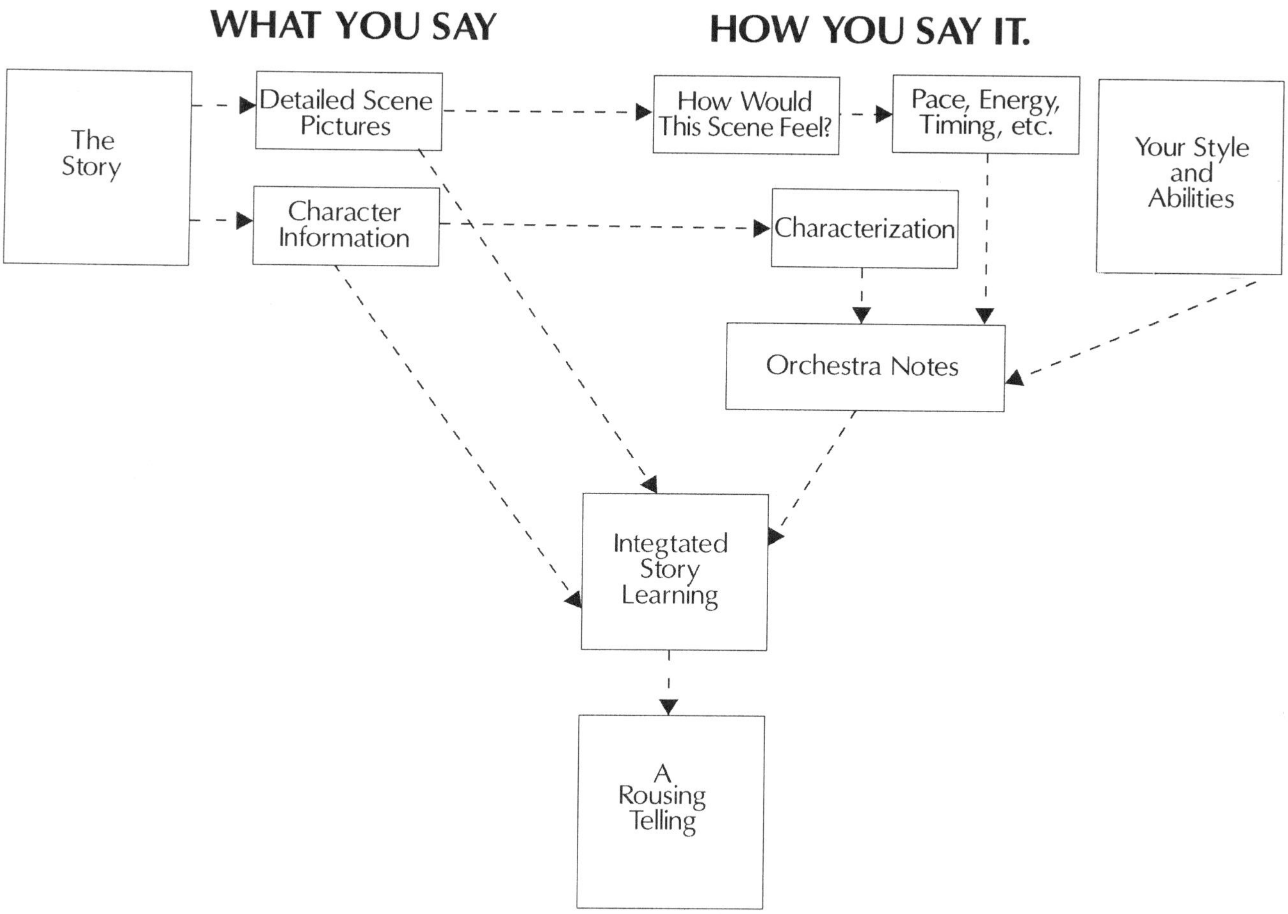

WHAT YOU SAY   **HOW YOU SAY IT.**

```
┌──────────┐    ┌──────────────┐      ┌──────────────┐  ┌──────────────┐      ┌──────────┐
│   The    │--▶ │Detailed Scene│----▶ │ How Would    │▶ │Pace, Energy, │      │Your Style│
│  Story   │    │  Pictures    │      │This Scene Feel?│ │Timing, etc.  │      │   and    │
│          │    └──────────────┘      └──────────────┘  └──────────────┘      │Abilities │
│          │    ┌──────────────┐      ┌──────────────┐                        └──────────┘
│          │--▶ │ Character    │----▶ │Characterization│
└──────────┘    │ Information  │      └──────────────┘
                └──────────────┘
                        ┌──────────────┐
                        │Orchestra Notes│
                        └──────────────┘
                        ┌──────────────┐
                        │  Integtated  │
                        │    Story     │
                        │   Learning   │
                        └──────────────┘
                        ┌──────────────┐
                        │      A       │
                        │   Rousing    │
                        │   Telling    │
                        └──────────────┘
```

The answers to these questions I call Orchestra Notes, a merging of the story with the teller's natural storytelling strengths, preferences, and tendencies. Orchestra Notes are filed in memory along with story details. Now when you tell, the key story information flows back into your conscious mind like a multimedia, multi-sensory slide show (just as it does during the telling of your own stories). With that story information come the appropriate Orchestra Notes, which direct the way you tell the story so that you effectively match how you say it to what you say and so that you stay within the comfort zone of your natural style.

Wow! Could it really be that easy? Could it really work?

Yes, and yes. Remember, you already know how to tell stories. You simply must make that process conscious so that you can extend it to stories that didn't happen to you and into situations that might not be completely comfortable.

That is the essence of the Super Simple Storytelling system. That's what Super Simple tellers do. The following sections detail exactly how they do it.

Remember, Super Simple Storytelling is not acting. You will not try to mimic the performance style of some other teller whom you have seen and whom you thought told their stories very well. You will not try to be the best, most versatile, and most powerful storyteller in America. You will not try to tell every kind of story even if it isn't comfortable for you. You *will* try to be the most effective and consistent storyteller you can naturally be while telling those stories that you feel you can effectively tell.

$\mathcal{M}$eet the Orchestra

KEY TOPICS IN THIS SECTION

> ❯ What your storytelling orchestra is and why you should care
> ❯ What the orchestra players do and how to ignore them

Earlier I mentioned one of the "big secrets" of storytelling: If the audience believes that you believe in your own story, then they, too, will believe. What information do they use to make this critical assessment? They study the *way* you tell your story. Do you appear confident, natural, and comfortable? Are you infusing your telling with a sense of energy? with enjoyment? Does the way you tell it emotionally match what you are telling?

These things we have covered before. But what *exactly* do audiences watch to make this assessment? They watch your facial expression, body posture, and movement, gestures, and nervous motion or action. They also listen to the tone, volume, pace, pitch, and variations of your voice. Those are the tools you use to tell a story just as a painter uses brushes, smears of acrylic paint, and canvas, just as a writer uses paper and words.

An analogy: Telling a story is like the performance of a piano concerto by a symphony orchestra in the spacious Hollywood Bowl. Picture the 86-piece orchestra wearing subdued black tuxedos, arched in wide semi-circles around a golden grand piano, 200 spotlights lighting it as bright as a second sun. The pianist is perched on his bench in flowing tails as you, the conductor, stand at the podium and lead with your flashing baton. An appreciative crowd of 10,000 is stuffed into chairs and packed along the hillside to listen.

If the piano played alone, it would sound a trifle thin—technically flawless and pleasant, intellectually stimulating, but lacking the depth, complexity, and substance to make the listener's heart soar. What amplifies, expands on, interprets, and fills out the piano is that 86-piece orchestra. It is that orchestra that lifts the music to the heavens and carries every heart with it.

In our analogy, the piano is the words of the story, *what* you say. The orchestra is *how* you say it. The two must flow together. But it is the orchestra that the audience emotionally connects with.

Now let's extend the analogy to describe how most tellers tell. You, the conductor, gather the orchestra three weeks before the performance date and say, "Listen, guys; gals, I have to work with the piano between now and the show, so I'm going to leave you on your own to rehearse. You're professionals. I trust you to be prepared. I trust you so much that I don't even have to give you the music to practice. You each show up and play what you think best."

As you raise your baton in front of an expectant crowd, the pianist begins to spin out his well-rehearsed part. (You say the correct words.) Each member of the orchestra, having been left on their own, begins to play: 86 different pieces in 86 different keys and at 86 different tempos. It sounds like abominable caterwauling. The audience boos and you sadly shake your head. "I trusted them and they let me down."

No. You let the orchestra down by not giving them sheet music to follow. But before we see how to successfully employ this orchestra without spending hours practicing in front of a mirror or taking acting classes, we should meet the members of your personal storytelling orchestra. Remember that they, like professional union members of the orchestra, have an iron-clad contract. You cannot perform without them and they *will* play loud and clear at every performance. It's in their contract. If you don't give them the music to play to match what you say, they will play whatever they feel like at the moment.

Your four-member orchestra consists of your voice, face, body, and hands. Professional tellers also have to consider the size and shape of their performance space, its acoustics and lighting, the distance from audience to teller, the shape and density of the audience, and the effect each of these characteristics of the telling space will have on how the story will be received.

You won't be as concerned with these considerations. Mostly you will tell in your classroom. You and your students are already intimately familiar with it. Most of the time you won't want to stop class to rearrange furniture for a story that was supposed to be a smooth-flowing part of a lesson block anyway.

Some teachers who hold regular storytelling times do pull the students forward in a tighter knot at the teacher's feet or gather them on a rug in the back of the room. Some dim the lights and close the blinds to block out the outside world during story time. These types of maneuvers can be effective in isolating storytelling time from the rest of the school day activity. But they are certainly not essential and I would recommend that you not spend much time and energy on the telling space until you are comfortable with and consistent in mastering the four main members of your storytelling orchestra.

Your goal is to become aware of what it feels like to use and control your orchestra. Learn what they feel like and what they do while you are expressing various emotions. *Then (and this is the real goal of all Super Simple tellers) learn how to ignore them while you tell but still have them play superbly.*

Your perpetual storytelling homework is to watch yourself and others around you to consciously see exactly what you do with your orchestra players to express each emotional state. Those conscious pictures will make it much easier to later forget all about your orchestra and still have them successfully perform their part of the story.

I have already introduced several exercises designed to help you become more aware of your orchestra and of your natural relationship with these players while you tell. Exercises 1.1, *The Wave Game*, and 1.2, *What'd You Have for Dinner?*, both serve this purpose. So do Exercises 3.2, *Stand and Watch* (page 142), and 3.3 (page 144), *Describe the Scene*. I have included nine additional exercises (3.4 through 3.12) specifically designed to develop a conscious awareness of what it feels like to control your storytelling orchestra.

I believe that the first three of these exercises—3.4, *Say It How?* (page 146), 3.5, *I Forgot My Homework* (page 149), and 3.6, *You Want Me To Go There.?* (page 151)—are particularly powerful and should be used to introduce the concept of orchestra control and manipulation for all new tellers and for all students. Every participant who tries these three simple exercises must be impressed by how expertly and perfectly their natural storytelling style is able to direct their orchestra to express even complex combinations of emotional and attitudinal states. I routinely see people laugh during the later stages of *You Want Me To Go There* and say, "I can't do this!" And yet their natural storytelling system successfully does it automatically and continually every day.

Exercises 3.7 through 3.12 are fun and effective exercises for understanding the function of the storytelling orchestra and for gaining more conscious awareness of it and control over it. They are not ordered as a fixed progression. Rather, they may be used at any time as tools to assist in gaining more conscious awareness of and control over the teller's orchestra and in becoming more comfortable with the process of storytelling and oral communication.

I have included one additional exercise in this section, Exercise 3.13, *Interrupter* (page 167), a fun and very telling game for you and your students to play. It is devised to isolate the partners' mental orientation and thinking about two stories into the two separate hemispheres of the brain. The first story being invented and told is obviously frivolous and mindless. It is just for fun and is pure right-brain activity. It is outlandish, non-sensible, full of energy and silliness, and is extremely fun to be part of.

Right-brain stories are like a kindergartner's stories: fun, energetic, and with absolutely no point. After 10 minutes of their impassioned ramblings you want to scream out, "What's the point?" The kindergartner will look at you as if you were crazy. To them the joy of telling is the point. That's all the point they need.

By changing the rules for the second round of *Interrupter*, the partners are made to feel responsible for their new story. That change shifts their thinking to left-brain logic and order. The resulting stories usually have more organization, cause-and-effect sequencing, and character development. They are also quieter, duller, and lack life and fun.

From the *Interrupter* game it is clear that the left brain controls the plot flow, facts, order, structure, and logic of a story. In other words, the left brain controls *what* is said. The right brain controls the energy, characterization, humor, passion, and emotion of a story, or *how* it is said. We need *both* to make our storytelling work. Your orchestra is the tool you use to project *how* a story will be told.

$\mathcal{M}$eet the Conductor

KEY TOPICS IN THIS SECTION

> Who your conductor is and what they do
> The rest of what you naturally remember
> How to successfully ignore conductor and orchestra while you tell

In the previous section I referred to you as the conductor. But are you? Do you consciously direct your storytelling orchestra while they play? The goal mentioned in that section was to become aware of the orchestra so that you could forget all about them while you tell and turn their control over to an orchestra conductor. But who is that conductor who decides when you will change tone, pace, or vocal pitch? Who directs your gestures and shifts in facial expression?

Not you. Not really. In *The Wave Game* and in *What'd You Have for Dinner?*, we saw that we are consciously unaware of those aspects of our storytelling. In *Say It How?* and in *You Want Me to Go There?* we saw how difficult it is to try to exert conscious control over this well-rehearsed orchestral machine.

Who, then, controls your orchestra and decides *how* you say what you say? Of course everyone grudgingly admits that they control their own telling, as if reluctantly accepting some onerous responsibility. However, that begs the question. How, *exactly*, do you do it if you really do control your orchestra?

Think back on the story I asked you to recall in the previous section. What did you remember besides scenic detail? *You also remembered how you felt at each moment as the incident unfolded.*

Now think about the job description for this orchestral conductor. What do they control?

How you say it.

Be more specific.

The conductor controls what the orchestra does to express an emotional state.

Correct. The emotion you express at each moment of the story is how you tell it. For successful storytelling, this expressed emotion matches the emotional state of the story characters and also expresses your (the storyteller's) emotional reaction to the story (confident, seemed to be enjoying yourself, natural—the reasons people voted during the *What Makes It Real?* game).

The conductor controls what your orchestra does to express an emotional state. So who is capable of accomplishing that feat?

Your emotional memory of an event. That's who.

You remember feeling scared during part of a story and so automatically portray being scared while you tell that part of the story. You remember being happy and automatically portray that emotion while you tell. That's why one of the conditions for successful functioning of your natural system is that the story had to happen to you. That gives you an emotional memory to serve as orchestra conductor. Having an emotional memory of the events in a story is the key to successfully engaging and directing your storytelling orchestra.

But what if you're telling "Hansel and Gretel," which certainly never happened to you? You weren't there and have no emotional memory of the story events.

Create one. Ask, "If this had happened to me, how would I feel?"

When a story happened to you, your emotional memory is vivid, explicit, and strong. It is easily capable of directing your orchestra to replicate the remembered emotions. The teller's job is to create an emotional memory for every scene of every story, whether it happened to them or not. Created emotional memories will never be as strong as actual memories. That's why the teller must become more consciously aware of their orchestra and of what their orchestra does to express different emotions. With the help of a conscious image of each basic emotion, even a created, or faux, emotional memory can successfully act as your storytelling conductor.

When you tell day-to-day stories that have happened to you, you turn control of the orchestra over to your conductor and don't think about them. You think about the story. When they tell a story from some other source, Super Simple tellers want to tell the same way, the natural way. Super Simple tellers create an emotional memory for each story scene and strive to build a conscious bank of what their orchestra naturally does to express each emotion so that they can forget about their orchestra while they tell and concentrate on remembering the images of the story.

How does Hansel's and Gretel's mother really feel when she decides to get rid of her own children? (Resigned? Distraught? Greedy? Does she hate all children?) How does Gretel feel following her father into the forest the next day? (Terrified? Hopeful? Unconcerned?) How does Hansel feel? (Angry? Confident? Unsure?) Scene by scene, ask how the major characters feel. If you aren't sure, decide how you would feel if that scene happened to you and use that as the way these characters feel.

With this emotional information in place and conscious knowledge of what their orchestra does to express emotions, a Super Simple teller can ignore *how* they are telling and focus on the story and on staying comfortable while they tell. That's what you naturally do.

The Super Simple System for Learning a Story

KEY TOPICS IN THIS SECTION

> ❯ The nine-step Super Simple Storytelling system for learning a story
> ❯ The significance and use of perspective
> ❯ How to use the Story Learning Note Sheet

Drum roll, please!

It's time to present the step-by-step nuts and bolts of the Super Simple Storytelling system for learning a story. Many readers were probably tempted to jump straight to this section and bypass the perspective provided in the previous pages. However, knowing your natural storytelling style and learning to organize your stories in a better way can do as much to improve your storytelling as any sequential system for telling a story.

The nine sequential steps of the Super Simple Storytelling step-by-step system for learning a story are listed in Figure 3.3 and are described in the following paragraphs.

STEP 1. UNDERSTAND THE MAIN CHARACTER

The character elements that define both a story and a character were well described in Part II, "Anatomy of a Story." The first task of preparing a story is to find and understand those core elements of the main character and enough of their other four layers to be able to see and understand this key character.

> ➤ What is the goal of the main character? Why do they want it?
> ➤ How can the teller make that goal and its associated suspense clear and important to an audience?
> ➤ What conflicts block this character from that goal?
> ➤ What risk and danger is associated with each conflict?
> ➤ How can the teller emphasize that risk and danger?
> ➤ How does the main character typically react? Why?

Figure 3.3. The Super Simple Story Learning Progression.

1. **UNDERSTAND THE MAIN CHARACTER**
   Who is your main character? What is their goal in the story? What keeps them from reaching their goal? Create a detailed sensory image of your main character.

2. **LEARN ABOUT THE SUPPORTING CHARACTERS**
   Especially for the antagonist, develop goals, motives, flaws and obstacles, risk and danger, personality, and sensory image.

3. **LEARN THE FACTUAL FLOW OF THE STORY**
   Name each scene and define its purpose. Learn the order of major story events. Use the Tell About and One-On-One-On-One-On-One games to cement this information into memory.

4. **REVIEW STORY PERSPECTIVE AND VIEWPOINT**
   Do you want to change them? Why? To what?

5. **CREATE DETAILED MULTI-SENSORY IMAGES FOR EACH SCENE**
   Use the Scene Game and other activities to expand and refine your image of story places and events.

6. **CREATE AN EMOTIONAL MEMORY FOR EACH SCENE**
   For each scene ask yourself, "How would I feel if this had really happened to me?" Your answer will act as the director for your telling of each scene.

7. **DEVELOP "HOW" YOU WILL TELL THE STORY**
   Use The Character Game and Be Your Character to develop a more detailed image of the sensory and personality layers of your characters.

8. **DEFINE ANY ESSENTIAL ORCHESTRA NOTES**
   Look for story moments requiring planned, extra emphasis or pauses.

9. **PRACTICE THE STORY**
   Practice to ensure that your preparation was adequate and to prove to yourself that you really know the story.

10. **YOU'RE READY FOR THE SPOTLIGHTS!**

➤ What is the personality of this character?

➤ How do they interact with other characters? Why?

➤ What is the sound and pattern of their voice?

➤ What significant, interesting, and unique information would your senses provide if you were in the presence of this character?

➤ What are the salient points of their history that make them think, believe, and act as they do?

➤ What characteristic habits, quirks, and activity do they have?

➤ What from this array of information does the teller want to use to create a memorable first impression of the main characters?

These are the questions that lead a storyteller into understanding a story by understanding the central characters. Once this character's information has been well digested, the rest of the story will fall into place behind it.

Not all of this information will be readily available in the text of a story. Some of it must be inferred by the teller based on what information is provided. Yet all of this information, explicitly stated or not, is important to understanding the central character and to being able to make that character seem real and interesting to listeners. Try to see central story characters in your mind's eye as well as you can "see" members of your own family.

STEP 2. LEARN ABOUT THE SUPPORTING CHARACTERS

The main character is not the only character who should seem real and compelling to an audience. Most stories have one or two other key characters and any number of minor characters.

The most obvious and important of these supporting characters is the antagonist, that character against whom the main character must struggle. The antagonist is the embodiment of the conflicts and problems that beset the main character. The antagonist's power creates the story's risk and danger, the central engine that drives excitement and tension.

The antagonist is as (if not more) important to the story than is the main character. The storyteller should therefore understand the antagonist as well as they do the main character and make that character as real and compelling as the main character.

➤ What does the antagonist want, and why?

➤ What do they care about? Why?

➤ Why are they opposed to the main character?

➤ What in their history has created this sense of opposition?

➤ What is their personality?

➤ What is their sensory image?

Minor supporting characters need not be as completely understood and may be defined by one or two key traits, tag lines (characteristic lines the character routinely says), body postures, or gestures. That is, define one or two unique characteristics for these characters that an audience can use to remember, understand, and recognize the character.

Exercises 4.1, *The Tell-About Game* (page 170) and 4.2, *One-on-One-on-One-on-One* (page 172), are excellent vehicles for developing a teller's images of any of a story's major characters.

STEP 3. LEARN THE FACTUAL FLOW OF THE STORY

Any story is about its characters. After they are understood, it is time to learn the sequence of events that unfolds their story. Make a list of the major story events and learn their order. This list is the backbone of the story and your memory of it.

Break the story into scenes. Make a copy of the story that you can write on. (It is legal to make one copy of any copyrighted material for your own use.) Physically draw a line between scenes on this paper and sequentially *number the scenes*. We have all seen enough movies, TV, and plays to have a sense for scene breaks. In general, scenes change when there is a shift in time, a shift in location, or when there is a major shift in the collection of characters present in the story.

If you draw some scene boundaries a little differently than I would, so what? This is a device to make it easier for you to tell the story. Break the scenes where it makes sense to you. If you find you have scenes that take much more than a minute to read, you will probably (but not always) be happier breaking them into two, shorter scenes. Shorter scenes will be less complex and easier to remember. If you find you have a string of very short (10- to 15-second) scenes, consider combining several. There will be fewer scenes to worry about and remember.

Create a name for each scene. Any name will do as long as the name itself dredges up an image of the scene in your mind. I write them first on the left-hand margin of the text and next on a Story Learning Note Sheet (see below). I tend to use very functional, descriptive scene names. ("Goldilocks busts in." "Goldilocks eats the oatmeal.") But I know tellers who find it is easier to remember cutsie alliterative names. ("Goldie gains ground." "Wrecking the rocker.") Remember, these are *your* scene titles. They are just for you. So any name will do as long as it is easy for you to remember and as long as it reminds you of the central events and images of the scene.

Next, in one short, simple phrase, *define the purpose of each scene*. (1. Hansel and Gretel overhear their parents plotting their demise. 2. H & G follow father into the forest. H scatters red berries (versions differ on what he scatters) behind them. 3. H & G wait in the clearing for their father to return. Both muse about their fate and their parents' feelings. 4. H & G retrace their steps home and discuss what they'll find and how their parents will feel, etc.)

For each scene ask yourself, what is so essential about this scene that it must be included in the story? Why can't you leave it out? If you could scrap this scene the story would be that much shorter and easier to remember and tell. Write this purpose both in the text margin under the scene title and on the Story Learning Note Sheet.

I have included two exercises designed to help you organize your thoughts about story characters and about the flow of events in a story. Exercise 4.1, *The Tell-About Game* (page 170), provides an opportunity to focus on any chosen aspect of a story and orally describe and explore that aspect as the teller describes it to others in a group and then answer questions from that group. This exercise can be used for the story line itself, for the story's obstacles and their associated risk and danger, for the main character, or for the antagonist.

Oral exercises are a valuable part of the development of a story to *tell* for several reasons. First, research shows that when you say something you force your mind to create a more detailed, vivid image of the thing you describe. The more often a storyteller describes the characters and events of their story, the more vivid will be the images of those story elements in the teller's mind when they actually tell the story.

Second, it is valuable to hear yourself talk about the story as well as practicing saying it. Justifying, discussing, and explaining various story aspects cements those elements much more firmly in your mind and improves your memory of the story. Third, describing aspects of the story that lie beyond the specific confines of the text makes the story feel more like your own story. The story becomes more a part of you and is thus easier to recall. Finally, describing the emotions of different characters and scenes improves your emotional memory of the story.

The other exercise that has proven itself to be extremely useful for the oral development of this stage of story understanding is Exercise 4.2, *One-on-One-on-One-on-One* (page 172). This is one of the most beneficial storytelling exercises I have ever seen. It is good for developing a strong sense of the general form of a successful story. It is excellent for honing natural storytelling styles, and it also happens to be an exceptional vehicle for developing a keener sense of almost any aspect of a particular set of story characters.

STEP 4. REVIEW STORY PERSPECTIVE AND VIEWPOINT

Now that you have a good sense of the story, it is time to consider the perspective from which you will tell it. The three major options are omniscient, third person, and first person.

Many storytellers never consider perspective, just as most student writers never consider it when crafting their stories. A story is written from a certain perspective and the teller assumes, without really pondering this decision, that they will tell it from the same perspective.

While a number of perspectives are possible, storytellers really need concern themselves with only three.

1. **Omniscient perspective** is told as if the storyteller were hovering high above the action of the story, able to instantly go anywhere, able to enter every character's mind and read their thoughts and feelings. Omniscient perspective is convenient: the teller never needs to explain how they managed to jump from place to place faster than a speeding bullet and learn what they needed to learn. Many folk and fairy tales are written in omniscient perspective.

    This perspective may be convenient, however, it is also the least exciting of all perspectives. No one's heart pounds while listening to a story told from an omniscient perspective.

    A teacher taking a storytelling class in South Carolina planned to tell the story of the old man and the old woman who wanted to make turnip soup for lunch. The old man walked to the garden and found a giant turnip but couldn't pull it up. He got the old woman and they pulled together but couldn't pull out the turnip. One by one they recruited a boy, then a girl, then a dog, a cat, a duck, a bird, and a mouse. The story was written from an omniscient perspective.

This teacher told me he must be doing something wrong in his preparation because the story was boring. I suggested he change perspective. He shifted to first person perspective as the turnip. By having the audience view the world through the eyes of a specific character—in this case, a turnip fraught with conflicting desires and loyalties—the story came alive and was electric in the telling. All he did was shift out of omniscient perspective.

2. **Third person** is told as if the teller were glued to one character and only reports what that one character sees, hears, and thinks. While third person limits the flexibility of the teller, it gains power by pulling the listener into that same perspective point and throwing them into the middle of the story's action.

3. **First person** is told as if the story had happened to the storyteller. Thus, the teller relates their own experience of the story to the audience. There is no reliable, factual eyewitness in a first person story. Everything is presented through the eyes, beliefs, interpretation, and thoughts of this character. This perspective is the most limiting and yet the most powerful. By pulling the listener into that same viewpoint, the story doesn't merely happen *around* the listener, rather it is as if the story happened *to* the listener.

So what's the point of considering perspective? If a story seems disappointing as you practice it, a perspective change might be the best way to perk it up. As suggested above, listeners are forced to place themselves in the same perspective point the teller uses to tell the story. The more a teller can pull the audience into the middle of the story's action by shifting to third or first person perspectives, the more immediate, exciting, and tension laden the story will be for that audience.

Perspective is a trade-off. You, the teller, need to be able to know what you need to know to effectively relate the tale. On the other hand, you want to pull the listener into the center of the story as much as you can. Shifting perspective usually means partially rewriting the story (as did that teacher while creating the turnip as a complex character). The question is, is the gained excitement worth the time and effort? Sometimes it is; sometimes, not.

I included a more complete discussion of perspective and viewpoint in my other book on working with stories, *Write Right!*, and would refer anyone who would like to read a more detailed discussion to that book. Super Simple tellers should ask themselves two groups of questions to decide on a story perspective:

1. Do you want to change perspective from that presented in your original source material? If so, change it to what? Why? How will that change affect your ability to tell the story? How will it improve your telling of the story?

2. Do you want to change the viewpoint character? (In first person and third person stories you must identify a specific character to be, or follow. That character is called the viewpoint character.) Which character would you change to? Why? How will that alter your ability to tell the story? How will it make the story more powerful?

I have included Exercise 4.3, *Where's the Camera?* (page 175), to demonstrate the effect of changing perspective. You will not want to change perspective for most stories: It's too much work. However, it is often worthwhile to consider a change when a story that you thought would be fun or exciting seems flat, dull, and boring as you begin to develop it. Those are the symptoms of a needed perspective change.

Please note that changing the viewpoint character almost always changes the story's main character. The turnip story I mentioned earlier is a good example. That teacher shifted perspective from omniscient to first person and defined the turnip as his viewpoint character. The turnip instantly replaced the old man as the story's main character. Now the audience cared about the turnip's goals, problems, and flaws. The old man became the antagonist and the teacher had to do some rewriting of the story to fill in the new gaps in story information.

STEP 5. DEFINE SCENIC DETAIL AND MULTI-SENSORY IMAGES

The multi-sensory details the teller creates for each scene, event, action, and character are the basis for remembering the story and are the images from which the story is told. Use Exercise 4.4, *The Scene Game* (page 178), to enhance the complexity of the details you create for your story. It is impossible to envision a scene in too much detail. The more details created, the easier is the memory of that portion of a story. Certainly tellers must create far more detail than they will ever express while telling the story.

There is a detail measuring stick tellers can use to develop a story without the assistance of a group (required for *The Scene Game*). Close your eyes and think about your own bedroom. Any details you know about your bedroom you should create for each scene in your story. But think for a moment about how much you know about your bedroom. You know the location, size, and color of every item. You know its history. You know where all the crayon smears and nicks came from. You know when and how light plays across the walls. You know what you would typically hear and smell in there at different times of day. You know if it feels drafty or stuffy. You know where the cat hair settles first.

In short, you know an incredible amount about that room. Create the same level of multi-sensory detail for the scenes in your story. It's easy to do. You simply make it up (or infer it) based on information included in the text of your story.

Do the same for each character in the story. Review the information you created in steps 1 and 2 for the sensory and history layers and search for aspects you have not developed in your mental picture of the characters. Use what you know about your own family as a guide to the information you should create for a complete characterization. What do they look and smell like? What do they typically say? How do they move, sit, stand? How do they enter and leave a room? What are their quirks and habits? Are there gestures and facial expressions that are characteristically "them?" What are their loves, fears, passions, and hates?

Jot down brief notes to help you remember some of the detail you have created. However, this is not a writing exercise. To be of value, these detailed images must be filed in your memory. Notes should be viewed as aids to be used only for those aspects of the scene that are hardest for you to remember and tell. You will not be able to refer to notes when you tell. If written notes become a crutch while you practice, it will be harder to set them aside during your storytelling.

STEP 6. CREATE AN EMOTIONAL MEMORY FOR EACH SCENE

For each scene in the story, ask this question of yourself: If the events of this scene had happened to me, how would I feel? Answer with a one-word, explicit, emotional state. Remember the difference between columns 1, 2, and 3 of the *Say It How?* exercise (3.4). Lean toward definite, garden-variety, strong, column 1 type emotions for these emotional memories you are creating. They are well defined, ones you probably regularly experience and are more consciously familiar with. They are also easier to portray and are more comfortable for listeners.

For stories where the main character is radically different from yourself, you can substitute the following alternate question: How does my character feel while the events of this scene are happening? This substitution produces a weaker faux-emotional memory, however, because you are distancing yourself from this emotional state by not claiming it as your own.

STEP 7. DEVELOP "HOW" YOU WILL TELL THE STORY

Now trust that you know the factual story and work to make the characters come alive. The best way to do that is to be the characters for brief periods of time. Remember, this is not acting and it doesn't matter if you physically do a good job of becoming your character. The idea is to create more detailed mental images and to explore how, and to what extent, you are comfortable portraying the characters.

Use Exercises 4.5, *The Character Game* (page 180), and 4.6, *Be Your Character* (page 184), to assist in this effort. The more you allow yourself to be silly and try to exaggerate the mannerisms and voice of your characters during private rehearsal, the easier it will be to convincingly and comfortably present engaging, compelling, and enjoyable characters to listeners when you tell, whether or not you include physical and vocal characterizations.

The question is often asked: "Do I have to act to tell?" The answer is definitely "no." An often-asked companion question is, "Do I *have* to do physical and vocal characterizations when I tell?" The answer again is "no."

There is nothing that you *have* to do to tell a story effectively. None of your orchestra elements is individually essential to successful storytelling. If you have concluded that you just can't jump around and act out a story—it just isn't plausibly natural for you—then don't do it. Being comfortable, natural, and real are far more important than physical personification of a story's events and action. If you have concluded that you simply can't do physical and vocal characterizations—it looks phony and silly and ties your stomach into knots—then don't do characterizations.

You *do* have to infuse your storytelling with enough energy and enthusiasm to spark the imagination and interest of your listeners. It doesn't matter which orchestra elements and what techniques you rely on to do that. Somehow you must get that central job done.

If you choose to set aside some of the orchestra players at your disposal because they make you uncomfortable, that's fine. But that puts more pressure on the remaining orchestra elements to accomplish the entire mission.

Kathryn Windham, from Selma, Alabama, is a powerful and delightful teller who specializes in true ghost tales. She does not physically interpret her stories. She does not move when she tells. She sparingly includes what story characters say and far more rarely shifts into vocal characterizations. She uses few gestures. Because she has set aside so many of her orchestra elements when she tells, the full burden for sounding real, compelling, committed, enthused, and natural all falls on the tonal quality of her voice. She happens to posses a powerful speaking voice and is one of America's most successful tellers. She gets the job done with the orchestra elements that are comfortable for her and that she knows will effectively carry the load.

You can do the same. You get to decide how you will hold true to your natural story-telling abilities and style and still effectively tell this story and make your listeners believe that you are excited to tell it. Trying to be the characters during story development is an excellent way to help make that decision.

STEP 8. DEFINE ANY NECESSARY ORCHESTRA NOTES

The Orchestra Notes I refer to here are for those few moments of special action, emphasis, or dramatic vocal change that you pre-plan for a story. For the vast majority of the story you will allow your conductor and orchestra to take care of themselves, as they have been taught to do. But occasionally there will be moments when you see that a particularly emphatic gesture will be effective, when a long pause will add dramatic power, when a certain look or facial expression will add important meaning for an audience. Jot down brief notes to help you remember any such action you want to remember.

A caution: Don't plan very many. The story will begin to look forced rather than natural, and these actions will detract from the effectiveness of your telling rather than adding to it.

STEP 9. PRACTICE THE STORY

Finally, practice to ensure that your preparation was adequate and to prove to yourself that you really do know the story. I have developed a chart to hold my notes while I practice a story. This Story Learning Note Sheet is shown in Figure 3.4.

I number each scene as I have divided them in my story text and list the numbers, 1 through whatever, in the left-hand column of the page. During Step 3 of the Super Simple sequence for learning a story, I write scene names and purpose in columns 2 and 3, respectively. I review these columns until I think I have memorized them. Then I set my notes and the text aside and tell the story into a tape recorder as best I can at this early stage of development. Any recorder will do, and, actually, the smaller and cheaper the better. That way, when you listen to the playback and hate the sound of your voice on tape, you can blame it on the poor-quality equipment.

Follow along in the text as you listen to the tape. Note the scenes you completely forgot and those you stumbled through badly. Re-read these scenes and the information you have already entered on your Story Learning Note Sheet. Adjust your column 3 notes if that will help you remember these scenes better.

During Step 5, I enter a word or two in the fourth column, Scene Picture, that will help me remember aspects of the scenic detail that I routinely forget. Some who are more visually based actually draw a small picture in that space. After reviewing these new notes on my Story Learning Note Sheet, I set notes and text aside and again tell the story into a tape recorder.

Again, I follow in the text as I listen to the tape, noting scenes that I described very poorly or stumbled through or whose order I confused. I then try to expand on and make more detailed my images of these scenes and add any necessary new notes in column 4.

Before progressing to Step 6 of the Super Simple story learning system, I enter a word or phrase in column 5 of the Story Learning Note Sheet to remind myself of any key character information contained in each scene. The core of a story, after all, is this character information. After reviewing this new column, I set notes and text aside and again record the story, listen to the playback, and work on my images of any scenes and characters that are still weak.

Figure 3.4. The Story Learning Note Sheet.

	WHAT YOU SAY					HOW YOU SAY IT		
Scene Number	Scene Name	Scene Purpose	Scene Picture	Character Info	Cute Bits	Scene Feeling	Orchestra Notes	Characterization
1.								
2.								
3.								
4.								

By this point I should be convinced that I know the basic story line and necessary core character information. If I am still forgetting anything in the story, it is probably some humorous, often-repeated, often-lyrical, non-essential bit that I think is soooo precious and cute. We routinely forget these cute bits because they are generally not part of the linear plot flow but are humorous asides. If you have any such bits and are prone to forget them, enter a one-word note in the Cute Bits column in every scene where the bit appears to help you remember. Study columns 1 through 6 of the chart and then tell the story again into your recorder.

Now it's time to move beyond the facts and images of the story and on to *how* to effectively tell the story. Step 6 of this progression asks you to create an emotional memory for each scene. I enter those under the Scene Feeling column in red ink block letters. They are that important and I want them to stand out when I review this sheet.

Again I tell the story into a tape recorder, listening during playback this time primarily to the emotional expression and pace with which I tell the story. I also listen for any moments that I feel need special emphasis in the telling and to how the characters come across when I tell about them. This prepares me to move to Step 7 of the Super Simple story learning progression, where I list notes in the Characterization column about how I present each character, and Step 8, where I list any consciously planned orchestra notes in the Orchestra Notes column.

For me, these Orchestra Notes primarily list intentional pace changes and pauses. Some tellers list primarily emphatic gestures at peak moments in the story. List only those few aspects in this column that you need as a reminder to your conductor.

Characterization notes are the only column that are not listed by scene. In this column I list each character and quick notes on how I want to present that character.

Again I tape the story and adjust my notes for any weak scenes, characters, and moments in the story. By this time I am ready to tell the story.

I recommend that you write the minimum essential amount on the Story Learning Note Sheet. I often have no notes at all for scenes I naturally tell well. It is not a contest to see how small you can write and how much you can cram onto one page. Your notes need not be clear enough for others to read and use.

This sheet has value as an organizational tool while you are learning a story and also as a review tool before you tell. One glance at this sheet and the key points listed on it should refresh your memory of the story and fix it in your mind for the next telling. If you have learned a story well, you will be ready to tell it at any time in the future after only a five-minute review of this sheet and one practice telling. Put on this sheet only what will help you the most in that quick review. I find that the more I write, the less willing I am to use the sheet and review it before I tell.

That is the Super Simple Storytelling system for learning and remembering a story. The Story Learning Note Sheet becomes a permanent reference page for that story, able to pop the story back into your head months, even years, after you have first told it. Remember that the general concept of this Super Simple approach to learning a story is to use this orderly progression to turn the words of a story into detailed sensory images and to create a workable emotional memory for each scene of the story.

Some tellers take the Story Learning Note Sheet one step farther by saying, "If I want to convert words to sensory images (pictures in my mind), why would I want to record my notes as words?" After completing a Story Learning Note Sheet, they draw a grid on a piece of paper, with one square for each scene, and draw a stick-figure picture of the scene in its box. Thus the last thing they look at before they tell isn't words but their page of simple pictures.

I have included three additional exercises that provide valuable information about how we learn and remember stories and about the effect of word choices a teller makes while they tell. Exercise 4.7, *The Retell Game* (page 186), shows how stories evolve and change as they are passed from teller to teller. Exercises 4.8, *Where Images Come From* (page 188), and 4.9, *She Entered the Room* (page 190), show how specific word choices a teller makes affect the images received and created by a listener. All three are valuable demonstrations for new tellers to experience.

The Great-Amazing-Never-Fail Safety Net

KEY TOPICS IN THIS SECTION

> What the Safety Net is and how to use it
> What causes most storytelling traumas and how to avoid them
> The real secret to avoiding storytelling blunders

Even the Great Garibaldi Brothers defying gravity as they soared high through the air of the Big Top had a safety net underneath them. The crowd still gasped and squealed at each death-defying leap and spin. But if they fell, a safety net was there to catch them. Super Simple Storytellers deserve no less.

There is no more need for you to fear forgetting while you tell a story than was there need for the Garibaldis to fear gravity. I can almost guarantee that, at regular intervals over the course of your storytelling career, you will forget.

So what? Who cares—besides you?

Why do we wallow in terror of forgetting even a few words of a story we learned from a book when we don't care one iota if we forget whole blocks of the personal stories we tell all the time? The Great-Amazing-Never-Fail Safety Net is designed to help you gracefully recover when you do forget and to alleviate the gnawing inner worry about forgetting.

The Safety Net boils down to four strategies to ensure that you never lose control and dignity in the midst of a storytelling nose dive. All of the specific problems you will ever encounter fall under one of these four umbrellas.

1. TELL ABOUT THE STORY

The most stressful telling of any story is the first telling. You won't have convinced yourself yet that you know the story. You don't know how listeners will react—whether the story will work as you had hoped it would, whether they will laugh when you want them to, whether they will bond with the story characters. You aren't sure yet if you have discovered the best way to tell the story. In short, every alarm and danger warning buzzer in your head will be loudly clanging throughout the first telling.

The problem is that your first telling of a story will most likely be the most important one, the real one, the one to your own class. The telling that you want to work the most will be the one with the most stress on you.

Your problems, however, aren't really with the whole story. They are only with a few parts of the story. There will be clusters of four or five scenes that you have down cold and solid. You *know* you will do well on these parts. You *know* your students will like them.

But there are other scenes and sections that stay a foggy mush in your brain no matter how hard you work on them. Knowing that these sections loom in the near future ties you into excruciating knots. That awful voice inside your head counts down the seconds until you reach these ever-so-tentative sections you struggle to hold together in your memory. "30 seconds to the part you don't know. You're gonna blow it. 15 seconds. Here it comes. Five . . . four . . . three . . . " Having to listen to that voice is enough to make you blow the parts you *do* know well.

Quiet the voice. Eliminate the tension.

Don't promise to tell a story, promise to tell about the story. You have changed the rules and the class's expectations.

Announce that you want to tell your class *about* a story. Then launch into *telling* the opening scene with all the enthusiasm and passion you ever dreamed of. Continue your rousing telling right up to the first section you are unsure of and reluctant to tell.

Stop, smile, and say, "Isn't that a wonderful beginning?" Then tell *about* the scenes you are afraid you won't remember and won't tell well. Provide a summary plot bridge to keep the class from getting lost while you skip the part you are unsure of. As soon as you pass that part and are back to firmer story ground, pause, smile, say, "Here is what happens next," and launch back into storytelling again.

Continue in this way—telling some sections, telling about some sections—right up to the glorious close you dreamed of while you were practicing the story. If you have more opportunities to tell this story, you'll find that on each telling you "tell about" less and "tell" more. But never will you have to tell parts of the story you aren't ready to tell.

By never forcing yourself to muddle through the sections you cringe at telling, you never pull your energy and confidence out of the telling. When you tell, you tell with passion and conviction. Listeners are swept into your excitement for your story. They only get the best of your storytelling, and they still get the story, albeit a slightly abridged version.

I have seen top-rated, main-stage professional tellers use this technique and even there it works. The audience didn't feel cheated. They feel that they were rewarded by being let in on a sneak preview. Telling about a story is a way to avoid most of the fear and trepidation you feel and give your audience the best you have to offer, which, after all, is what they deserve.

2. DO THE OPPOSITE

During any storytelling, a teller periodically starts to tighten, to feel nervous and less sure of their story and their telling. At these moments every teller tends to drift into their nervous, destructive habits. Some speed up and talk in a blur to get the story over with. Some slide into a whispered monotone, hoping no one will notice that they are still telling. Some turn overly animated and leap frantically about the stage to hold the audience's attention. Some nervously pace or shift back and forth. Some merely let their eyes rove aimlessly around the ceiling and walls, pretending that no one is there to listen to them.

These are the nervous habits we discussed earlier. When you feel yourself drifting into these nervous habits, pause, smile, take a deep breath, and do the opposite. If you tend to talk fast when nervous, intentionally talk overly slowly and deliberately for a few sentences. If you talk softly when nervous, belt out the next few sentences.

The effect is instant and dramatic. It jerks both you and the listeners out of your stupor and gets you back on track with the story. Some experienced tellers advise that all tellers should periodically pause, smile, breathe, and check to see if they might be drifting toward their nervous habits as a safeguard.

3. THE PART YOU REMEMBER YOU FORGOT

You're blithely telling and, with a lightning jolt of terror realize that, earlier, you left out a whole hunk of the story. Relax. Every teller periodically forgets part of a story.

The solution is to convince yourself that it is no big deal when you do forget. It's just not a significant problem if you happen to do so.

Study the informal stories you tell and hear. People forget parts all the time and, when they realize they left part out, merely stuff it back in whenever they remember it. All listeners are fully capable of resorting the story information and images in their head to accommodate this new information without getting lost. We naturally tell stories in a jumbled, non-sequential fashion anyway, so we're all used to it.

The only actual mistake you can make at these moments is to cringe, grimace, and mutter dire curses at yourself. That announces to listeners that you made a mistake. Like sharks at a feeding frenzy, they will now ferociously devour every word you say until they find it.

The key to recovering is to neither look nor act as if you have done anything wrong (which you haven't). I know this is difficult to believe when the hunk you omitted contains all the information your listeners need to understand the next story event and sentence. But even then it's true.

First, pause, smile, breathe, and nod, as if you were taking a moment to relish this, your favorite part of the story. Then say "There's something I haven't told you yet" and tell them the part you earlier forgot. Perfectly true. You haven't told them yet because you forgot it. Or say, "There's something you need to know before we go on." Again true. They need to know it because you left it out. But it is fine for them to think that you planned to hold it back for this moment in the story.

If you aren't sure, say, "Now, did I tell you that?" If they nod yes, answer, "I just wanted to make sure because this is where it's going to become important." If they blankly shake their heads, say, "I didn't think so, but I better before we can go on."

Either way, they will feel that you are taking extra-good care of them and enjoy the story all the more. No one but you will suspect that you made a mistake (and actually you didn't make a mistake) and your storytelling will take a great leap forward.

4. WHAT COMES NEXT

Probably the greatest imaginable speaking terror is to suddenly realize you have no idea what to say next. Thirty faces stare expectantly at you, "Well? Go on!" Your brain crackles to a terrifying blank.

You're sure you just blew it. But the truth is you haven't goofed at all. That is, not unless you *act* as if you had. The truth is, no damage has yet been done because no one but you knows you don't know what comes next and you have plenty of time to recover if you hide that fact from your listeners.

So relax. Pause, smile, breathe, nod your head as if this were your favorite part of the story. Chuckle softly to yourself as if you can scarcely believe how much you like this part. Breathe again, deep and slow.

Right there, there's a good 10 seconds you can buy without having to say a word. Ten seconds is a long time to think about what comes next. If you remember, simply proceed with the story. They'll never notice a thing.

If the story hasn't reappeared in your mind yet, you need to verbally tread water and hold your spot in the story while you mentally reboot the story. How?

1. **First, repeat the last line.** Repeat it with all the enthusiasm you can muster. "They walked out the double French doors onto the patio." Again, pause and smile and breathe. Repeat the line a third time as if it were a prophetic turning point of the story. "Yup. The two of them . . . side by side. . . . They walked right out those polished French double doors. . . . *Both* of them . . . just . . . marched right out those doors and onto the patio."

    Bamm! There's another 15 seconds for your mind to use to reconstruct the story and where you are in it. If your mind is still a blank, buy more time. How?

2. **Describe the scene you are in.** We rarely mention more than a salient bit or two of the cornucopia of details we have created and stored in our minds. Let your mouth wander randomly around the scene, mentioning every detail for every sense it can recall while your brain tries to figure out what happens next. Describe the weather, the sounds and smells, the flying and crawling insects, the kinds of plants and flowers, the weeds that have crept up. Any detail that comes easily to mind about this setting is fair game.

    It is easy to buy another 30 seconds with this description. You have now bought almost a minute—plenty of time for you to begin a systematic, orderly reconstruction of the story.

    How? No matter how fried your brain has become, you will not forget numbers. Begin with scene 1. What is the title? What happens? Scene 2. What's the title? What happens? Scene by scene you proceed down the Story Learning Note Sheet until you reach the scene you are stuck on and reboot it in your mind. Once the next scene has been recaptured, proceed with the story as if nothing unplanned ever happened. No one will suspect.

    If, however, it becomes obvious that your listeners are tired of description and are ready to find out what happens in this well-defined setting, and you still don't have a clue as to what happens next, relax! You are far from trapped and out of fallback positions. As a teacher telling in your own classroom, you have options main-stage performers do not have.

3. **Ask them.** It is common for you to periodically pause during your presentations to discuss the material with your class. Students are used to it, even expect it. Do that now. Stop and say, "Before we go on, I want to make sure everyone understands where we are in this story. Who can tell me what's going on in this story?" Let them argue it out while you sneak back to your desk and glance at your Story Learning Note Sheet.

    If you didn't bring your note sheet, or if your mind is now so frazzled you can't remember which story you're telling and so nothing seems to help, don't panic. Instead, smile, breathe, and say, "Very good, now who thinks they know what happens next?"

If they have heard this story before they'll spill the beans every time. If not, they're intelligent story listeners. They can use previous story events to logically forecast future happenings. Let them guess for a while. Even if no one hits the mark, one of their guesses might trigger some spark of recognition in your brain. If nothing they say helps, you still have three more options.

4. **The fast close.** Take any suggestion they make and use it to jump to a one-paragraph quick end to the story. Your students will be a bit confused ("Nice story, but it sure didn't end the way I thought it would.") but you'll have successfully exited the spotlight. That night you rework the story and retell it the next day saying, "Do you remember the story I told you yesterday? There are several versions of that story. The one I told yesterday is not a very common version. Today I want to tell the version you'll most often hear."

    They'll never suspect what really happened and, as a side benefit, they learn that stories can have more than one version, which is a valuable concept for them to absorb.

5. **Brutal honesty.** Tell them that you can't remember the rest of the story and that you are going to stop until you've had a chance to review your notes so you can tell it correctly. It's valuable for them to see both that their teacher isn't infallible and that a storyteller can forget and still survive.

6. **The ultimate fallback.** If all else fails, the ultimate fallback is to say in an eager and excited voice, "All right, all right. Let me finish the story because this is my favorite part. Now, as soon as. . . . Oh, look at the time! We don't have time to finish the story today. Story time is over. I'll have to finish it tomorrow. Now please pull out your math books."

    You're off the hook and have a one-day reprieve. More important, each student will mentally write the balance of the story that night because we hate it when we are left hanging in the middle of a story with no resolution.

    The real point of the Safety Net is this: As soon as you *believe* that you can extract yourself from a potentially troublesome spot and save face in the process, you will. Actually, you won't get into trouble in the first place because it is the fear of forgetting that makes you forget. Disarm the fear and the problem evaporates.

    The trouble isn't forgetting. We all do that. The trouble is the mind-numbing panic many tellers experience when they forget. As soon as you realize that forgetting is an occasional and natural part of storytelling and that it is easy and natural to recover, you won't forget as much and it will stop being such a traumatic event when you do.

PART IV

TELLING TIDBITS

𝒯ips for Telling a Story

Some tips to help your telling:

1. **Just before you tell:**

   ➤ Review the Story Learning Note Sheet. Mentally walk one-by-one through the scenes to make sure the scene images jump sequentially into your mind.

   ➤ Rehearse the opening and closing paragraphs as the last thing you do before you tell. These are two of the places where tellers are most likely to stumble. Often tellers rush into a story before they are really ready to begin and blow the opening.

   As a teller nears the end of their story, they think, *Alleluia! I'm going to make it. Only a couple of paragraphs to go.* And their mind rushes prematurely back into their seat, abandoning their mouth and body, which must stumble unguided through the close. Mistakes on that final scene leave a bitter taste in the teller's mouth.

2. **Pause before you start.** After you stand and announce that you are going to tell a story, pause, breathe, and smile while you check to make sure that the images for the first scene are there and ready to use.

3. **Pause when you finish.** Don't move when you finish the story. Stay standing where you are, breathe, smile, and acknowledge the adulation of the crowd. Only then may you sit down, pick up papers, or allow your mind to turn away from the story. This will help prevent those embarrassing last-paragraph blunders.

4. **Stand to tell.** Many beginning tellers feel conspicuous, presumptuous, and excessively formal when they stand to tell. However, sitting ties up part of your orchestra and makes many gestures and all body movements awkward.

5. **Focus on the story.** While you tell, focus on the story, not on your performance of it, not on what you look or sound like telling it. Pretend you are *living* the story and are aware of nothing else. I have seen it happen hundreds of times. A teller is doing a wonderful job and suddenly becomes aware of how well they are doing. Their mind slides off the story to their superlative performance of it and, bamm!, they blow the next line. When you feel yourself become consciously aware of your own performance, pause, breathe, smile, and concentrate on the next few story images before you continue.

6. **Avoid stories in the round.** Keep the audience in front of you. Avoid gathering your class into a circle or placing listeners behind or beside you. When you tell you want to look at your audience. If they are all around you, your head has to bounce from side to side faster than at a sizzling tennis match.

7. **Pause regularly.** Regularly pause, smile, and make sure the images of the next scene are ready to go in your mind. We usually rush stories and adding pauses is good both for the audience and for you. Also, intentionally pause periodically to see if you are slipping into any of your nervous, destructive habits. When you feel them coming on, pause, smile, and do the opposite.

8. **Ignore yourself while you tell.** You can't afford to think about whether you look silly or whether your shirt is coming untucked in the middle of a story. The more you think about yourself, the less you are focusing on the story and the less energy you are putting into your telling. Focus on the story as if you *were* the story and the characters. Whatever your orchestra does when you are deeply focused on the story will be just fine.

9. **Be aware of listeners.** The only thing you should ever be aware of while you tell—other than the story—is the audience. Are they locked into the story, mouths dropped open, eyes glazed over and turned inward to watch the wondrous movie they are creating in their minds? Are they growing restless? Are you going too fast, or too slow, for their needs? Do they need review and explanation? Clear up their concerns and launch back into the story, repeating a paragraph or two to help them re-settle into the adventure.

10. **Celebrate your successes.** Remember that the first telling of a new story is always the most stressful. It is still a new story. You want the first telling to go well, and it will. But it won't be perfect. Rather than being overly critical of your performance and revisiting each mistake, identify what worked and what both you and the audience liked as much as you search for the aspects of your story that need revision.

11. **Never apologize for a story or your telling of it after you finish.** Never tell your audience all the things you think you did wrong. The audience doesn't want to hear it. You will discount their experience of the story, which might be very positive. They will suddenly feel swindled and cheated, instead of gloriously satisfied with you and your story.

All Those Who Are Creative, Stand Up

The Super Simple Storytelling system assumes that each teller possesses a sizable modicum of creativity. Do *you* feel like a creative person? When I ask groups of teachers, usually more than half claim that they aren't creative.

Nonsense. Of course they are. If you are a living, breathing human being, you create. Period. It isn't possible for a human to *not* create, just as it is impossible for a living human to *not* think.

At the root of this misconception is our misunderstanding of the word *creativity.*

The dictionary defines creativity as the ability to bring something into existence, to transcend traditional views or modes of thinking. Many in our culture have slipped a quality qualifier into their personal definition of creativity. For them creativity requires that the thing they bring into existence is of exceptionally high quality, of professional caliber. Creativity has nothing to do with quality. Quality comes with time, focused practice, and sustained effort. Creativity has only to do with the act of creating.

Virtually nobody is "exceptionally good" the first few times they try anything. Most successful storytellers were mediocre at best when they began to tell. Many were downright embarrassing. The-awful-things-you-used-to-do is a popular topic when storytellers gather.

I view creativity differently. *Creativity is the natural result of two qualities: the willingness to look foolish and the persistence to do it over and over again.* Painters paint terribly when first they smear color on paper, writers write miserably, and beginning sculptors slip and crack their hunk of marble. No dancer looked creative the first time they tried a plié at the dance bar. No cellist ever sounded gifted while still trying to learn the scales.

Natural human creativity takes time to develop, to train the fingers, feet, and brain to perform what the creative mind envisions and dreams up. The creativity is always there. The rest of our bodies just need time to learn how to let it get out undamaged.

You, too, are creative.

Storytelling and Copyright

You're thinking, *I'm not going to write anything, or even copy anything, so why do I need to think about copyrights?* Because one of those copyrights is the right to perform (tell) the story, and it belongs exclusively to the copyright holder.

A copyright is a bundle of five rights society grants to the person who creates a work. These exclusive rights are the right to:

➤ *Reproduce,* or make copies of the story

➤ Create *derivative works,* or change the story

➤ *Perform* the story for a live audience or in a recording studio

➤ *Distribute,* or sell the story

➤ *Promote* the story

No one can legally do any of these without the copyright holder's permission.

Any time you tell a copyrighted story you automatically run into at least two of these rights: performance and creating a derivative work. (You always change a few words in the telling.) Stories are either covered by a valid copyright or belong to the public at large (you); the latter are called *public domain* stories. You need permission to tell stories covered by a valid copyright. You may tell public domain stories anytime you like because you own them. Virtually all folk and fairy tales are old enough to be in the public domain.

How does a well-meaning teacher-teller know? Here are the questions to guide you to your tell/no-tell decision.

1. **Is the story covered by a copyright?** This is, unfortunately, not as simple-minded a question as it sounds.

   ➤ If your source is an unpublished work or on the Internet, the copyright notice (©) must appear on every copy of the work and should be near the front. If there is no copyright notice on your copy, you can tell the story on the assumption that it isn't copyrighted. If there is a notice, the story is covered by a copyright.

   ➤ If your source is a published book, look on the back of the title page to see who holds the copyright and when the work was copyrighted. A copyright does not necessarily mean that your story is copyrighted. You have to ask several more questions.

   Has the copyright expired? All copyrights expire after a certain number of years (the exact number has varied over time as the copyright laws have changed). Current law extends a copyright for the life of the author plus 50 years. If a story was written by someone who died before 1950, those stories are now *public domain* stories.

   What does the copyright cover? This is the real problem. You don't know. The copyright means that "everything *original* to the author in this work is copyrighted." However, a writer could change five words in an old folk tale and slap a copyright notice on the story. Only those five original words are covered! A copyright notice only tells you that something inside is covered. It could only be the typeface and layout!

   So what does a copyright symbol mean on a newly released collection of old folk tales? You can't tell from looking at the book. The copyright might have nothing to do with the story itself. There is no sure way to tell without *comparing various versions* of the story to see how they differ. Many professional tellers have spent months tracing back through stacks of versions and copyrights of a story only to find that as many as half a dozen copyrights might have some claim to the specific wording, phraseology, and characterizations of a particular, current version and that the actual story has existed in a slightly different version in the public domain for a century.

   ➤ The test. Here are the ways to circumvent a printed copyright notice:

   * If you can find a public domain version of a story, you are free to tell it without permission.

* If you can find three different versions of the same story, even though they are each individually copyrighted, you are free to tell the story without permission.

2. **What do you do if a story is copyrighted?** Simple. If a story is covered by a single, unambiguous, valid copyright, get permission to tell it from the copyright holder. Write or call. As a teacher telling in your classroom you will normally have no trouble gaining the right to tell the story.

3. **What will happen if I violate someone's copyright?** Here is what *can* happen. If you perform a copyrighted story and are not paid specifically to tell that story (you are not, you are paid to teach), the worst the copyright holder can legally do is enjoin you from telling the story again. That's it. The copyright holder can go to court and spend several thousand dollars to have a judge issue an injunction forbidding you from ever telling the story if that person is irate enough at having you promote their book and their story by telling it to your students. Decide for yourself what this means to you.

    After years of wrestling with this issue, the storytelling community has decided that the most important thing is to be *ethical*. If the story was written by a living writer, get permission. For *all* stories, give credit to your source. Tell listeners where you found the story.

estures

Watch a group of people talk. You can tell who's talking by watching each person's hands. The hands of the talker will be in motion. Gestures are a natural part of all oral communication. Gestures:

> ➤ Add a sense of natural comfort

> ➤ Add tremendous amounts of energy to a storytelling

> ➤ Provide an important form of detailed, visual information

> ➤ Make the teller appear more confident, comfortable, and natural

> ➤ Contribute to how a story is told

It is fine to say, "Create detailed images of each scene and character and gestures will take care of themselves." However, just as a canary will be the first victim of noxious gas in a coal mine, so, too, gestures are typically the first victim of nervousness. A teller's hands always want to run and hide at the first sign of stress and discomfort. The more you know about gestures, the less likely your hands will be to succumb to their own cowardly urges.

What are gestures? Movement by hand, body, or face intended to provide information to an audience. This definition excludes nervous gestures, ticks, and habitual movements, which provide either no information or counterproductive information to a listener.

> ➤ As visual elements, gestures pack far more information into each second of story time than do words—*gestures communicate efficiently.*

> ➤ Being visual, gestures translate more directly into specific, powerful images in the listener's mind than do words—*gestures communicate effectively.*

➤ Gestures engage different sensory organs than words and can be transmitted simultaneously with words to create a complementary cacophony of densely packed information to flood the listener with imagery and energy—*gestures communicate powerfully.*

There are five ways a teller can use gestures:

1. *Information gestures* provide basic descriptive information (size, place, shape, position, direction, etc.). Information gestures are the result of detailed images in the mind of the teller.

2. *Character-related gestures* show how a character moves, postures, thinks, and acts and provide powerful character personality and sensory information for listeners. Character gestures spring from vivid images of story characters in the teller's mind.

3. *Action gestures* depict the action and events of a story. Action gestures arise from the teller's detailed images of the settings and events of the story.

4. *Emphasis gestures* add emphasis to specific moments in a story and are usually pre-planned and listed in the Orchestra Notes column of the Story Learning Note Sheet.

5. *Audience asides* are gestures and facial expressions tellers use to convey their own feelings and reactions to listeners outside the context of the story. It is as if the teller steps outside of the story for a moment and visually comments on the story to listeners.

Watch how you and others naturally weave these five types of gestures into everyday speech. Pay particular notice to which of these categories of gestures you use extensively and which you tend to omit from your own speech. While none of them is essential to the effective telling of a story, it is important to know if you naturally shy away from one or more types of gestures so that you can plan around them during story preparation.

Also watch to see if you frequently use gestures that do not fit into one of these five categories. Such gestures are probably counterproductive nervous habits and worth breaking.

I have included Exercises 3.8, *Mum's the Word* (page 155) and 3.9, *Gesture a Word* (page 159), to help you and your students become more aware of gestures and to explore the limits of effective gesture use. These are both fun storytelling games to play, but also effectively demonstrate what gestures are capable of doing.

Natural gestures spring from strong, detailed images of the scenes, characters, and actions. For the most part, don't worry about gestures when you tell. Learn the story well, plan characterizations and Orchestra Notes. Then focus on the story, not on your performance of it, and your gestures should admirably perform their role in an effective storytelling.

$\mathcal{P}$rops, Costumes, and Other Extras

It's decision time. You're going to tell Little Red Riding Hood. But should you pack your big red scarf to drape over your head when you tell about Red? Should you take an ax and hold it when you tell about the woodsman? Why not take a painting of a cottage in a forest clearing? Should you wear a period costume to put the class in the mood for this story?

Should you really drag this clanking mound of junk to school just to tell this one story? Should you dutifully pullout your props at the appropriate times during the story? Won't they enhance and heighten your students' experience of the story? Won't they make it seem more real?

The answer is an unwavering "maybe." To decide if these props are worthwhile, you must add up the pluses and minuses of props and costumes.

THE MINUSES

1. **Gathering props and planning their inclusion in a story takes time.** The time you spend dashing around the neighborhood gathering props and washing, sewing, ironing, and polishing them so they will look decent could have been spent working on the story. Each teller must decide how their time will be best spent.

2. **Your prop usually won't be exactly right for the story.** As the woodcutter bursts into Granny's cottage, you reach under your desk and pull out . . . well, okay, it's really just a hatchet because you don't have an ax and had to scrounge through most of the neighborhood to find this stubby thing. It is rare that you will find a prop that exactly matches what you think the thing should look like.

3. **Listeners don't need props.** The whole idea of storytelling is that listeners imagine the story inside their heads. The more props you pull out the more you keep them from doing their part.

4. **Props always pull listeners out of a story.** As you flourish a new prop every listener stops imagining vivid scenes and characters of the story and is pulled back into the classroom to stare at this thing you hold. They are pulled out of the story and it will require some effort on your part to push them back in.

5. **Listeners stop listening while they study a new prop.** Instead of listening to your story, listeners are now examining the prop. Is that thing really sharp? How much did that thing cost? Is that a wood handle or just plastic? I wonder how heavy that thing is. Could you really cut with it? Etc., etc. Everything you say while this detailed assessment is in progress will be ignored. They just won't hear it.

6. **Listeners' imagined props are always "wrong."** If there is a significant difference between the "real" prop and what they imagined, younger children will tend to think, "Oh, I was wrong." They will accept your prop as correct and will reduce, or stop, imagining other objects and elements of the story for fear of making similar mistakes.

Add it up and you'll find that your listeners pay a hefty price whenever you pull out a prop during a storytelling. To be worth this price, that prop had better be essential to the story and to your telling of it.

THE PLUSES

1. **The prop is essential to understanding the story.** If your story can't be told, or understood, without a prop, then using that prop is a big plus. "Crictor the Boa Constrictor" falls incredibly flat if the teller doesn't have a six-foot stuffed cotton snake in their hands as Crictor learns to form his body into letters and numbers. The story simply won't work without Crictor as a prop.

2. **The prop is essential to understanding a character.** A prop might be such an integral part of a story character that you can't present the character without using the prop.

3. **Unfamiliar items.** If there are important items in the story with which your students cannot possibly be familiar, the story will fail miserably unless you can show them what these items are and do.

4. **Curriculum links.** There may be props you can introduce as part of the story, which are being used for the sake of the subsequent curriculum teaching points rather than for the sake of the story. Without the props, you won't be able to effectively transition between story and your content material. It works for any subject area: numbers, alphabet, math, geography, history, science. You design props to use during the story because they reinforce your teaching points.

MINIMIZING THE COST

Even well-justified props don't come for free. Be sure you really need them before you ask listeners to pay the price for their inclusion in the story. How? Try telling the story without the prop. If the story flops without the prop, you need to use it. Now manage the introduction of that prop so as to minimize the price listeners pay for its use.

1. **Introduce the prop before you tell the story.** Then leave it out in plain sight through the entire story, using it when needed and returning it to its visible spot, so that its introduction and reintroduction during the story won't pull the audience out of their images of the story.

2. **Create an introduction spot.** If you first introduce a prop during the story, find—or create—a slow spot for its introduction. Find, or create, a moment when little is happening, when the audience isn't in a frenzy to keep up with the images they are creating and watching, when they won't miss any critical information while they check out of the story to check out the prop. Either include non-essential story information during this introduction spot (background, assides, extra detail) or plan to repeat any important information after listeners have gotten used to the prop and have returned their attention to the story.

3. **Don't rush the prop's introduction.** Give the audience time to see the thing and to run through their laundry list of mental questions about it.

   Of course, you can't simply stand there and say, "Okay. Here it is. Take a good look. I'll wait." You have to appear to continue to tell the story. But because you know that no one is listening to you for a moment, you'll wisely pad the story with non-essential fluff or with story information you plan to repeat later. It's like verbally treading water while they absorb this new visual element before leading them on with their swim.

4. **Don't overemphasize a prop.** It doesn't matter that you consumed 18 hours painstakingly making the thing, or that you spent six years scrounging through the backroads of Bolivia to find it. While you tell a story, the story must be the central focus. Gush over the prop before or after you tell. But during a story, it must be the story that holds center stage.

COSTUMES

Costumes are simply props you don't have the luxury of setting aside when you don't need them. If you wear a character's costume, you are stuck in the role of that character. Whatever costume you squeeze into for one story you are stuck in until recess or lunch. Character costumes are almost as dramatic and effective if you bring them in on a hanger. It's also a lot easier on you because you're not stuck in the costume all day.

Storytelling costumes are a little different. Many teachers have a hat, a vest, a coat, an apron, or a shawl that they wear whenever they tell stories and only when they tell. The first time or two they pull these costume elements out, their class pays the same attention price that is paid for any prop. But as it becomes familiar, the item ceases to distract and becomes an aid to preparing the students to listen to a story. It acts to isolate story time from the rest of the world. Like a bell for Pavlov's dogs, it prepares them to dive into a story.

PUPPETS

Puppets are the ultimate prop. They always upstage a human. Always. Drag out a raggedy old puppet and stuff it onto your hand and that puppet instantly becomes real, important, and the center of everyone's focus. They will no longer watch you. They will study every nuance of the puppet's action.

This means that you had better be proficient in manipulating a puppet before you bring it to class because any deficiencies in your puppetry skills will be greatly exaggerated by the attention the puppet commands. This means lots of extra practice with this upstart attention grabber after you have learned the story. But those who have watched good puppet shows know the effort can be well worth it.

Audience Participation

When most people think of audience participation stories, they picture a room full of children dutifully droning out a quickly rehearsed line on command from the storyteller. Many children enjoy having an assigned part in a story. However, studies have shown that what children remember from such events is their participation and *not the story*. If you are telling this tale just to allow the audience to participate, fine. But you are asking them to pay a significant price for the privilege of participation. Their minds will be so focused on their part that they will not develop strong imagery of the story. They sacrifice the story, itself, and the glory of receiving a well-told story for the sake of their one, repeated line.

There are two types of audience participation, however, which we should differentiate.

1. **Spontaneous, voluntary audience participation.** This is when audience members spontaneously, verbally react to story situations or call out to story characters. Everyone does the former, young children often do the latter.

   A teller can encourage, even plan for, spontaneous participation. Tell stories with repeating character lines. Add fixed gestures and body movements to reinforce the pattern of those lines. Say the lines slowly and rhythmically while smiling at the audience. By the second or third appearance of these lines, the audience will jump in all on their own. There is no need to assign the task to them.

   You can also tell stories the audience knows and have a character stumble over well-known lines. Younger audiences will always spontaneously dive in to make sure the characters get it right. If your Big Bad Wolf says, "I'll puff.... No, wait. Huff first. I'll huff, ... and I'll, ummmm . . . " you can be sure many audience members will shout out the correct line, without any direction or prompting on your part.

   Spontaneous participation adds energy and humor and doesn't pull listeners out of the story because they are commenting to story characters within the context of the story.

2. **Assigned participation.** If you want to assign the audience a line to periodically say during a story, first make sure you have a strong reason to shift their attention away from the story and onto this one phrase, which they will repeat. Introduce and rehearse their line before the story starts. That way the story won't grind to a complete halt while you accomplish this task during the story.

   Next, minimize the disruption at each occurrence of their line. Don't stop the story and shout out, "This is your line! Everyone together now!" Those words aren't part of the story and simply pull listeners farther out of their experience of the story to do their part.

   Instead, pause expectantly at the beginning of their line and, with a broad smile, start slowly into their line yourself, waving your arms like a conductor directing the players to stay on time and with the tempo. It also helps to nod a time or two as if giving them permission to blurt out their line. In this way listeners are allowed to hold onto their images of the story through the advent of their assigned participation. They'll enjoy it more and, who knows, they might even remember the story as well.

The Sore Throat Blues

Throughout this book I am encouraging you to speak forcefully for extended periods—without any break, without even an extended pause. It's like running long distance races. You have to get the appropriate muscles into shape or you risk getting into trouble halfway through your event. For storytelling, those muscles are in your throat and if you don't take care of them when you tell, you're asking for a case of the sore throat blues.

Teachers often get sore throats during the first several weeks of school while they struggle to whip their voices back into shape after long summers off. Most teachers write off these recurring, minor annoyances as being a standard hazard of the job. However, the vocal stress of storytelling is a giant step beyond what teachers normally experience. So three tips on avoiding the sore throat blues are in order.

1. **Breathe better.** The best way to reduce stress on your vocal cords and the muscles that control them is to breathe better. More specifically, stop asking your neck and throat muscles to assist in your breathing. Put the thumb and forefinger of one hand on the sides of your throat slightly above the collar bone. Expand your chest, sucking in a quick, deep, full breath. Feel those neck muscles tighten? You have to engage your neck muscles when you expand your chest to breathe. The problem is that some of those same muscles help modulate your vocal cords when you speak. By using them to breathe, you make them pull double duty, often trying to pull two ways at once. They rebel and you get a sore throat.

    Now place one hand on your diaphragm (just below your rib cage). Breathe normally and you probably won't feel your hand move much at all. That's because we are taught to breathe with our chest instead of with our diaphragm. Now breathe again, expanding your chest, pulling in a full breath. As you exhale hold your chest expanded and stretched. Don't allow it to collapse and compress. You will feel your diaphragm cave inward as you exhale. Continue to hold your chest artificially expanded. When you want to breathe you will have to use your diaphragm. Feel your hand rise as you pull air in from the bottom of your rib cage.

    Now try it with your chest compressed. Exhale fully, squeezing all the air from your lungs. Your chest will compress in on your lung walls. Consciously hold your chest tightened in this way. Eventually you will have to breathe. If you hold your chest in, you will *have* to breathe with your diaphragm and feel your hand rise out past your ribs.

    Get used to breathing with your diaphragm and you'll avoid most sore throats.

2. **Warm up.** Pretend you are a sprinter at the Olympics. Lounging in the locker room on a pile of bean bags in front of a whirring fan, you sip ice tea and say, "I'm not going to get hot and sweaty and waste all my energy on warm ups. I plan to save myself for the race." Everyone would say you were crazy, that you can't expect muscles to function properly until they've been warmed up.

    The last time you had to do a lot of talking, did you warm up your vocal muscles? I bet not. Want to prevent sore throats? Warm up before you begin to tell. Stretch your tongue out as far as you can. Stretch your face and mouth, exaggerating every possible facial expression. Roll your head to stretch your neck. Sing scales with vowels and with two letter syllables (ba, ca, da; fe, ge, he; etc.). Slowly increase the volume and range of these warm ups. The isolated privacy of your car on the way to school is an ideal place for these potentially embarrassing vocal gymnastics.

3. **Don't chill your muscles.** Again, picture yourself as an Olympic sprinter in the 100 meter finals. The starter calls, "On your marks." With a final kick of each leg you ease down into the starting blocks beside the other eight finalists. The crowd grows hushed with explosive anticipation. You rise up on fingers and toes as the starter calls "set."

    At that moment your coach rushes out and splashes a bucket of ice water across your legs. Everyone would agree you both were out of your minds. Ice water will tighten your legs. You'll pull a muscle before the race is half over.

    However, most speakers guzzle ice water not only before they speak, but during their event. The effect is the same. The muscles of your neck tighten and are much more likely to grow sore. Get in the habit of sipping warm or hot liquid—tea, coffee, lemon water, or plain water—before and while you tell. Your voice will last a lot longer.

PART V

STORYTELLING IN THE CURRICULUM
Putting the Magic to Work

*T*eaching with Telling

Why teach with storytelling? Telling stories eats up precious class time. Isn't the telling of stories during serious class time an attempt to turn school into an entertainment center? The answer couldn't be a more emphatic "no!"

I have previously mentioned research that supports the fact that storytelling is a powerful, efficient, and effective teaching tool. Factual and conceptual information is learned faster and better, and will be remembered longer, recalled more readily, and applied more accurately when that information is delivered as part of a well-told story.

But there is more. Storytelling, like an effective keynote speech, focuses student effort and attention and provides a common reference point and framework for the subsequent study. Storytelling motivates and excites students and creates more incentive for study and research. After all is said and done, storytelling is a more effective, efficient, exciting, motivating, and entertaining way to convey information and concepts.

That's why storytelling should be a standard teaching tool of every person who needs to teach—teach anything to anybody—or to motivate.

In the following sections I separate the discussion of using storytelling to teach into two parts: language arts teaching, where the form and structure of the story and the use of language are of primary teaching concern, and other curriculum subjects, where the content of the story is the core teaching vehicle. Certainly a single story can do both. But the successful methods for extracting pertinent information are different.

Teaching Language Arts Through Stories

Stories demonstrate powerful and effective use of language and contain the best use of dramatic structural elements. Stories contain effective and persuasive argument and logical development of ideas and themes. There is no aspect of effective language use (other than those associated with tightly formatted and metered language such as poetry and song) that cannot be effectively demonstrated through stories.

You will never want to tell all the stories you present to your class. Some you will want them to read. Some you will read to the class to preserve the author's exact wording. When you choose to tell a story, you will demonstrate the sound, rhythm, and pattern of effective oral language and create more vivid, detailed, powerful, and personal images of the story in the listener's mind. The best stories to take the time to learn and tell are those you want your students to spend the most time tearing apart and analyzing. Telling the story arms students with a greater vested interest in their images, impressions, analysis, and recollections of the story than will any other means of story delivery.

However, reading or telling a story to your class doesn't automatically teach the language arts lessons available in the story. Listening to an oral story *is* a valuable experience for students. But that is a small fraction of the teaching potential you have set in motion by priming students with the energy and excitement of a powerful story.

The problem is that *too many* individual concepts and techniques are being modeled at the same time for students to pick out and critically assess each one, just as it's harder to assess the third viola's technique while the whole orchestra is playing. You want music students to hear and revel in the glorious totality of stirring orchestral arrangements. You also want them to appreciate and learn individual technique.

The same is true for stories in a language arts program. No one wants to pull out a string of modifiers, action verbs, out-of-context epiphanies, character profile information, similes, or foreshadowing clues as a substitute for sharing the whole story. Still, it is those very elements of the story that your students need to master.

What is needed is an orderly and rational progression of constructive activities to lead students through story assessment in a positive and exciting way; a progression that assists students in more deeply understanding and learning from the stories you read and tell.

The Super Simple Storytelling progression of activities is a composite set of activities to use before, during, and after a story presentation. In fact, this progression is itself a string of exercises. Because of the logical flow from activity to activity, I thought it better to describe the majority of them in the text rather than refer to a prolonged sequence of individual exercises. While there is a logical flow from one to the next, it is neither essential to employ all 20-plus activities for every story you share nor to use them in strict sequential order. Use those that are grade and topic appropriate for the concepts you want your class to address and master.

PRE-STORY ACTIVITIES

Any discussion or activity to better prepare students to recognize and appreciate the specific language concepts you want them to remember is a worthwhile pre-telling activity. Define and discuss the purpose of a particular language element (action verbs, foreshadowing, characterization, goals and obstacles, scenic details, etc.). Then model its effective and also its ineffective use through improvised story mini-snippets. Have students experiment with this particular language element in exercises. (Exercise 5.1, *The 30-Second Story*, page 192, is an excellent vehicle for this type of student exploration.) Now the class is primed to recognize, observe, and appreciate the effective application of this particular language element in a story you present.

I have found four general topics universally worthy of pre-story discussion time. Individually and collectively they will assist students to hone their story skills. These four are:

1. **What makes a story fun to listen to?** Is it the story? What specifically about the story? Is it the way it's told? What about the way it's told? Is it a combination of both? Which elements are more important? If the class is unable to separate storytelling's contribution from that of the story itself, ask them what makes a story fun to read. This will focus on the story-related aspects. When you return to the original question, they will be adding back in those elements that relate to the way a story is told.

   Exercises 1.3 through 1.6 and 2.2 are all designed to support an exploration of this question. Stories are structured and shaped as they are, and told in the manner in which they are told, specifically because they make the material more enjoyable and interesting to receive. By critically studying what makes a story fun to hear or read, students are really beginning to analyze the effective use of all of the available language tools.

2. **What makes a story seem real?** Exercise 1.4, *What Makes It Real?*, directly addresses this important story aspect. Most students take for granted that the stories they read will seem believable enough to make them want to create vivid images of the story in their minds. Yet that very quality is one they struggle most to include in their own stories.

   On the surface, it is details that create reality. While that is true, it is also beneficial to examine these details more closely. Do *all* details seem real? Do more details always make a story seem more real? Are some kinds of details more effective than others? No detail-related exercises are included in this book. However, there are three and an accompanying discussion in my companion volume, *Write Right!* I would refer anyone to that book for assistance in guiding students toward a better understanding of effective details and their use.

3. **Review the core elements of a story.** Part II of *Super Simple Storytelling* is devoted to assessing the core elements that act as the driving engine for a story. Review these elements with your class. Use Exercise 2.3, *The Big Three*, to reinforce the central importance of these story-defining character elements. The more often students reinforce their new habit of thinking about character instead of plot when they think of the theme, purpose, and defining elements of a story, the better able they will be to both create their own stories and understand and analyze other stories.

4. **Create a perspective for the story.** Fiction stories (myth, legend, folk tales, genre fiction, fairy tales, etc.) are not created in a vacuum. They were created in a specific place and time. Neither are they set in places and times devoid of governing principles, values, beliefs, and laws based on those of the country of origin for the story. Review the historical, cultural, and geographical context of a story with your students before telling it. What were the concerns, struggles, problems, and hopes of the country when this story was created? What was the state of their technology and science? What were their beliefs and societal structure? How are these cultural elements reflected in their stories? The more students know about a story's context before they hear it, the better they will interpret, appreciate, and understand the story.

DURING-THE-STORY ACTIVITIES

It is easier to demonstrate how some elements of story information are presented while that information is still incomplete; that is, *during* the story, while listeners are still searching for some of the needed information, rather than after the story, when all necessary information has been successfully delivered.

I have discovered four questions that have sufficient teaching value to merit your stopping a good story to discuss them with your class. Luckily, teachers, like parents, routinely establish a pattern of momentarily interrupting a presentation for comment or analysis. Students won't mind as much when a teacher stops in the middle of an exciting story to ask a question.

Don't interrupt every story with these assessment questions, and I recommend that you don't explore more than two of these questions during any one story. The discussions will digress too far from the story before you can steer students back to the text for the next installment. However, don't overlook the value of studying a story's structure while its threads still dangle loose and unwoven in the minds of your students. There is great understanding to be gained from these discussions.

Stop periodically during the telling or reading of a story to ask students one or more of the following questions. I most often stop three times during a story and ask the same one or two questions each time. I try to stop once early on before the core story information has been provided, once mid-way after the conflicts and goals are known but not developed and resolved, and once just after the climax when all that is left to learn is whether the main character finally completes their quest for the story's goal. Let students debate their answers, using story information to support their beliefs.

Insert an extra-long pause into the story when you stop for discussion. Give your students time to complete and cement their final story images before the break. Then begin the chosen discussions.

When you return to telling the story, begin your telling with a summary review of the story up to this most recent interruption. Then begin your telling by repeating the last paragraph or two of the story from just before the point at which you stopped. This will help both you and the students sink back into your images of the story and into its flow, pace, emotion, and events.

The four questions I recommend for use during the telling of a story are:

1. **Who's the main character, and why?** This question forces students to compare information on all story characters and decide for whom they have the most relevant core story information. It is not always obvious. Antagonists are occasionally introduced and developed before the main character. A few stories open by following a side character that leads the story to the main character. Some stories delay development of the core story conflict. Thus the answer to this question during the early stages of many stories is anything but obvious.

    More specifically, this question forces students to decide which story character has an explicitly stated goal and problems that block them from that goal. This is the definition of a main character. In the absence of this core information, the students will assume that the character for whom they have the most information will become the main character.

    The value of this discussion comes not from *identifying* the main character, but in having students *justify* their answers with supporting story material. This discussion helps all students learn to identify key character information and to more readily recognize it in future stories.

2. **How will the story end, and why?** Stories end when the goal of the main character is either realized or forever abandoned. Always. That goal is the purpose of the story and the source of story suspense. The story cannot satisfactorily end until that question is resolved.

    However, students cannot successfully answer this question until they identify the main character and that character's goal. Character goals are routinely omitted from student thinking and from student stories. It is valuable to draw attention to this important character aspect while there is still doubt about a story's outcome.

    Note that goals are often implied rather than overtly stated in stories. In such stories, students will have to identify the central conflict to infer a goal and the possible resolutions that can become plausible story endings. Again, it is important for students to justify their answers using story information.

3. **What will happen next, and why?** This question calls on students to use cause and effect logic to assess the flow of the recent story events. They must assume that past and current story events are the causes that will inevitably create the next actions in the story. Realizing how they rely on cause and effect in stories they read and hear will help students avoid events that simply "happen" in their own stories and will help them become more proficient at structural analysis for their own writing efforts.

4. **Is it a story yet, and why or why not?** This is perhaps the most valuable question of all. Exercise 2.2, *Is It a Story Yet?*, is an example of this question in action. The first sentence of a story does not itself constitute a story. Somewhere along the flow of scenes, actions, problems, and plot twists, sufficient information is provided so that a listener will say that it *has* become a story.

    Stop several times before the critical pieces of information have been provided and, when most say that, no, it is not yet a story, ask them to explain why it isn't a story and to identify what essential information is still missing. Encourage students to challenge each other's answers, using story information to support their arguments.

    This question requires students to ponder what distinguishes a story from other narrative forms and what information they really need to call something a story. In short, it will ask them to identify the core elements of a story and to learn to recognize them when woven into the fabric of a story.

    Collectively, these four questions can be used to investigate and reveal virtually all of the major structural elements of a story and to demonstrate how they are typically ordered and presented in a story. They form a powerful assessment tool and, if treated like a mystery to be solved based on existing story clues, will be a fun addition to your story presentations.

POST-TELLING ACTIVITIES

The story is over; satisfied smiles linger on the faces of your students. You want to jump straight to a detailed assessment of how tension and suspense were maintained throughout the tale. Instinctively, you sense that your class will resist this leap to analytical probing. There is an awkward pause as you try to glean the best route to drag them toward your myriad of technical teaching points.

Begin the assessment process by helping students to make their images of the story firmer and more specific in their minds. Until they do, each individual's images are rather fragile and easily replaced by outside images just as your delightful images of character and setting from a book are so easily swept aside by the screen images when you later see the movie.

1. **Verbal reprocessing.** Following are four quick activities to help students cement story events, characters, and images in their minds. Students need to be paired for the first three activities. For the fourth, they should be grouped into teams of four to six.

    A. **Each student tells their partner about their own experience of listening to the story.** Allow 45 to 60 seconds per student. What went through their mind while they listened? What were they thinking about and picturing while this story was being told? What images and events did they focus on? Emphasize that there are no right or wrong answers. Whatever was actually on their mind is what they need to report.

    Hold a general class discussion in which students share with the class what they told their partner. You summarize and paraphrase what each student says and show that their comments all fall into the following four categories:

    > ➤ *Evaluation of the story* (form, content, performance). Many will have noted any pre-telling discussion elements and how they blended into this story. Many will have watched various aspects of your performance technique and style: your use of characterization, gesture, vocal changes, etc.
    >
    > Virtually all students will have, at some point, paused to critique and evaluate the story and its major elements. Some will have paused to decide if they thought the story still made sense or if they could find logical flaws in its information. Others will have paused to evaluate story details. Most will have assessed the core character elements and the major story characters to decide if they were appealing, relevant, interesting, adequate, and appropriate.
    >
    > All such observations fall under the story evaluation category, which, typically, occupies most of their time and attention.

    > ➤ *Comparison to other stories.* It is natural for listeners to sift through their previous story experiences for comparisons while they listen to your story. These comparisons can center on stories about the same topic or theme and which contained the same types of characters or humor, were from the same country or culture, were about the same character (How many stories about Jack have *you* heard?), were by the same author, or which were delivered with similar performance style.

    > ➤ *Relating this story to their own life and experiences.* Most students will periodically compare these story characters to their own life experiences or to those of friends and relatives. How did *they* react when they were in a scary situation or when they were tempted to steal or cheat? Did someone in their family face a situation similar to, or containing many of the same elements as, that described in the story?

> ➤ *Unrelated thoughts.* Finally, all listeners have complex, demanding lives outside of the confines of this story. Periodically, concerns related to those lives will intrude on story images. Often the intrusions are triggered by story events. Often, however, you will find that they appear during moments when the teller struggled the most, was the least sure of their story and their telling of it, and poured less energy and conviction into their telling.

All four items are valuable elements of a listening (or reading) experience. They are the ways in which we humans understand, interpret, and internalize story information. More important, the act of recalling and describing their own images and recollections of the story will help them permanently fix images of the story in their minds for later use during story assessment exercises.

B.   Each partnership quickly (in 30 seconds for older students, in several minutes for primary students) draws or sketches the story. Only one picture is allowed for each team. Either one or both partners can do the actual drawing but they both decide on its content. The time limit is designed to keep students from holding back on their imagery because of a lack of artistic skill. In 30 seconds everyone will scrawl stick images on the page. Their focus should be on the story and the choosing of appropriate images, not on the drawing itself.

Have students share what they drew and describe both what they pictured and why they chose that element to represent the story. It is valuable for students to see what others chose to single out as central story themes and elements.

Typically, these drawings will focus on underlying story themes, major plot sequencing, character relationships and feelings, and physical setting. Some will try to map the story. Some will picture the climaactic scene or final resolution. Some will depict the story's conflict. In every case the students are revisiting their experience of the story, reviewing their story images, and making those images and memories stronger and more permanent.

C.   Each pair retells the story to each other. One student begins and tells for 30 seconds. The other student takes over and continues the story for 30 seconds, then the first takes over again, and so forth. You time the tellings and call "Switch!" at 30-second intervals.

Students should use their own wording and their own emphasis when they retell the story. If one student can't remember what happened next, they are not excused from telling. Instead of moving forward, they repeat the last scene during their 30 seconds. If one student is truly stuck, they can ask their partner for a hint. However, discourage prompting. Part of the value of this exercise is for each student to remember and claim their *own* experience and version of the story.

Typically this telling will focus on a left-brained, factual plot summary and will omit much of the story detail, dialog, character motive, character feeling, and characterization. Discuss as a class what aspects of the story students omitted from their telling, what they included, and what they changed.

D. **In teams of four to six, students act out the story.** One tells the story as the rest of the team acts out each of the mentioned story elements (sound effects, actions, setting elements, etc.). Discuss as a class whether students were better able to picture the scenes, events, and characters after participating in the process of physically recreating each of these story elements.

2. **Reviewing and analyzing story characters.** Any story assessment should begin with a review of the most central and basic single component of any story, the story characters. Following are seven activities that allow students to review and assess the story characters and how they were constructed and presented.

A. **Rank the characters.** Ask the class the following questions. Allow time for students to discuss and debate their answers.

➤ Who is the *main* character? Why?

This question calls on the students to conduct a factual investigation of the story's information and to formalize their definition of a main character. Some might think that the main character is the one in the most scenes or the one with the most lines. This is often (but not necessarily) true, but they have the relationship backwards. It is not that lines makes the character but rather that a character may be expected to have a lot of lines or to show up in many scenes *because* they are the story's main character.

Some might argue that a character is the main character because more character information is provided for that character than for any other. However, the main character (protagonist) is a structural, factual position within the story. *The main character is that character whose goal is resolved at the story's end.* The goal of the main character defines the purpose of the story. With rare possible exceptions, the plot of a short story is about the efforts to overcome the jeopardy facing the main character. Novel-length stories can deal with the struggles and jeopardy facing several characters, so struggle and jeopardy are not guaranteed to be true indicators of the main character.

Students should sift through story information to both identify the main character and support their assertion. Make sure that there is agreement before continuing because disagreement here implies a difference in opinion about the structure, goals, resolution, and purpose of the story.

➤ Who do you think is the *most important* character? Why?

This question allows students to combine their subjective assessment of the characters with an objective evaluation of each character's contribution to the story. There can be honest disagreement as to the character who best fills this position.

Some will say that the main character is the most important because the story is about this character. Some could claim that the antagonist is the most important. Stories are about conflict and struggles. The antagonist is the embodiment of both.

Some other character may provide critical information or motivation and thus hold some claim to being the story's most important character. The value is not in assigning the crown but in having students use story information and story structural concepts to support and argue their positions.

➤ Who is your *favorite* character? Why?

This is seemingly a purely personal and subjective interpretation. That is only true in part. In part, authors and storytellers pick viewpoints and structure character information, story events, and delivery gestures, facial expressions, and vocal tones to force listeners to identify with certain characters and to dissociate themselves from others.

First allow students to express their personal opinions using story information and events to explain their selection. Then have the class examine the story and its presentation for techniques the author and/or teller used to direct listeners toward the character selections they made.

B. **Assess the story's core information.** Return the discussion to the main character and analyze their role in defining and shaping the story. What did they want to do or get? Why? Why didn't they already have it? What stood in their way? Was there any risk or danger to them if they tried to achieve their story goal? Specify this jeopardy. What was the source of this jeopardy? What did they do to try to achieve the goal? Did they have to face the potential risk and danger? When? (mostly during the climax scene). Did they succeed? How do these pieces of character information define the beginning point, ending point, and story line of this story?

Core character information does not come out of the story. The story comes out of this information.

C. **What creates an interesting character?** Have your students list what they know about the main character. Begin by asking them what makes the main character of this story an interesting character. Be careful to separate factual information stated in the story from conjecture, assumption, and opinions of the students. You want them to list only actual story information.

As students identify specific information, you will need to help them divide it into the five possible layers of character information. Show them that the story has woven key information from each of these layers into its ongoing events to make listeners understand and appreciate this character.

D. **Assess other story characters.** Have students compare how much they were told about the main character's five layers of information with what they learned about other characters. Begin with the antagonist. Did they learn any of the antagonist's core layer of information and the motives behind these goals and obstacles? How well did they learn the antagonist's personality, history, and sensory and activity layers?

Move on to supporting characters in the story. What kinds of information did they learn about each of these? Can your students begin to draw conclusions about the kinds and amount of character information they were given as a function of the character's role in the story?

E. **Interrogate the characters.** Often listeners are left with lingering questions about one or more of the characters after a story is over but don't have a way to ask the questions and gain the information they want. There seems to be no one to ask.

As a class, decide to invite one of the story characters into the room and interrogate them to find out all you and your students would like to know. Have students answer these questions: If you could bring one character in to this room and grill them with questions, who would you bring? Why? Who should ask the questions (you—the listener—or another character in the story)? What questions would you want answered?

After you've agreed on a story character to question, use Exercise 5.2, *Interrogate the Character* (page 196), to bring the character into the classroom and provide the answers your students need. This is a fun and valuable exercise in helping students identify both the kinds of information they want about a character and the value of that information in making the character seem more real and interesting.

F. **Judge the characters.** Because the central story characters must struggle against grave jeopardy, they often do things that, technically, are illegal, ethically and morally wrong, or at least very suspect.

Use Exercise 5.3, *Judge the Characters* (page 198), to put story characters and their actions on trial. Hold real in-class courtroom trials. Students love the courtroom drama and get a valuable opportunity to evaluate complex character behavior and its relationship to the students' own world. During this exercise students focus on the ethics of a character's actions rather than on their legality.

G. **Create shadow voices for major story characters.** This is an excellent activity for older students (especially middle and high school). We humans do not think and speak with a single voice. There seems to be an army of different voices screaming at us from inside our own heads, each demanding that we do what they think we should. Sometimes one voice reigns supreme, at other times another of the voices rules. It is a valuable lesson in the makeup of story characters to identify the major voices that speak to a character and to watch how they influence and befuddle that character's actions.

Exercise 5.4, *Shadow Voices* (page 200), is designed to allow your class to construct and observe these voices in operation. Listeners are typically much more sympathetic toward a character after they have seen the inner turmoil caused by these competing voices.

3. **Reviewing and evaluating the story.** This initial review and evaluation should be completed by extending student consideration beyond the central characters to encompass other story-wide aspects. Following are three activities that help students identify and recognize the major construction blocks for a story and place this story within some greater context.

A.   **Review the story.** Have students draw pictures, maps, and flow diagrams of the story, its characters, its settings, and the major events to fix the flow, relationship, and pattern of events in their minds. Have them search for patterns in the story's events. Have them search for cause and effect in this pattern. What is the cause for each event and how did each event later become the cause for some other event? Have them search for repetition. What was repeated? Why? How often and in what pattern?

B.   **Find the significant parts of the story.** Have your students identify each of the following parts of the story, recall when and how they were presented in the story, and put them in the order in whichthey appeared in the story:

> ➤ Goal of the main character
>
> ➤ Perspective and viewpoint
>
> ➤ Problems and flaws faced by the main character
>
> ➤ Conflict
>
> ➤ Risk and danger to the main character
>
> ➤ Setting and time of the story
>
> ➤ Climax (Also have them define the climax: the moment when the main character confronts the final obstacle blocking them from their goal.)
>
> ➤ What comes after the climax?
>
> ➤ Foreshadowing that hints at the climax and builds toward it
>
> ➤ Resolution
>
> ➤ Character reactions (an important component of character information)
>
> ➤ Tension and excitement

The only items in this list they will not be able to locate physically in the text of a story are tension and excitement. These are not physical elements in a story but rather are feelings created in the listener by the risk and danger associated with the story's conflict. Conflict is produced by the problems and flaws blocking a character from a goal.

If students complete this list for several stories, patterns will emerge in how and where some of this information appears. The climax is followed by either one or two short scenes that always contain the story's resolution of the main character's goal. Risk and danger are introduced after (and about) the conflict problems and flaws blocking a character. Risk and danger can be, and often are, gradually increased up to the climax. Tension and excitement track with the level of risk and danger. The main character's goal was stated or implied early in the story. Observing these types of successful patterns in stories your students have enjoyed will assist them in structuring their own stories.

C.   **Place this story.** Compare and contrast this story with others of the same period, on the same subject or theme, about the same character or type of character, presented in the same mood or tone, or by the same writer or culture. Have students search for aspects that are unique to this story and those it holds in common with other stories. Have students search for values, attitudes, and beliefs that reflect the time and culture in which the story was created. This will help students both understand basic story structure and develop their own stories along classic plot lines.

4.   **Extending the story.** Before breaking the story into individual building blocks and writing elements, it is valuable to examine the effect of major, story-wide decisions an author or story-teller makes. Following are eight extension activities that virtually any grade level can use.

A.   **Retell the story, *but* change the perspective and viewpoint character.** Who else could tell this story? How would the story change? How would a listener's view of the characters and events change? What is the importance of defining a perspective and viewpoint?

B.   **How else could this story have ended?** Have students sift through early story information to detect other plausible endings. Have them support their ideas with story material. A story's resolution is tied to the goal of the main character. That character either achieves their goal or has to abandon the goal forever. However, within these two plausible outcomes there is a wide range of specific possibilities.

C.   **What happened next?** Have students extend the story beyond its current ending point. Be sure they support their extension ideas with information from the existing story.

D.   **What happened before?** Have students use story events and character attitudes and relations to build a picture of events that could both explain and lead up to the story as told. What they are really doing is creating a history for the main character that explains the goals, beliefs, hopes, fears, attitudes, and relationships of this character that exist as the story starts.

E.   **Retell the story, *but* change the setting and/or time.** Have students imagine how these changes will alter the characters and sequencing of the story.

F.   **Retell the story, *but* change character personalities and goals.** Major story events must stay the same, but the character interactions and event outcomes all change. This is a classic way to alter fairy and folk tales. (How many versions of the "Three Little Pigs can there be?" Answer: as many as anyone can imagine.)

G.   **Have each student answer this question:** If it were *my* story, how would *I* end it? Why? Make sure that their answers are consistent with existing story information. What would they have to change in the story to support the ending they chose? Have them use story information to defend why they think theirs is the best ending for the story.

H.   **Use "What if . . . ?" questions to change the story.** ("What if BB Wolf had a sore throat and couldn't huff and puff and blow down even a straw house?") Let students create a series of plausible what-if's for the story you told. Then let them rebuild the story from that point on in small teams and compare how the what-if questions changed and redirected their version of the story.

5. **Digging below the surface.** Now fine-tooth combing of the technical aspects of the story is appropriate. Focus the class on those specific techniques and concepts of successful story building you want them to master through this story. But even this process of tearing into individual techniques and aspects of a story can be divided into three tiers.

A. **Macro-structure.** Study the placement of major story information and its order of presentation. How and why did the first few paragraphs make you want to hear the rest of the story? What did you learn in that opening scene? What makes listeners (or readers) become interested in the characters and in their fate? How was tension created and maintained throughout the story? What information was held out to keep listeners in suspense?

   What and when was the story's climax? How did the story build to that moment? *What* built to this moment of climax? (Most students will think that it is action that builds to the climax. But action occurs in spurts throughout a story. It is tension that faithfully builds toward the climax.) How soon did students know what this climax would be? Why? How was this event foreshadowed?

B. **Micro-structure.** (For this assessment each student needs a copy of the story.) Study paragraph length and the variation in that length. Does paragraph structure correlate with anything else (like action or tension)? Study transitions—between scenes, between thoughts, across gaps in time. How did the transition keep listeners from getting lost or confused during the jump? Study sentence length and variation and try to correlate it with other story parameters.

   Look for powerful writing forms like epiphanies and ironies. Identify plot twists and surprises and decide how the story set up and created them. Have students search for any aspect of story creation and presentation that extends over a significant portion of the story.

C. **Micro-micro-structure.** Study the effect of specific word choices in the story. How did specific word choices affect the images students created in their minds? How were places, characters, and events described? What forms of detail were used in this story? Were similes and metaphors used? Were they effective and memorable? How did a select few bits of detail create whole vistas in a reader's mind?

   Where do those mental images come from? Which kinds of words create images? Use Exercise 4.8, *Where Images Come From* (page 188), to show that, in general, nouns create images, modifiers provide visual richness and detail, and verbs create motion, emotion, and action to connect individual images.

   Which details were and, in general, how much detail was, included in the story? What was left out? Study the verbs used in the story. How many were specific action verbs? How many were general or vague? How many were verbs of state? Which were more effective in creating images of story events?

Stories in Other Curriculum Areas

Stories are valuable for language arts teaching because of their ability to reinforce and develop an understanding of the form and structure of story and of the use of oral language. In other curriculum subjects, stories are valuable for their ability to increase student understanding and retention of content information. As a teacher, your focus has shifted from the form to the content.

Still, stories are stories. Yes, you want to emphasize the content material. But you still must create a story, and those stories must still be character based and focus on character goals, conflicts, and struggles—even if it is the final discoveries, accomplishments, and triumphs of those characters you want to teach. The established value of using stories to teach curriculum material has already been discussed.

Because stories naturally focus on struggles, they also effectively teach and demonstrate the *process* of human activity—the process of doing science or of other human endeavor that is routinely overlooked by teaching methods that focus only on final outcomes.

The worlds of science, history, math, and art abound with spellbinding stories about the people who have developed their respective fields and the process of their activity. There are countless other stories—both fiction and nonfiction—that effectively depict principles and concepts in each of these fields. All of these stories are capable of teaching. *Telling* any of these stories adds the extra enchantment, motivation, and enthusiasm inherent in the process of storytelling.

The central purpose of *Super Simple Storytelling* is to provide a detailed guide to understanding and *doing* storytelling. The possible schemes and plans for weaving storytelling into the curriculum are as varied as the storytelling styles of individual teachers. However, there are four particularly effective models for using storytelling as a teaching tool, which can be generally applied in most lesson blocks in most subject areas.

UNIT INTRODUCTION STORIES

In the late 1970s I was asked to deliver a keynote speech to open a scientific conference on potential changes to the Environmental Protection Agency regulations covering off-shore oil production for parts of the California coastline. (I was working as an oceanographic research scientist at the time.) I wasn't enflamed by any relevant passion I wanted to impart to the participants. I wasn't even sure what a keynote speech was supposed to say and do. In desperation I centered my short talk on two rambling poems that humorously looked at how we believe in the great value of environmental protection—until it begins to inconvenience us. One compared the value of the fishes in the sea to what "my electric blanket means to me."

I struck a chord. For the next two days comment after comment and discussion after discussion used this poem as a reference point and yardstick for the comparisons and comments participants wanted to make. That poem provided a common perspective, a way for the participants to view and approach their work at the conference.

That was the most effective keynote speech I have ever given. I have given many that were funnier, more eloquent, and more stirring. But never have I given one that so unified a body of people and gave them a common perspective and understanding of their upcoming work. That speech set the tone for the conference. It introduced the key questions and themes in a way that made them relevant to each participant on a human level. It gave purpose and focus to their subsequent deliberations and efforts. It initiated their thought processes.

Those are the characteristics of a good keynote speech. They are also the list of the benefits and advantages you accrue from using a story to introduce a block or unit of instruction. The story becomes an effective keynote speech for the subsequent unit. Why *tell* the stories you use to introduce a unit block of study? Because it is a more powerful means of delivery. Because telling produces more vivid and detailed images of the story. Because the factual and conceptual information in the story will lodge more deeply in your students' minds.

A story as unit introduction creates relevant purpose and focus for students' study, just as a goal for the main character creates purpose and focus for the events of a story. This model of using stories to teach is presented diagramatically (think picture outline) in Figure 5.1 (page 90).

Unit introduction stories are used as you first introduce a new unit of study to launch students into this particular study and to create a common reference point or perspective for that study. I'll walk through the steps of this most common and effective model with two examples.

STEPS OF A UNIT INTRODUCTION STORY

A second-grade teacher introduced a science unit on what makes things grow by telling the Frog and Toad story "The Garden," by Arnold Lobel. In the story Frog, fearing his seeds are afraid to grow, tries to encourage his garden by singing to the seeds, playing music, shining lights at night, etc. It is a delightful story.

1. This teacher first (step 1 in Figure 5.1) identified the theme (how plants grow) she wanted to use as the focal point for this unit.

2. Second (step 2), she found and told an appropriate story. (I describe the characteristics and potential sources for these stories later.)

3. After telling the story she asked (step 3), "Do you think Frog was right in what he thought would make seeds grow? Do you agree with him? What do you think makes a seed grow?"
   She listed all of their doubts, questions, disagreements, and ideas relating to this story in question form on the board, prodding and probing as needed to keep her students thinking about the story and the beliefs and actions of the characters. She then looked for similar themes and ideas in these questions that she and her students could group together.

4. From these groups of similar questions they identified (step 4) their own set of hypotheses about the science facts in the story. A hypothesis is simply a supposition or a statement of belief. This teacher and her class condensed their list of questions into five hypotheses, such as, "We do not believe that singing to and playing music for seeds or plants will make them grow better and faster," "We do not believe that watching and talking to seeds or plants makes them grow faster and better," etc. Note that these hypotheses are not simply statements of the students' beliefs about what makes a plant grow. Rather they are statements about whether the students believe the facts of the story. The teacher wants to teach the content material. Students want to check out the story and see if it is plausible.

Figure 5.1. A Story as a Unit Introduction.

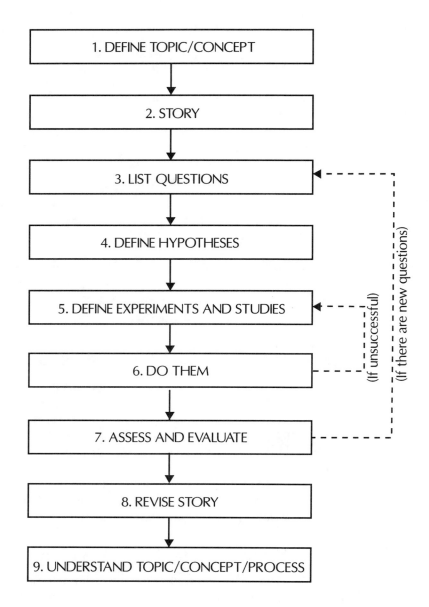

Examples:
- "The Commissioner of Ballons," by Kendall Haven
- Frog & Toad, "The Garden," by Arnold Lobel
- Mother Goose, "What Little Boys Are Made of ..."
- "Bembleman's Bakery," by Melinda Green

Characteristics:
- Usually from literature
- Usually fiction
- Focus is on the application of a concept

5.   Next (step 5) the teacher asked her class, "How are we going to find out if we are right?" Some said they could read books to find out. (The teacher said that there was information in their textbook they could use and lots more in the library.) Some said they could conduct an experiment and grow their own plants to see. (She agreed that they could.) Some wanted to watch a video. (She agreed that they would search for a good one on the subject.) Note that the activities the students suggested are exactly what the teacher was going to do anyway during this unit block of study. All that had changed (and significantly increased) was the motivation for her students to participate in this study.

   The class was split into teams that would conduct each of the experiments and studies the students identified. Each study was specifically designed to assess one of the students' hypotheses and through that hypothesis to establish the scientific veracity of the story.

6.   Over the next several weeks the studies and experiments were undertaken (step 6). The teacher gave additional lectures and presentations on the subject, as she always had. But the students discussed plant growth in terms of Frog and Toad. The story had become a successful focusing vehicle for their efforts and learning.

   Experiments, especially, have a way of not working correctly and of identifying new variables rather than answering the original questions. Many of the experiments had to be restructured and repeated because they didn't successfully refute or substantiate the hypothesis they were designed to address.

7.   As each study was completed (step 7), the students assessed the corresponding hypothesis. Was Frog right or was he wrong? What makes a plant grow? Often the studies would also identify several new questions the students hadn't thought of before. New questions would spawn new hypotheses and new studies or experiments.

8.   Finally (step 8), the teacher and her students concluded their research and decided to revise the story to include the information they had learned. The students were happy because they now knew if this story was true.

9.   Their teacher was happy because (step 9) they had eagerly, aggressively, and enthusiastically learned the material she wanted to teach. As an important side benefit, they had walked through every step of the scientific method. They had "done" the process of science and now also better understood how to conduct major studies.

A high school teacher at my nephew's school conducted a unit on revolutions in which he wanted his students to both learn the facts about a number of important revolutions in history and also to study the forces that generate revolutions and how they build to explosive power.

He told a story by Jay O'Callahan, a marvelous Massachusetts storyteller, about a father and teenaged daughter who were locked in their own private war, which led to her threatening to revolt. He had his students discuss the character of the daughter and decide if they agreed with and could support what she felt and said and if they thought that these forces related to the societal forces that fueled revolutions.

Their lists of questions, opinions, and ideas were converted into hypotheses listing the forces these students believed were the driving forces of revolutions. The class rushed into their study—not because they wanted to learn about world revolutions, but because they wanted to learn if their hypotheses based on the experience of one girl in a story were correct. They completed their study and concluded that Jay O'Callahan had done an excellent job of presenting the major revolutionary forces through the struggles of one girl. Along the way, they thoroughly learned the unit material and also learned how to conduct a major study.

SUCCESSFUL UNIT INTRODUCTION STORIES

The preceding are two typical examples of the power and potential of unit introduction stories. What kinds of stories work best for unit introduction? There are three keys to identifying successful stories.

1. **There is no need for the stories to be *about* the unit subject matter (science, history, math, etc.).** But the struggles of the characters must deeply involve the unit subject and theme, even though the characters are not aware of it and never mention it. This link between story events and unit theme must be strong enough so that follow-on student questions (step 3) about the story will also be about the unit subject matter.

   My 45-minute story, "The Commissioner of Balloons," is a good example. A boy wants to buy a special birthday present for his mother. In a desperate, last-ditch effort to earn the needed money, he grabs a job at the fair selling helium balloons. Excessively eager to earn lots of money fast, he blows up too many balloons, so many that they lift him off the ground. He flies with a handful of balloons. It is a delightful and powerful story, but it is not about science. Still, it has been used at a number of schools to introduce a science unit on gasses. (The questions—step 3—that are typically generated include: Can you really fly with helium balloons? With how many? Why do helium balloons fly? How high will they fly? What happens to helium balloons that rise into the sky? Why is helium lighter than air? What is air? Are there other lighter-than-air gasses? Are there lighter-than-helium gasses? Why not use those for balloons? If helium is so light, why is a helium tank so heavy?) The story characters and their struggles lead students to wonder about some aspect of the intended subject matter, in this case gasses.

2. **The story characters and their goals, jeopardy, and struggles must be powerful, captivating, and relevant enough to your students so that they will want to ask and answer questions about the characters and story.** Most successful unit introduction stories are fiction because only fictional characters are willing to do whatever they must to maximize story risk and danger and to act in such a way as to maximize the mesmerizing power and drama of their struggles.

   The story must be captivating and it must involve central concepts and themes of the unit you plan to teach, but need not contain any accurate factual information. (In "The Garden" Frog is wrong—from a second-grade perspective—on every page and with every thought about what makes seeds grow. Still the story works because it introduces those themes and questions. Students at a high school or college level discover that what Frog did *does* have a positive influence on plant growth.)

Because the story will influence activity over an extended period of study, there is no need to require that the story be short. "The Commissioner of Balloons" and the Jay O'Callahan story mentioned previously are both nearly an hour in length. Many powerful and appropriate unit introduction stories are in the 15- to 30-minute range. On the other end of the scale, the story "Brian and the Worms" (listed in Exercise 2.2, *Is It a Story Yet?*) is less than a minute long and has been used to introduce primary biology units. The Frog and Toad story, "The Garden," is about five minutes long. I have met teaches who used the Mother Goose poem, "What Are Little Boys Made Of?", to introduce units on human physiology. The students spent their time both confirming that there are no puppy dog tails in a boy and trying to decide what differences between boys and girls might have made the author think that there were. They walked away knowing something about literature and lots about human physiology. The unit introduction story had done its magic.

3. **The final key to a successful unit introduction story is that it must be a story you feel you can comfortably tell.** A central *Super Simple Storytelling* premise is that every story you tell must fit with your storytelling style and abilities. This is still a story. We are still talking about telling that story. All the concepts of storytelling mentioned earlier still apply. Even though you want to pick the story that best fits with the theme of your curriculum unit, it won't work unless you can also tell it well. That is the most fundamental mandate of storytelling. If you can't comfortably and successfully present the story so as to excite your students about these characters and their struggles, its value will be lost.

How do you find stories that meet all three criteria? Luckily you need not grope blindly through endless stacks of literature hoping to stumble across a suitable story. A number of thematic guides exist that link existing stories to theme, subject, and grade appropriateness. Given a unit theme and grade level, the guides will identify a short list of potential stories for you to review. Every public library and many school libraries carry a number of them. I have listed my favorites in the "References." These guides are all currently available and have worked well for many teachers.

DAILY THEME STORIES

Within the flow of a general unit, there will be a number of specific themes and teaching points you want to emphasize for your students. Many of these can be effectively housed in stories. This use of stories is more tightly focused than are unit introduction stories. Your goal will be to use a story to demonstrate, enliven, and clarify a specific concept, principle, or event, or to make those who produced some historical event seem real and interesting.

Unit introduction stories are designed to excite curiosity and wonder, to generate questions, to present strong and compelling characters, and to involve the process of the unit's central material. Daily theme stories are used to provide specific information, to answer questions, and to demonstrate concepts and principles. The most common in-class, curriculum-based use of stories is as daily theme stories.

The general model for using stories to amplify such daily themes is shown in Figure 5.2 (page 94) and described in the following seven steps.

Figure 5.2. The Story to Amplify and Clarify a Daily Theme.

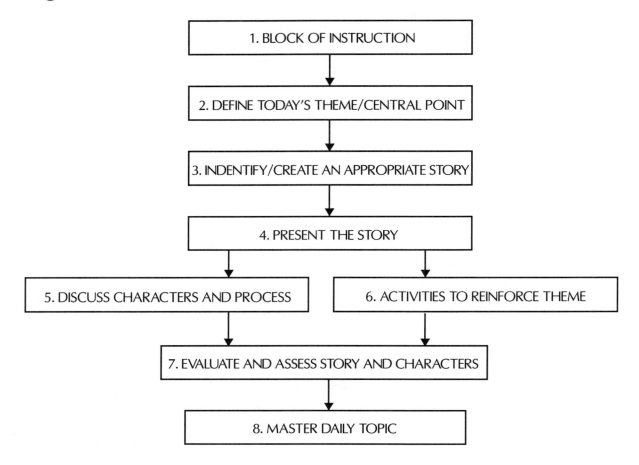

Examples:
- "Marvels of Science: 50 Fascinating 5 Minute Reads," by Kendall Haven
- "Mathematicians Are People Too," by Wilbert Reimer
- Math curriculum stories

Characteristics:
- Short—10 minutes or less
- Usually nonfiction (but can be fiction)
- Focus is on the person and the process

1. First specify the flow and key concept of a unit of instruction (step 1 in Figure 5.2)

2. Identify a concept, principle, event, or individual you want to emphasize as the central theme of that day's lesson (step 2).

3. Identify or create a story that clarifies or demonstrates this theme or its creator and their process of creation and development (step 3).

4. Present (read or tell) the story (step 4).

5. Follow the story with student discussions (step 5) that expand on and reinforce the process and character involved . . .

6. And with activities that demonstrate and clarify the daily theme (step 6).

7. Use the results of student discussion and activity to assess character and story (step 7), and then . . .

8. Allow this assessment to assist students to more fully understand the theme of the daily lesson (step 8).

Daily theme stories are simpler and more direct than unit introduction stories and have a much more limited role to fulfill. Some examples may be helpful. Lorrie Spindler, a Pennsylvania fourth-grade teacher, used an African origin story about how the stars and moon came to be in the sky as a unit introduction story for a unit on the solar system. It is a funny, lively story and set her class to wondering about the origins of the solar system and galaxy.

As one part of that unit, Lorrie wanted her students to consider the difficulty of making extensive and accurate observations for early astronomers and the social and political upheaval early discoveries caused. She read a story I wrote about Copernicus in my book *Marvels of Science* (Libraries Unlimited, 1994), to her class to begin one day's study. Yes, she read the story instead of telling it. No one will tell every story they present to a class and daily theme stories are far less important to tell than are unit introduction stories.

The story describes Copernicus's growing anxiety as he discovered that his findings contradicted the belief of every other scientist in the world and the stated position of the all-powerful Catholic Church, which was housing and feeding him and paying for his work. The more firmly he became convinced that he was right and the rest of the world was wrong, the more terrified he grew of the anger and retribution of the Church when he released his results. In the end, Copernicus became so frightened that he put in his will that his results could not be released until 25 years after his death.

Lorrie led a brief discussion about why Copernicus might be condemned instead of praised for his discovery. Her students had been compiling a list of major astronomical discoveries. She asked them to find out what was believed before each of those discoveries had been made and to try to list who might have been upset by each discovery and what beliefs were shattered by each discovery. She later used a story about Galileo to introduce a discussion about the effects of the limits of technology on the kinds of discoveries astronomers were able to make.

In both cases these daily theme stories were told to demonstrate a specific concept and to act as a model for her students to use in their subsequent efforts to uncover similar information about other astronomers and discoveries. The story answered rather than generated questions and modeled the students' subsequent behavior.

Similarly, stories about Revolutionary War and Civil War generals and leaders have been used to make those historical figures seem real and important to students and to demonstrate various aspects of period life and military tactics. I have also helped several teachers create fictional stories to demonstrate the steps and process of various math procedures (multiplication, division, working with fractions). In all cases the stories were meant to model and supply information that would assist student study rather than to initiate that study.

SUCCESSFUL DAILY THEME STORIES

Daily theme stories are typically shorter than unit introduction stories and rarely exceed 10 minutes. Daily theme stories must include a clear, unambiguous presentation of the information you want to convey. While unit introduction stories are most often fictional, daily theme stories are most often nonfiction (to provide more factual and conceptual information).

NONFICTION STORY SOURCES

Effective nonfiction stories include those describing the people who created knowledge, discovery, and advancement, significant events in history, and relationships in nature. The availability of suitable nonfiction daily theme stories varies substantially by subject matter.

Science

Science stories are the most available. Certainly nonfiction nature stories about different ecosystems, species, and relationships abound. Even more valuable, I believe, are the growing number of stories about the people who have produced significant scienctific advances. These stories not only describe the people and discoveries but also reveal the look and feel of the process of doing science. Themed collections of stories about scientists (women scientists, black scientists, astronomers, chemists, etc.) are now commonly available. You can often find historical stories that include key information on the process, discovery, or concept you have selected as a daily theme. Historical science stories are so successful because science naturally contains all of the motives and intrigue of the best soap operas. Think of the incredible stress on Copernicus. Seventy years later Galileo was placed under permanent house arrest by the Italian Inquisition Board of the Catholic Church for confirming Copernicus's findings.

Isaac Newton didn't simply invent gravity one sunny afternoon. No. He had been tormented for years by his failure to understand why the moon didn't fall down to Earth and why Earth didn't fall to the sun. It almost drove him mad before his young nephew, while playing with a ball on a string, showed Newton that the moon really *does* fall toward Earth but that the moon's momentum counteracts that force by trying to make the moon fly off into space. It is a great story. But the story isn't Newton's laws of gravity and motion. The story is Newton's struggle. Science discoveries are a long and continuous trail of struggles—struggles against ignorance, struggles against societal beliefs, struggles against other scientists.

There are no silver and bronze metals in the world of science. It is a winner-take-all endeavor. Newton was not the first to develop the principles of calculus. But once he published his papers and was proclaimed the father of calculus, the German scientist who had previously developed many of the same principles was forgotten. Less than two weeks after Alexander Graham Bell announced the development of his telephone system, a scientist working for Western Union completed work on his system, which worked as well as Bell's. That scientist's name is lost in the dust of history.

Five research teams around the world were racing to discover the shape of the DNA molecule. Secret offers and counteroffers of collaboration were telegraphed between teams. Francis Crick and James Watson won the race (by using information stolen from one of their competitors). Crick and Watson gained instant fame, prestige, and fortune. The other teams received nothing for their efforts and several lost research support for failing to win the race.

Stories focus on these problems, flaws, risk and danger, and struggles of characters. The history of science is stuffed with enough of this jeopardy to make almost any science story gripping. The problem is that most histories focus on accomplishments and ultimate success instead of on struggle and jeopardy. Figure 5.3 (page 98) contains a list of many of the flaws, problems, and personal goals that are common throughout the history of science. As you read literature about science, search for these elements and you will find that it is easy to convert mundane histories into gripping science stories.

History

History is, virtually by definition, a story. The problem is that we so often skip the story (character, goal, and struggles) to jump straight to historically significant accomplishments. Try Exercise 5.5, *The History Game* (page 202), with your class. This exercise clearly shows that we have learned the identity of significant events in history but are hungry for character-based information that can convert fact into story.

Unfortunately, I have found far fewer collections of short, tightly focused stories about political, social, and cultural history than I have about science. There are good collections on explorers and on medical sciences. However, most history writing has tended toward either complete biographies of one person (which may contain the material for dozens of stories); epic narratives tracing an entire nation, period, or culture; or detailed and complete histories of an event (the Civil War, the Teapot Dome scandal, the Oklahoma land rush, the Indian wars, the California Gold Rush, etc.). These all require the teacher to perform extensive editing and rewriting to whittle them down into suitable daily theme stories. The best general sources for history stories is often the biography section of the children's library. These book-length biographies often contain a string of connected stories about the chosen individual.

Math

Nonfiction math stories aren't nearly as popular as those for science and history. The focus of math is often exclusively on application (teaching students how to do the math manipulations) and ignores the history and development of those numerical processes. I have only seen three accurate collections of stories about the history and development of math. Fictional math stories that clearly depict the processes of math are more popular and often more useful.

Figure 5.3. Elements of Science Story Characters.

The following is a list of common, frequently occurring character elements for historic characters in science stories. Search available information for these, and other, unique elements that will bring your science stories to brilliant life.

1. **CHARACTER GOALS:**
   Knowledge
   Understanding
   Fame
   Wealth
   Truth
   Power
   Altruism
   Desire to help humanity
   Thrill of discovery
   Need to solve a problem
   Revenge

2. **CHARACTER FLAWS:**
   Lack of understanding
   Lack of knowledge (ignorance)
   Lack of self-confidence
   Overconfidence
   Bull-headedness
   Arrogance
   Insecurity (Indecisiveness)
   Selfishness
   Lack of ethical standards
   Envy
   Greed

3. **CHARACTER PROBLEMS:**
   Lack of support (peer, public)
   Lack of funding
   Competition
   Peer pressure to conform
   Technical and equipment limitations
   Public opinion

FICTION STORY SOURCES

Fiction stories can be effectively used as daily theme stories, as long as the story clearly presents the informational material related to the daily theme. Fiction stories have the advantage of being designed around the characters. So if the story includes the requisite content information, it is sure to include the necessary story elements to create a successful story experience.

Published sources for daily theme stories include myths, legends, origin stories, nature stories, *por qua* stories (which describe why things are as they are), animal stories, folk and ethnic tales, and period stories. The real challenge is to sift through the mountain of available stories searching for ones that match the specific daily theme you plan to emphasize and that are grade appropriate for your audience. Published thematic guides linking existing stories with subject, grade, and curriculum theme are the fastest and surest way to identify the stories you want to use. Such guides are available in every public library system and in many school libraries.

It is often difficult to find a story that presents the exact process you want to teach through a story. However, it is relatively easy for you to create your own fictional daily theme stories that do. Identify the one concept, principle, process, or idea in the lesson plan that would benefit most from clarification, personification, and illustration through a story. Create a main character for this story by turning a related noun into that character. Any noun can become a character in a story. Any relevant verb can become an event, action, or goal for this character. The story then centers around this character learning to do their assigned job.

As an example, I helped a third-grade teacher create a quick story about Ms. Multiplicand, who needed to find her place in the multiplication process. She was pushy and bossy by nature and wanted to do and control everything, saying, "Oh, I'd just rather do it all myself." No one liked her or was willing to work with her. The king of numbers was frustrated because no multiplication was getting done. Ms. Multiplicand's friends had to talk her into cooperating with others (Mr. Product and Mr. Multiplier). To create a truce and some cooperation, they had to create a treaty stating exactly what each would do. That treaty, of course, detailed the process of multiplication the teacher wanted to teach to her students that day.

THE ONGOING STORY

An ongoing story combines some features of unit introduction stories and daily theme stories. Like unit introduction stories, ongoing stories are designed to stimulate questions and action by students and to provide perspective and purpose to their subsequent study. Like daily theme stories, each ongoing story is tightly focused on one small element within an overall unit of instruction.

To accomplish these dual tasks, an ongoing story is broken into individual segments or episodes. Like a chapter in a book, each episode features the same main character and overall story goal but deals with the character's attempt to overcome a specific problem of the day. Each episode of the story acts like a rousing unit introduction story for the specific daily theme. As each daily theme is mastered, a new infusion of energy and motive is injected into the unit by the next episode of the story and next element in the unit.

Ongoing stories are always fictional and are created by the teacher because each episode must be tailored to the sequential themes a teacher wants to emphasize in a unit of study. The process of creating an ongoing story, however, is much easier than it might seem. The flow diagram (think picture outline) for ongoing stories is shown in Figure 5.4 (page 100) and summarized in the following eight steps.

Figure 5.4. The Ongoing Story.

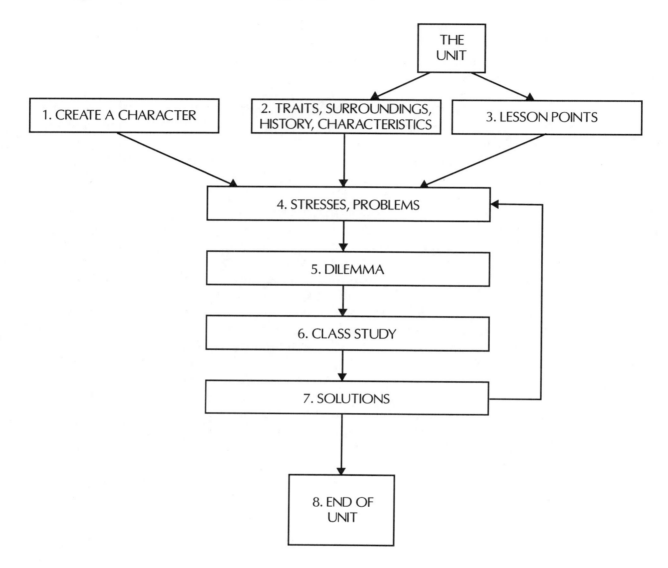

Examples:
- Uncle and European geography/culture
- Puppet in the Blue Box

Characteristics:
- You create character and story situations
- Focus on flaws and problems
- Historical fiction style

1. You invent a main character (step 1 in Figure 5.4), a first impression for that character, an overall story goal, and initial elements of a character personality and profile. The nature of the unit of study may help shape this character because you must immerse their problems into the unit's subject matter.

2. Create surrounding events and setting for this character that will immerse them into the unit subject matter (step 2).

3. Block the unit into a sequential series of key concepts or study areas you want your students to focus on (step 3).

4. Create a problem (step 4) for the main character that can only be solved by understanding the first of the unit's key concepts.

5. Bring the story up to a climax point where the main character has to make a decision or answer questions or take action based on the first key point (step 5). Make sure that this character does not understand that point and is in desperate trouble in making their decision.

6. Stop your telling of the story and have your students complete this story episode (step 6) by mastering the key lesson point of the story and of the day.

7. Once student study creates a correct solution for the dilemma facing the main character (step 7), add a new problem to the story that requires the character to progress to the second key point of the unit, thus looping back to step 4 on the picture outline.

8. Once the unit has been completed (step 8), end the story by achieving the main character's goal.

An example may be helpful. California fourth-grade teacher George Markham wanted to use an ongoing story for his unit on European geography. First he created a character and an overall story. His students loved murder mysteries, so he created a fictitious uncle of his who lived in Canada and had been accused of murdering the rich heiress on whose property he lived.

George decided that it would not be realistic for him to tell the individual episodes of the story. He decided to bring them in as letters from the uncle and read them to his class. He coerced a neighbor into writing the final draft of each letter so that they wouldn't be in George's handwriting.

In the first letter George described the heiress, her vast estate, and the three other people who were there on the night of the murder: the owner of a golf course next to the heiress' estate, a free-loader nephew of the heiress, and a friend of the heiress who had fallen on hard times and had just been forced to sell her beautiful family estate. He also listed three clues: a barking dog, some muddy footprints, and a half-empty glass of wine.

George had no idea how those clues fit into the mystery or even who committed the murder. His uncle had found the body and called the police, who accused him of the vile murder. George ended the letter by saying that the uncle was terrified of going to jail and so had fled to England to escape from the police while he proved his innocence. However, he hadn't had time to plan the trip and appealed to George for immediate assistance. He needed information on English geography, culture, economy, customs, and currency. Would George gather the information and send it to him so he could better fit into English society?

George's class was instantly hooked, eager to research England to do their part in solving a grand murder mystery. The story provided no pertinent curriculum information, but rather created motive and purpose for their study beyond mere academic mandate from their teacher.

Within a week the class had compiled an impressive profile of England. George thanked them and said he would get it to his uncle. The class refused to be brushed off so easily. They insisted on mailing it themselves. George packaged the reports, addressed them to a fictitious post office box in a small town near London he had found on a map, and marched the class to the post office.

Two days later another letter arrived from the uncle. Interpol had been breathing down his neck in England. He had fled to Denmark. Could George provide the same kind of excellent information for Denmark? The letter included several clues to the murder and more character information on the uncle and on each of the other possible suspects. (George had been developing this information all week.)

George sent a note home to parents explaining his study plan and telling them that the story was fiction and simply part of the unit. That note never seemed to dim his students' enthusiasm, as he feared it might.

The unit marched on as George's uncle fled across Europe. George found that he could model his mystery after a Sherlock Holmes story he found and so modeled the clues in each letter after the clues Holmes received.

The students reveled in their involvement in such a grand murder case, developing profiles of each story character and deciding who they thought did it. Soon they began to suggest places the uncle might want to hide by finding European countries they wanted to study.

George completed the unit and found that he had one more important task to undertake. He had to successfully end not just the unit, but also the story. The uncle finally wrote that the golf course owner had been arrested. He had killed the heiress because she found out that he had illegally placed two of his fairways across her land and altered the property deeds to cover it up. However, the uncle was still too traumatized to return to North America. He moved to Australia but vowed to visit the class and thank them for keeping him out of jail as soon as he dared return.

The class was thrilled. Many of those students returned to school four and five years later to inquire after George's uncle and to say that that unit was their favorite part of school.

George was thrilled. That class put more effort into their studies and turned in more complete and well-documented reports than had any previous class.

Ongoing stories work well for any unit with sequential or progressive daily themes to use as the focus of individual story episodes. Note that there is no need to directly connect the overall story (character, goal, and jeopardy) to the curriculum unit. Unit material, however, must be an integral part of solving the story.

I helped a second-grade teacher create "The Minister of Multiplication" as an ongoing story. The new Minister knew nothing about multiplication, which he figured was all right because no one else in the kingdom did either. Most people actually believed that multiplication was a myth. The Minister grabbed the job only because he wanted an easy, stress-free life and figured a cushy government job was just the thing. During his first audience with the king, he solemnly stated that it would take him many years just to discover if there was such a thing as multiplication.

Then an evil wizard threatened to flatten every tree, wither every field, and dry up every stream in the kingdom unless the king opened his castle gate on the correct-numbered trumpet blast. The "correct" number was given as a multiplication problem.

The king called for the Minister and told him to solve the riddle or lose his head. The Minister bowed and dove into a deep bout of severe panic. He had only two days to solve a problem he didn't understand! Luckily, two castle children who had great common sense and logic power offered to help the Minister. Together they devised three possible solutions to the multiplication problem, detailing each step in each solution system. The time was up and the Minister had to announce his solution to the king.

The story stopped and the teacher turned the problem over to her students. Which scheme was correct? They had to master the day's multiplication concept to decide which scheme was correct.

Exhausted by his panicky efforts, the Minister retired to his chambers to, he hoped, live out a life of stress-free ease. Next day, of course, the wizard threatened to strike again and the poor minister was back in the thick of it. On went the story through a series of math techniques. Over time, the personality of the Minister developed more fully, as did those of the supporting characters in the castle. The class loved the stories and willingly dove into the math concepts.

These are ongoing stories at work.

SPLINTER STORIES

Splinter stories take a different approach from the three previous models. Instead of you providing a story to inspire students, splinter stories allow students to compile their own story.

A major problem with most student reports is that they present only the overview facts and plot summary of the events they describe. They tend to omit the character-based story information. In part this is because the encyclopedia is the students' model for such historical and factual reports. In part it is because they simply didn't think of including other types of information. In part, however, it is because most report topics are too broad for them to do otherwise.

Being asked to "write a report" on George Washington, Alexander Graham Bell, Michael Jordan, the Civil War, The Depression, the development of steam power, the Louisiana Purchase, or the Crusades, or on virtually any other topic, is too vast an assignment for any school-aged student to prepare in story form.

The options then are to accept encyclopedia-style factual reports or radically narrow the focus of each student's assignment so that they can dig out the essential story ingredients. That is the idea behind splinter stories, shown in picture outline form in Figure 5.5 (page 104) and described below.

Splinter stories are a simple, straightforward, five-step process:

1. Within a curriculum unit, identify the one central character or event you want students to focus on for their research and writing (step 1 in Figure 5.5).

2. Splinter that topic into small, bite-sized pieces, one per student (step 2).

3. Individually and in teams, students research and draft their splinter of the total class story (step 3).

Figure 5.5. The Splinter Story.

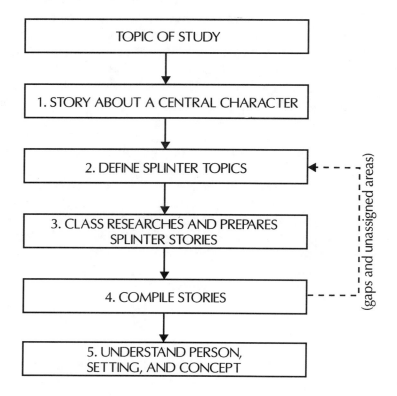

Examples:
• Hour/day/week in the life of: (topic being studied)
• Friends/enemires/competitors of: (topic being studied)
• Fears/hopes/dreams/problems/goals of: (topic being studied)

Characteristics:
• All character based
• Nonfiction
• Original story must make character important and intriguing

4. Individual reports are presented and compiled into a unified whole (step 4). This process often identifies gaps and holes in the gathered information, which must be reassigned for additional research.

5. From researching one splinter, from hearing and seeing the other splinters, and from seeing how the splinters interconnect and merge into a single whole, students gain a deeper understanding of the character or event (step 5).

You will likely be able to assign only one splinter story for any one unit because students will need several weeks to research, write, and compile their individual contributions into a total class report.

The key to splinter stories is the way you choose to splinter the general topic. Topics may be divided by space, time, function, or character information to reach individual student assignments.

An example may help. A South Carolina teacher decided to assign a splinter story during a unit on rain forests with her fifth graders. She divided her students into five groups, each group having five students. The resulting splinter assignments were:

GROUP TOPIC	INDIVIDUAL ASSIGNMENTS
Native Human Activity	Daily life of a child; daily life of a woman; myths, stories, beliefs, and fears; and predators of humans, how they survive.
Water Cycles	Seasonal variations, sources of water, rain, rivers, lakes, and marshes.
Canopy Layer Ecosystem	Each student had to pick one animal and one plant species and describe both a "day in the life" and a life cycle for both. (The group had to include at least two predator and two prey species.)
Mid-Level Ecosystem	Same assignment.
Ground Level Ecosystem	Same assignment.

This was a functional splintering of the general topic of rain forests. Each group had to coordinate the format and accuracy of their individual reports before presenting them to the class.

The teacher could have splintered by:

➤ *Time*—season, day/night, time of day—and have each student describe what typically happens during their assigned time slot.

➤ *Function*—into ecosystem niches (inorganics; grasses, bushes and trees; browsers and grazers; predators and top predators; fish; birds; and decomposers)—and have each student describe a day in the life of one member of one species in their functional niche.

➤ *Geographic location*—type of ecosystem environment, country—and have each student describe events in their particular geographic area.

➤ *Character information*—for a given species describe characteristics, goals, problems and obstacles, and the daily struggle. Have each student describe only their assigned type of information for several species.

Any division that gives each student a small enough piece to be able to include some character information and story details will improve their combined report. I have met teachers who splintered a major scientist. (Four students created a framework by researching goals, problems and flaws, risk and danger for a given period in the scientist's life. Other students were then assigned one hour of the day to write a typical "day in the life" account that specifically dealt with the goal, problems, and struggles identified by the first group of students.)

I have seen the Revolutionary War splintered by time (year of the war), by function (each student takes one type of person—housewife, merchant, infantry man, general, politician, child, etc.—and researches what they are doing, thinking and feeling during the assigned time period), and by geographic location (different students describe conditions, attitudes, and events in different colonies).

The value of splintering is that it allows students to focus on a topic narrow enough for them to be able to include key character and story information and still, through the class composite report, gain an overview of some major event.

PART VI

TEACHING STUDENTS TO TELL

$\mathcal{T}$he Value of Student Storytelling

KEY TOPICS IN THIS SECTION

> ❯ Student storytelling develops critically needed oral communication skills
> ❯ Student storytelling develops self-confidence, enthusiasm for learning, and all four major language arts skills
> ❯ Student storytelling programs are sprouting across the country

Storytelling is a powerful teaching tool for you to use, but why use valuable class time to teach students to tell stories? Earlier I mentioned the experience of teacher Peggy Buzanski and of several students who had been part of student storytelling programsr. Their reactions were included in this book because they are typical of the reactions of all students and teachers who have been involved with student storytelling projects.

In 1993 and 1994 surveys by major national polling organizations, between 93 and 94 percent of adult, working respondents said that, to successfully do their job, anyone would depend more on their ability to communicate orally than in writing. That means that 19 out of 20 jobs in this country depend more on oral communications ability than on written ability. Compare that overwhelming affirmation of the importance of oral communication with the percentage of language arts time spent on oral communication in your school. Most state frameworks devote well over 90 percent of their effort to reading and writing.

Having students tell stories develops all four language arts skills. Earlier I mentioned studies that concluded that storytelling was the most effective single activity to develop student oral communication ability and self-confidence.

Elementary schools across the country are forming storytelling clubs and groups. Public libraries and civic groups are sponsoring student storytelling events. Volucia County, Florida, libraries, in conjunction with the schools, hold annual elementary storytelling championships. The program is incredibly popular with students and teachers. The city of Boise, Idaho, sponsors a city-wide student storytelling program through the schools whose winners get main-stage time at a major area festival. East Tennessee State University holds a national championship for middle and high school students. High schools across the country are forming touring storytelling troupes. One of the most active and successful is at Hanford High School in the California Central Valley town of Hanford. Kevin Cordi, the storytelling teacher and coach, has linked his group with over 80 other high school storytelling troupes across the nation.

School after school and district after district are finding that creating a storytelling unit is a positive, fun, effective school program that produces not only improved language skills for participating students (an essential to a successful work life) but also a growing sense of self-worth and self-confidence and a blossoming enthusiasm for learning and studies. Storytelling is a powerful, effective use of student school time.

*T*eaching Students to Tell the Super Simple Way

KEY TOPICS IN THIS SECTION

> The Super Simple progression for student storytelling
> Student storytelling activities and exercises
> The "tellability" of different types of stories

Isn't teaching students to tell stories the same as teaching yourself?

Yes . . . and no.

Yes. . . . The same concepts, the same three Super Simple Storytelling pillars, the same nine-step system for learning and remembering a story, and the same orchestra exercises that apply to you apply to your students.

No. . . . Elementary, middle school, and even high school students have not accumulated the years of experience and practice at speaking in front of a live audience (classroom of students) that an adult teacher has. Students need more entry-level activities and more practice with the component parts of storytelling.

You don't start a car in fourth gear. You don't start a football team with an important conference game and then go to practice. For each activity there is an appropriate progression of activities that leads to some end goal. The same is true for student storytelling. Many think the way to develop student storytelling skills is to have them tell stories. But that's the end goal, the final step. First a teacher must lead students through a progression of activities to sequentially develop the necessary awareness and understanding that ultimately lead to successful storytelling.

Figure 6.1, "Student Storytelling Progression," summarizes the seven steps that lead to successful student storytelling. Telling a story is step 7. This group of seven steps is not linearly sequential as was the story learning progression in Part III. While there is a natural flow from the simpler early steps to the more complex later steps, in reality steps 1 through 6 could be intermingled to meet the unique needs of a specific classroom.

Figure 6.1. Student Storytelling Progression.

1. YOUR TURN
You tell stories to them.

2. INTRODUCTORY ACTIVITIES
Introduce students to being, moving, speaking, and acting in front of the class through selected theater and storytelling games.

3. STORY-FORMING ACTIVITIES
Introduce students to the process of forming, developing, and telling stories through the One-On-One-On-One-On-One exercise.

4. REFINE SKILLS
Use the 30-Second Story and other focused exercises and games to develop specific oral communication skills.

5. SPECIAL PURPOSE GAMES
Augment storytelling exercises with general-purpose theater games to develop confidence and broad-based skill areas (e.g., physical characterization, gesture, or vocal intonation).

6. ORAL PRESENTATIONS
Have students give oral reports and tell improvisational stories to their own class.

7. TELL A STORY
Now students are ready for formal storytelling.

1. YOUR TURN

Model effective storytelling for your students. Make storytelling (formal storytelling and informal day-to-day stories) part of your normal routine. Weave stories into the curriculum as examples. Improvise stories around lesson points if you are comfortable with improvisation. Prepare and tell formal stories. While this is valuable for your students, it does create one risk. They will be prone to try to mimic you and tell stories the way that you tell them. Use the activities and exercises listed in Part I, "Natural Storytelling," and those listed below to send students in search of their own style for telling stories.

Discuss story form and structure and the key elements that create a story with the class and search for solid examples in the literature they have recently read. Use the "During the Story Activities" activities listed in Part V. Especially, stop a story and ask, "Is the story finished?" When they answer no, ask, "How do you know?" Play devil's advocate and force them to analyze the story's structure to convince you that it can't possibly be finished yet. The more they hear, work with, and argue about the form of a story, the easier and more natural it will be for them later to perform stories.

2. INTRODUCTORY ACTIVITIES

Many students have an initial reluctance and unease about the process of formal oral presentation. Use introductory activities to allow them to gain more experience with oral activity and with consciously forming information into a story. Exercises 6.1, *Sneak Them In* (page 204) and 6.2, *The Circle Story* (page 206), are good for this purpose for younger students. Additionally, Exercises 2.1, *What Is a Story?* (page 131), and 2.2, *Is It a Story Yet?* (page 133), may be used as part of this introductory effort.

3. STORY-FORMING ACTIVITIES

Exercise 4.2, *One-on-One-on-One-on-One* (page 172), is especially well suited for the double-barreled job of getting students used to making oral presentations and getting them used to forming information into effective story structure. Exercise 1.4, *What Makes It Real?* (page 125), is also effective for this purpose and, as a side benefit, introduces students to the concepts of The Golden List of audience needs. Finally, use Exercise 2.3, *The Big Three* (page 137), to create the habit of relying on character-based information to create basic story structure. Exercise 2.3 may be extended into more of an oral storytelling exercise by allowing students to improvise and complete the story created by the three exercise questions.

4. REFINE SKILLS

Use exercises to introduce students to their storytelling orchestra, to help them to become conscious of how they naturally use those orchestra players, and to consciously experience the feel of manipulating their orchestra. Many of the *Super Simple Storytelling* exercises are well suited for this purpose, including Exercises 1.1 through 1.3 and 3.4 through 3.13. Additionally, Exercises 6.3, *Pass the Picture* (page 208), and 6.4, *Ruler of the Island* (page 210), are designed for this use. Search for comedy improvisation games and books on theater games for additional suggestions.

Finally, use age-appropriate elements of Part I, "Natural Storytelling," to gently investigate each student's natural style and nervous habits. Make this process an exciting "exploration of discovery" and a "fun game" to arm students with an understanding of how they can best make their stories work.

5. SPECIAL PURPOSE GAMES

Hone student telling skills with focused storytelling exercises to emphasize and develop individual aspects of the process. Exercise 5.1, *The 30-Second Story* (page 192), is the most flexible and most powerful of these games. Any aspect of telling a story, any aspect of orchestra manipulation, any aspect of natural storytelling style, and any aspect of story structure may be singled out as a special requirement for a round of *The 30-Second Story*. Use *The 30-Second Story* to address and develop whatever your students struggle with and need to improve upon.

Exercises 4.8, *Where Images Come From* (page 188), and 4.9, *She Entered the Room* (page190), may also be helpful in demonstrating for students the effect of their storytelling word choices. Finally, Exercise 6.5, *Stage Coach* (page 212), is a fun and raucous storytelling game that can be used to hone student skills on identifying and forming key story informational elements.

6. ORAL PRESENTATIONS

Increase opportunities for students to practice oral skills through oral reports, debates, presentations, and discussions. Oral presentations may be made to groups within the class if time does not permit for them to be made to the class as a whole. Every opportunity to speak in front of others gives students a chance to practice the oral skills they are developing.

7. TELL A STORY

Finally it's time to combine all of the individual techniques and skills students have been learning by orchestrating them into the formal telling of a story. Two questions are routinely asked:

> ➤ What are the best stories for students to tell?

> ➤ What is the best way to prepare them for their storytelling?

THE BEST STORIES

There are no such things as "the best stories" for students to tell. "Best" depends on the age, inclinations, and natural storytelling style and strengths of the student. I can, however, list the pluses and minuses of different types of common stories and assess their net "tellability" factor. The key words that differentiate each type of story are highlighted in each definition.

FAIRY TALE   A story for children about fairies, or about *magic and enchantment*.

Pluses: Usually great jeopardy, rapid pace, and the potential for easy development of vibrant characters (if characters aren't fully developed in the version a student is using). These are usually fun stories.

Minuses: Usually too long to tell without major editing. Editing, however, tends to make the story read more like a plot summary and less like a character-based story. Characters may not be developed (written versions often, themselves, read like plot summaries) and some character work is required.

Net: Good to tell *if* a short enough version can be found.

MYTH   A traditional story concerning fabulous or *supernatural beings*, giving expression to the early beliefs of a people and often serving to *explain natural phenomena* and the origins of peoples, places, and important things.

Pluses: Most myths are stuffed with all of the character flaws, risk, danger, and intrigue you could ask of a great soap opera. Goals, obstacles, jeopardy, and struggles are all boldly laid out. Often myths end in a clever twist that explains some natural phenomenon.

Minuses: Again, myths are usually too long for a student storytelling. The student will have to search for one segment of the entire myth that can stand alone and tell just that one part, being sure to include all necessary character information.

Net: Myths are great stories to tell *if* the student can find short myths or segments that make sense standing on their own.

LEGEND   A story, handed down from the *past*, which lacks accurate historical evidence but has been, and still may be, popularly *accepted as true*.

Pluses: Legends sound like real-life events and so have a ring of truth that myths and fairy tales lack. Legends usually feature strongly defined and developed characters and goals.

Minuses: Some legends ramble on about many side characters and historical places that only tangentially affect the story. Most of these can be cut for a student telling. Many are too long to tell and typically can't be cut down as easily as myths.

Net: If the length is right, legends make for great storytelling.

PARABLE   A short story *designed to teach* a moral or religious principle by *suggesting a parallel* (a metaphor).

Pluses: Parables are punchy, to the point, and have strong moral dilemmas for the central character.

Minuses: Parables often have very poorly defined characters and are often too short to form into a story without considerable work to flesh out the characters and develop the scenes.

Net: If a student can make the characters work, parables are quick, easy stories to learn and tell.

FOLK TALE   An *anonymous*, traditional story, *orally transmitted*, the subject *rarely being tied* to a specific time or place.

Pluses: Folk tales are usually short and written in a conversational style and so are closer to the right wording for telling than any other story form. They usually feature a quick pace and are peppered with humor. They are typically easy to learn and easy to tell.

Minuses: The only minus to folk tales is their lack of overt character development. The student teller must do a little work to be able to see the characters in their mind's eye before they can make the story come alive for others.

Net: The most reliable, fun, easy set of stories for students to tackle.

CLASSIC FOLK TALE   Folk tales *well known* by the general population (e.g., "The Three Little Pigs," "Little Red Riding Hood," "Jack and the Bean Stalk," "Hansel and Gretel").

Pluses: The teller already knows the story lines, so they are easy to learn. The teller is freer to focus on the characters. The audience already knows the story and so will not get lost in the telling even if the teller omits part of the story line.

Minuses: The audience already knows the story and so may tire quickly unless the teller develops some original interpretation or especially appealing performance technique to hold their attention.

Net: Great stories to change around and play with. (See "Extend the Story" techniques in Part V.)

TALL TALE   A *deliberately fantastic falsehood*; an impossible story told with tongue-in-cheek humor to entertain.

Pluses: Good humor. Fast-paced story lines. Usually short enough to tell without much cutting.

Minuses: The story focus is often on the outrageous events of the story. The teller must still create enough character information to carry the story. Younger students often don't relate well to the tongue-in-cheek nature of the humorous exaggerations and tend to over-tell the stories.

Net: Sure winners if students can avoid overplaying the comic exaggeration.

"POR QUA"   Often called "Just So" stories, these short, *humorous, tongue-in-cheek tales* claim to *explain some physical phenomenon* of the world.

Pluses: Usually short, with strong character goal, flaws, and problems. Usually humorous and fast paced. Good twist endings.

Minuses: No general problems.

Net: Good stories to tell.

ETHNIC TALES   Stories of or relating to a people whose unity rests on *racial, linguistic, religious, or cultural ties*. Folk tales from another culture.

Pluses: Ethnic tales share all the pluses of folk tales. Plus they represent some other country and culture.

Minuses: Much of the cultural symbolism and significance will be lost on student tellers from a different culture. Tellers must take care not to trample on cultural concepts from the source culture in the way they develop and present the story characters.

Net: With a little cultural source crediting before the story and a bit of cultural research, these are consistently successful stories to tell.

PERSONAL   Stories written in the *first person* so that, when told, they appear to be stories about the teller.

Pluses: Powerful, engrossing stories because of the chosen perspective. Typically plenty of character development and jeopardy.

Minuses: The story must plausibly have happened to the teller to make the perspective work. With rare exceptions, personal stories are copyrighted and authors are less willing to grant permission than for other stories.

Net: Good stories *if* the teller can make them sound plausible.

ORIGINALS   Stories, fiction or nonfiction, *written by the storyteller.*

Pluses: Easy to learn. Will always be told with extra energy and enthusiasm. The story's wording fits with the natural style of the teller.

Minuses: The student has to write a good story and then stop rewriting the story and figure out how to tell it effectively. Many students keep rewriting right up to show time and never work on *how* to tell it.

Net: Good stories to tell *if* a story already exists and works well in its current form. Original stories are a poor choice, though, if a student has to write the story *and* learn to tell it all in the time planned for simply learning the story.

MODERN FICTION   *Recently written and released stories* about any subject, set in realistic settings and times, which convey some facet of life, character, or the world.

Pluses: The subject matter and language are typically more appealing to modern student tellers. The pace will be fast and the stories will abound in visual detail.

Minuses: Outside of picture books, few sources for telling-length modern fiction exist. Most sources are intended for adult audiences and may not be appropriate for younger tellers.

Net: Good stories *if* a student can locate an appropriate one. (Picture books are listed separately below.)

PICTURE BOOKS   Modern fiction written in book form that *relies heavily on accompanying pictures* to explain, augment, and complete the story's text.

Pluses: Illustrations create ample visual detail for tellers to use when learning scenes and stories. Stories are usually strongly character-based and provide ample jeopardy to drive the story. Detail will abound, both in words and pictures. Always short and an appropriate length for telling.

Minuses: The text carries only a small fraction of the total story detail and not all of the key story information. Tellers will have to search the pictures for important information not included in the text and add that information to the story before they tell it. Substantial story editing will be required.

Net: Good stories if the teller is willing to integrate illustration information back into the text of a story.

Each of these categories of stories exists in every culture on earth and is a rich and vibrant way to compare cultures or explore new ones. The real problem students will have is selecting a story from the myriad of available ones.

THE GENERAL PROCESS

Teachers can ease the burden of a student's selection process by assigning a *type* of story to each student so as to limit the scope of their search. Have each student read five stories in their assigned type and pick one they want to tell. You should establish basic criteria for these stories. I recommend three for students' first storytelling experience.

> ➤ The story should be a maximum of five minutes long when read. (It will grow longer during preparation for telling.)

> ➤ A maximum of three important, central characters. (Additional bit characters who do not need to be developed are okay.)

> ➤ No props or costumes allowed. (Their focus should be on their telling. They can use props with future stories.)

Students should report to you (in writing or orally) naming the five stories they read and stating why they selected one to tell over the other four. Note that they will not be saying that this is their favorite story or the one they *most* want to tell. Rather, they will be saying only that this is their favorite of the five they read.

The truth is that they could adequately tell any story compatible with their natural style. For their first story, it is better to focus on the process of learning and telling a story than on the search for a perfect story. They can search for all-time favorites for future tellings.

Follow the Super Simple progression presented in Part III to guide students from story selection to initial tellings. You may simplify the progression for young tellers, omitting, for example, consideration of perspective (step 4) and Orchestra Notes (step 8). You could also simplify the Story Learning Note Sheet by omitting words and creating one box for each scene in which the student draws a quick illustration of the scene and a stick-figure face in the upper right-hand corner showing the scene's emotion.

After students have completed the preparatory exercises listed in the Super Simple progression, they should be ready to tell their stories first in small groups and then to the class as a whole. Students will now be ready to dazzle listeners at assemblies, evening parent gatherings, or other classrooms or other schools.

*E*valuating Student Storytellers

KEY TOPICS IN THIS SECTION

> ❯ Criteria for evaluating student storytellers' performances
> ❯ Judging scores for storytelling performances

If student storytelling becomes a curriculum activity, at some point these students must be graded, or judged, on their storytelling. As with music, dance, and painting, storytelling is an art. Some have more innate talent and will always do better. For some, merely standing in front of a group is a struggle. Many teachers find grading the quality of student art-related work difficult if not repugnant and prefer to base grades on effort and improvement. However, some students have more natural ability in science and math and no one has qualms about grading students on the absolute quality of their work in these areas. Math is either done correctly or it is not. There is no A for effort. Grades are reserved for the quality of performance.

If storytelling groups or troupes form at a school and storytelling performances and assemblies are held, some judging must take place to select the few who get to perform from the much larger number of school student storytellers. To some that selection should be based on performance ability alone: Put your best tellers on stage. For others, effort and improvement should be the keys that trigger selection, with less regard for the ultimate quality of the student's storytelling performance: Give the kids who try the hardest a chance.

The question of *whether* to grade and judge student storytellers is not germane to this book. The question of *how* to do it is. If students are going to be judged or graded on their storytelling work, specific criteria for that assessment are needed. Figure 6.2 (page 118), "Student Storytelling Evaluation Criteria," lists the areas to evaluate during a storytelling and the relative weights to assign to each area.

First, a storytelling can be divided into two aspects: preparation and performance. I would rate them 30 points for preparation and 70 for performance. It is not that performance is that much more important. Rather, most of the performance categories reflect the degree of preparation. Thus a sizable share of the performance score really reflects the student's preparation.

Preparation can be divided into two categories: story selection and story learning/editing. Learning/editing may further be subdivided into (1) the development of story characters and (2) learning and developing the scenes and "how" to tell the story.

Similarly, performance can be divided into the specific telling of this story and a more general category of stage presence. While stage presence reflects in part the degree of preparation, it transcends any particular story and is a characteristic of the individual teller and their style of telling.

In Figure 6.2 I have divided the specific performance of a story into seven elements reflecting the focal elements of the *Super Simple Storytelling* system: Introduction and Exit, Voice, Wording Choices, Pace, Gestures and Poise, Characterizations, and the Use of Story Time. Rating these individual elements will produce an accurate and representative evaluation of the student's performance and identify those areas for the student to concentrate on for future stories.

Figure 6.2. Student Storytelling Evaluation Criteria.

The following criteria involve considerations appropriate for the evaluation of the merit of a storytelling performance. Relative weights for each area are shown based on a 100-point total.

1. **STORY SELECTION (5 pts)**
   - Is the story an appropriate length?
   - Are its subject and content appropriate for the teller and intended audience?

2. **LEARNING/EDITING (25 pts)**
   - **A. General (10 pts)**
     - Has the teller thoroughly learned the flow and sequencing of the story?
     - Did the teller struggle to recall scenes or lines? Did they forget parts of the story?
     - Have they comfortably incorporated "how they tell" the story with "what they tell?"
     - Has their editing of the story enhanced or detracted from your enjoyment and understanding of the story?
     - Is the perspective appropriate and consistent?
     - Is the climax satisfying and well developed?

   - **B. Story Characters (15 pts)**
     - Is the main character "real," specific, and interesting?
     - Are there clear goals and motives?
     - Are story obstacles real, relevant, risky, satisfying? Are conflict and struggle clear and compelling?
     - Is the antogonist interesting, compelling, and worthy?
     - Can we see, hear, etc., each character?
     - Do characters express relevant and appropriate emotions?

3. **THE TELLING (55 pts)**
   - **A. Intro/Exit (5 pts)**
     - Were the introduction into, and the exit from, the story smooth? Was the close and exit awkward or forced?

   - **B. Voice (15 pts)**
     - Was diction clear? Were word choices appropriate?
     - Did the language create strong, vivid images?
     - Was the telling grammatically correct? Was inappropriate slang ("So, ya' know ...," "like ... like" etc.) used?
     - Could the teller be heard clearly? (Was volume appropriate?)

   - **C. Wording (15 pts)**
     - Was vocabulary varied, appropriate, and interesting?
     - Was the wording concise? Did the teller needlessly repeat? Was excess description included?
     - Were scenes, characters, and events adequately described? Was strong detail chosen? Was the detail visual and specific?
     - Were the chosen verbs strong and forceful?

   - **D. Pace (5 pts)**
     - Was the pace of the story appropriate, varied, and effective? Did it support the content and style of the story?
     - Did the teller effectively use pauses?

   - **E. Gestures (5 pts)**
     - Did the teller make effective use of gesture? Did gestures enhance or detract from your enjoyment of the story?
     - Did the teller effectively use their face, body, and hands to match and support the flow of the story?

   - **F. Characterizations (5 pts)**
     - Did the teller use vocal and/or physical characterizations?
     - Were all characterizations consistent throughout the story?
     - Were characterizations appropriate for the characters and the story?

   - **G. Use of Time (5 pts)**
     - Did the teller run over their allotted time?
     - Did the teller effectively use their allotted time to develop and present their story?

4. **STAGE PRESENCE (15 pts)**
   - Did the teller maintain eye contact with the audience?
   - Did the teller appear at ease and confident?
   - Did the teller seem excited by their story? Did they seem to be enjoying the process of telling a story?
   - Did the teller seem relaxed and poised?
   - Did the teller exhibit nervous habits that detracted from the story?

PART VII
SUPER SIMPLE STORYTELLING EXERCISES

Super Simple Storytelling Exercise 1.1

THE WAVE GAME

Explore our natural focus while speaking

❯ **APPROPRIATE GRADES: Second and up**

❯ **TIME REQUIRED: 10 minutes**

GOAL:

Effective storytelling involves both what a teller says and how they say it. However, our natural tendency is to focus exclusively on content (*what* we say). The Wave Game is a fun way both to demonstrate this natural tendency and to introduce the tools with which we communicate (voice, face, gesture, body).

DIRECTIONS:

This is a great introductory exercise that introduces several important storytelling concepts while appearing to be an ice breaker game. Tell the students that, because they are going to spend some time working on storytelling, they should say "hi." Tell them that, literally, that is exactly what you want them to do.

Starting with yourself and progressing one person at a time around the class, each person will say "hi" to the person on their left. That person must try to *exactly* mirror (or mimic) back to that person the way that person said "hi" to them. Then this new teller turns and says "hi" to the person on their left. And so on around the class. The only rule is that each person must say "hi" differently than anyone who has gone before.

Do not repeat or elaborate on these instructions. Begin by waving with one hand and saying "hi" to the person on your left. Make sure they mirror your version of "hi" back to you before turning to say "hi" to the next person.

Your job is to keep track of two things: first, the number of people who actually say "hi" and, as instructed, change the *way* they say it, versus the number of people who change *what* they say (the content) in violation of the rules. Second, watch how effectively and completely each person mirrors the previous teller.

Stop about halfway through the class and discuss the results up to that point, using the teaching points listed below as a guide. By the fourth or fifth teller in most groups, students begin to change *what* they say and de-emphasize *how* they say it. From then on, the vast majority violate the rules by changing content (what they will say) and, to a large extent, ignore how they say it.

As an option for the second half of the class, have each student not merely mirror how the previous student said "hi," but also *exaggerate* everything they can when being the mirror. You can also discuss which aspects of *how* each student said "hi" were noted and successfully exaggerated during mimicking.

TEACHING POINTS TO EMPHASIZE:

Two key concepts are demonstrated in The Wave Game. First, as speakers, we naturally focus on content, trying to learn and master *what* we will say. However, as listeners, we just as naturally focus on *how* something is said, concentrating on vocal tone, facial expression, etc. This discrepancy is a potentially major problem for beginning tellers.

As a demonstration, sneer at one student. Let your eyes roll in disgust and say, voice dripping with sarcasm, "Oh, don't you look nice today." Was it an insult or a compliment? Have the class vote. Unanimously they will agree it was an insult. Yet the words, themselves, were complimentary. Gush radiant warmth at one student and coo, "I hate you." This will always be interpreted as a playful statement of endearment.

When there is a discrepancy between *what* is being said and *how* it is being said, we *always* believe the form, the way it is delivered, over content. Always! Storytellers must learn that content alone will not carry a story. An audience must accept and be enthusiastic about how the story is being said before they will seriously listen to content. Luckily, effectively delivering "how" the story is being said is far easier to do than it sounds.

Second, the mirroring typically is woefully incomplete and imprecise. Gross hand gestures are generally imitated. Vocal tonal patterns are generally mimicked. Only rarely does one student note and mirror how another student held their legs, whether they sat up straight or slouched, how they held their shoulders, when they breathed, or even whether or not they smiled and established eye contact. Never have I seen someone consciously record eyebrow position, how individual fingers were held, or subtle body movements. No one notices the discrepancies between teller and mimic because none of the tellers consciously knew what these various body parts were doing when they said "hi" in the first place.

What does this mean? As speakers we are not consciously aware of what our body, face, hands, and voice are doing to project the words we plan and say. We don't *consciously* record these elements when we watch someone speak. Rather, they are subconsciously recorded. We also don't consciously control what our face, voice, and hands do while we talk. They are also subconsciously directed. That's why they are hard to replicate. Becoming an effective storyteller means gaining conscious control over *how* we tell to match the conscious control we exert over *what* we tell.

Super Simple Storytelling Exercise 1.2

WHAT'D YOU HAVE FOR DINNER?

Explore how we naturally approach storytelling

> **APPROPRIATE GRADES: Third and up**

> **TIME REQUIRED: 15 minutes**

GOAL:

Storytelling is not a new and alien art form. We all naturally tell stories as part of our normal conversation. The place to begin to developing effective storytelling skills is with a conscious understanding of one's own natural storytelling style and tendencies. In this way individual strengths and weak areas can be identified and honed into an effective style of story presentation.

DIRECTIONS:

Each student must choose a partner and find out what that partner had for dinner last night. Give students a minute or two to complete this exchange. Now group students into groups of six. (Groups of five or seven will do if that makes the groups come out even.) It is preferable, but not essential, for partners to be in the same group.

Number the students in each group (1 through 6). Arbitrarily pick one number and have that numbered student in each group describe, in one minute, the meal told to them by their partner *as if it were their favorite meal in all the world*. This teller may not alter the content of the meal. Their goal is to convince every person in the group that this is a truly delightful meal fit for their next special party or occasion.

After these students have finished, pick a second numbered student, who will describe the meal described to them by their partner as if it were the worst excuse for food in the history of civilized dining, as if they wouldn't serve this slop to a cockroach. Again, the teller may not alter the content of the meal. This teller's goal is to turn the stomach of each listener with *how* they tell their description of this meal.

It may help both of these tellers to pretend that they are describing a meal served to them at someone else's house.

Finally, pick a third numbered student in each group to describe the meal told to them by their partner as if the individual elements of the meal were all right, but they made for a terrible combination. (Peanut butter and corn flakes are both fine—but not together!)

Feel free to change the assigned attitude of each teller to ones that you think would better match the interest and abilities of your students. It is, however, critical that each teller be given an assigned attitude and motivation for their telling.

Following these three tellings, lead a class discussion by asking the following list of questions:

1. **For the tellers:** *What were you focusing on and thinking about while telling?* On just getting through this silly assignment? On the facts of this meal? On your audience? *How did you feel while telling?* Nervous? Embarrassed? Apologetic for misrepresenting both your own and your partner's actual views of this food? Uncomfortable? Bored? Exhilarated? Playful? Did you "get into" the telling? Do you remember how you felt during the telling, or was it just a blur?

2. **For the listeners:** *What did you see?* Anything? The food? The plate and setting? The room? The characters? What did the teller do to make you see these elements? Could you smell, feel, and taste the food as well as see it? Why? Would you have liked to have been led to see more, or were you satisfied? *Were you convinced by the telling?* What did the teller do to make you believe or not believe the attitude they were assigned to represent? *Were you engrossed by the telling?* Why or why not? Did you laugh? What did the teller do to make you laugh? Did you hang on every word? Did you find your attention wandering to other groups?

3. **For the tellers:** *Did you include information about the characters as well as the menu?* (Successful stories center around characters, not things.) *Did you get a laugh during your telling?* (There are few forms of praise higher than a laugh.) Do you remember what you did to get a laugh? Did you *try* to get a laugh and fail? Do you remember what you did to fail to get a laugh? *How did you physically amplify the words of your story?* Did you use your face? Gesture? Add vivid details? Use multiple senses? Do you remember if you used any of these storytelling tools? *Did you expand the story beyond the specifics of the menu?* Could you see the scene and characters in your mind, or just the food, or just the words? Did you embellish the story? How? Why? Did you try to lead your audience, guide them through a visceral response to the menu?

TEACHING POINTS TO EMPHASIZE:

This activity, as does any opportunity to tell and listen to story snippets, allows each participant to identify their natural styles and tendencies during telling. What do you do when you become nervous or unsure while telling? What do you do when you sense that an audience is interested? Or uninterested? How do you naturally approach the process of organizing and preparing story material?

Some of each person's natural styles and tendencies will be constructive and support effective telling. Some will be counterproductive and tend to undermine a telling. The first step toward consistently effective telling must be to become consciously aware of one's own natural style and tendencies, to become aware of our lifelong subconscious habits and patterns. It is impossible to change natural tendencies that don't work until the teller both knows what they are and knows what they feel like when those tendencies take over.

Second, this type of exercise allows each listener to identify the story and performance elements and tendencies that draw them into a story. Each teller may then compare their own patterns, habits, and tendencies to what, as a listener, they want in others. Compare these lists with those generated in Exercises 1.3 and 1.4.

Super Simple Storytelling Exercise 1.3

YOUR FAVORITE STORY

Explore what attracts a listener to a story

> **APPROPRIATE GRADES: Third and up**

> **TIME REQUIRED: 20 minutes**

GOAL:

Why is one story more effective than another? Why is one telling more appealing and memorable than another? Knowing what draws an audience into a storytelling experience is the first essential step towards developing effective storytelling habits.

DIRECTIONS:

Create a stressful situation for which your students could make up a wild story. Why they don't have their homework. Why they were late to school. Why they flunked a test. Why they were late getting home. What they would do if they had to take care of their boss's pet bat for a week. Why they can't return their boss's pet bat (which died during the week they cared for it). Etc. Virtually any situation with the potential for stress will do.

Give students 15 or 20 seconds to invent a story they would tell to explain their way out of the situation. Gather students in groups of three. (A four-person group will do if you have an odd number. So will two-person groups if you don't have very many students to begin with.) Within each group, each student, in turn, tells their story to the group. Once all stories within the group have been heard, the group votes for their favorite. Each group *must* pick one of the stories they heard as their favorite. They may not combine elements from several to create a new super-story.

Lump students into super-groups by combining three original groups into one super-group. Within each super-group there are three students whose story won the first round of telling. Each of these students repeats their story for the super-group and the super-group then votes for their favorite story.

Combine super-groups into mega-groups of three super-groups each and repeat the process. Continue in this way until the class as a whole listens to and votes on the final round of storytellings.

After a thunderous round of applause for the tellers, it is time for discussion. There are two topics worth exploring. First, *Why did you vote as you did?* Every student voted at least three times for their favorite of three stories. Have them articulate what made them vote for one story over another.

The second discussion topic is ***How did the stories change over time?*** The finalists' stories were told at least three times. How did those stories evolve over the course of three tellings? The best people to answer this question are not the tellers, but those who listened to the winning stories all three times they were told.

The key points for both of these discussion topics are described below.

TEACHING POINTS TO EMPHASIZE:

Make a list of the reasons students used to decide their votes. Their tendency will be to concentrate only on the final vote and on votes in which they voted for the teller who "won." Counter these tendencies by repeating that "It doesn't matter who you voted for. But over the course of three (or four) votes, what made you decide to vote for one teller over the others?"

You will find that everyone votes for the same few reasons, which can be divided into elements having to do with the story itself and elements having to do with the telling of the story. Elements relating to the story itself typically include details, interesting plot (twists and surprises), humor, and information about the feelings, motives, and reactions of the characters. Elements that relate to the telling of the story typically include enthusiasm, energy, confidence (eye contact, gestures, tone), humor, characterizations, and "the teller seemed to have a good time with their story."

Both are short lists. There aren't many things that an audience really needs from a teller to become enthusiastically swept-up in a story. Notice that the elements relating to the telling of the story revolve around the confidence and comfort of the teller. When comfortable with both the story and the audience, a teller naturally pours their energy and enthusiasm into a story. Learning to be a consistently effective teller requires above all else that each teller learns how to make themselves comfortable with the process of telling and confident in the stories they plan to tell. That is actually much easier to do than it might seem.

Note that one important element is not on this list. No one ever voted for a story because the teller "got all the words right." Yet, as tellers we tend to focus on memorizing and correctly repeating a fixed string of words. It is never the specific words a teller says that matter to an audience. It is the *way* those words are said that matters most.

Save a copy of these "Why did you vote" lists to compare with the lists generated during Exercise 1.4, *What Makes It Real?*

Have students who heard the same winning stories told at least three times describe how the stories changed over the course of those tellings. Typically, the stories grew longer, more detail was added, humor was increased, and characterizations were expanded; the teller's timing, confidence, and enthusiasm improved; and those story elements that worked once got emphasized and expanded while those that didn't work were eliminated or reduced. Typically, the stories got better with more tellings. It's a natural process we all use while we develop stories.

Storytelling is never a static, rigid activity. Naturally, both story and telling flow and adjust to become more successful. Note that the list of story and telling elements changed over time is very similar to the list of reasons students voted. Listener and teller are naturally tuned in to the same elements of a story.

Super Simple Storytelling Exercise 1.4

WHAT MAKES IT REAL?

Explore what makes a story seem real to an audience

❭ **APPROPRIATE GRADES: Third and up**

❭ **TIME REQUIRED: 20-25 minutes**

GOAL:

By turning a review of what makes a story sound real into a game, students are compelled to sift through a story for all possible clues without even realizing that they are creating a short list of elements to include in their own stories to make them sound equally real. They will quickly discover that specific, relevant story details create a sense of reality more than anything else a student can put in their story.

DIRECTIONS:

Divide the class into groups of either three or four. Give each student a moment to recall a personal (real) story on whatever topic you assign. Use simple, broad topics—something funny that happened to you, or something scary. Even a topic as broad as something that happened in your family will work well. These personal and family stories should have happened at least three years ago and should *not* have been previously shared with other students in the class.

Each student shares with their group the bare-bones summary of their remembered story. Some students will want to drift into elaborate storytelling here. Don't let them. These should be 20- to 30-second summaries. Give the group a total of two minutes and task them to keep on time.

Have the group choose one of these stories that they think makes the best story or the one that is their favorite. They cannot combine stories to create a new super-story. They must pick one of the stories told by a group member. Give them 30 to 45 seconds to accomplish this.

Proceed only after every group has picked their story. Have every member of the group learn that one story they picked well enough so that they could tell it as if it had happened to them. This means that each group member has to question the person to whom it really happened to uncover the information they will need to tell the story.

At your option, you can prompt them about what kind of information they need to master. ***When and where did it happen? Who was there? What happened? Why? How did the characters feel? Why?***

Be sure to tell them that they may adjust the physical reality of the story to be plausibly consistent with their own history. For example, if the story happened between the teller and a brother, a student who doesn't have a brother could say the story happened with a cousin. Who would know they don't have a male cousin?

If the story happened when the teller lived in Atlanta, and the other students never lived in Atlanta, they can say it happened where they really lived at the appropriate time. If Atlanta were important to the story, they would then say it happened while their family was visiting someone (grandmother, friend, etc.) in Atlanta. Again, who would know it wasn't true?

Give the groups two minutes to gather whatever information they need.

Pick one group. The members of that group line up at the front of the class and, one by one, tell the complete story, claiming as they do that it really did happen to them. Instruct each teller that their goal is to say and do whatever they have to do to convince every person in the room that the story really *did* happen to them. That's their job.

The job of the audience is to figure out to whom it really happened. Don't allow any pause for discussion between tellers. As soon as teller #1 finishes, say, "And now the story from teller #2."

As soon as all the tellers have finished and the thunderous applause has died away, have the audience vote by show of hands for the teller to whom they think the story really happened. Do not allow any discussion before this vote. Every student must commit themselves and vote.

Usually the biggest vote-getter is not the person to whom the story really happened.

This is a fun game and does develop oral storytelling skills. But the real value of this exercise comes from the follow-on discussion. Ask the class, "***Why did you vote the way you voted?*** It doesn't matter if you voted for the right person or not. I still want to know why you thought one story sounded more real than the others."

Write the responses you get on the board, spatially dividing them into two groups: those comments that relate to the story itself and those that relate to the way the story was told.

Discuss the elements that made the story seem real enough to vote for. These are extremely powerful story elements for each student to remember to include in their own stories.

As you repeatedly use this exercise, vary the story theme. Any commonly available experience will do: summer vacation, a time they were scared, something that happened on a bike, disasters with a pet (theirs or someone else's), etc.

TEACHING POINTS TO EMPHASIZE:

Everyone votes for a story for the same few reasons. It doesn't matter whether they are first graders or teachers, fifth graders or college seniors. Even more amazing, almost all groups mention their reasons for voting in the same order.

First is always the *details* in the story. One teller included more details and their story sounded more real. One teller included impossible or unlikely details and so sounded less real. Details create reality.

The second aspect mentioned usually has to do with the *way* the story was told. One teller overacted, or hesitated and seemed to be making it up. One teller put more expression in the story, or seemed more confident and so was more believable. One seemed more natural and relaxed. One seemed stiffer and more halting. The general impression created by the way they told the story seemed more real or less real and so they were either voted for or against.

Next mentioned is usually something about characters and the amount of character information one person included. Next is usually humor. Make a list of all the reasons your students mention. It will be a very short list. There are not many things an audience needs to enjoy a story.

Compare this list to the one generated in Exercise 1.3, *Your Favorite Story*. You'll find that they are virtually identical. What makes a story enjoyable are the same few elements that make it sound real. Alone at the top of these lists are *story details* and *that the teller seemed comfortable with, and enthused about, their own story.*

Super Simple Storytelling Exercise 1.5

WHAT DO YOU REMEMBER?

Explore what creates memorable images in a listener's mind

> **APPROPRIATE GRADES: Third and up**
> **TIME REQUIRED: 10 minutes**

GOAL:

It is important for every new teller to hold a firm, concrete understanding of what listeners need in order to become engaged in the act of story-listening. This exercise reinforces students' understanding of this list of audience needs.

DIRECTIONS:

Have each student choose a partner. On your command, one partner tells the other about their experience of . . . (whatever topic you assign) . . . for 45 seconds. The topic can be any experience readily available to every student. Ones I have seen used include lunch yesterday, getting out of the house to school today, something that happened last weekend (or evening, or summer), something that happened at recess, at a dance, while eating out, etc.

The second student in each partnership now has 45 seconds to tell their experience on the same topic.

Have students switch partners. Assign a new topic and have students repeat the exercise. Following this second topic you must talk (lecture) for at least three minutes and preferably five minutes. Talk about the noise level in the room during the tellings. Talk about how we all regularly tell informal, day-to-day stories. Talk about anything. Your mission is to distract students from the stories they just heard and to put some temporal distance between each student and these stories.

Finally ask students what they remember from the two stories they heard. Do they remember *anything* without prompting? *What* do they remember and why? If they don't, why don't they? What did the teller do to make them remember or not remember?

As a show of hands, ask students how many of them remember a ***moment of stress*** (conflict, embarrassment, trauma, etc.)? How many remember ***specific sensory details*** from the stories? How many remember ***humor*** (something that made them laugh)? How many remember some ***characterization or character information?*** How many remember a moment when the teller put extra ***energy or passion*** into their telling?

Now ask if they remember any other moments or aspects of the stories. They probably don't. The five areas listed above are the key elements of The Golden List of audience needs. Most of the student memories probably center around one or more of these few elements. Have students list other things they remember and see if they, too, relate back to one of these five elements.

TEACHING POINTS TO EMPHASIZE:

An audience has relatively few needs from a storytelling. That is, it takes few successful story elements to effectively engage a listener and have them create vivid, memorable mental imagery of a story. It is important for a teller to clearly understand what these key elements are so that they can become the focal points of the process each teller uses for learning, rehearsing, and prepping a story.

Everyone is drawn into a story for the same few, simple reasons. The five biggest are listed in the questions above. If a teller provides these specific elements for an audience, they have maximized the probability that the audience will become involved with the story.

Super Simple Storytelling Exercise 1.6

WHAT MAKES IT FUN TO LISTEN TO?

Explore what your students think
makes a story fun to listen to

> **APPROPRIATE GRADES:** All

> **TIME REQUIRED: 10 to 20 minutes, depending on how much discussion you want to pursue**

GOAL:

Everyone has a concept, an idea of what makes a listening experience enjoyable. What students think they like in stories they hear, they will try to recreate in their own stories. A major problem arises when the terms and the vocabulary students use to describe what draws them to stories lead them down a very unproductive, in fact, *counter*productive path when they learn and tell their own stories.

It's worth exploring what they really like and why they like it. The place to start is with their initial impressions.

DIRECTIONS:

Start with a broad question to your class as a whole: *What makes a story fun to listen to?*

List their answers (preferably one or two words each) on the board in a column as they are given. Accept five or six and then stop. Look for two separate, but related, groups of answers:

> ➤ Those that relate to the story. This list will probably include words like *action, exciting, adventure, humor,* and *scary.*

> ➤ Those that relate to the way the story is told. This group will include expression (their catch-all term for emotional variation and presentation), vocal and physical characterization, and energy and enthusiasm.

Go back over the list one response at a time. Ask the questions: *What makes action (for example) fun to listen to? What makes scary parts fun to hear?*

Let the student who first proposed the word respond first. Your role is to push the class into examining what *really* draws them into each of the items they have listed. Ask, "why?" to each response you get. (Example: "Action is fun because it's exciting." "Why? What makes it exciting?") Have the students use specific examples and passages from stories they have read if possible. Your goal is to push students toward connecting plot-related items they have mentioned (action, scary, adventure, etc.) to characters. In truth, it is not abstract action students enjoy. It is the fact that thet action represents risk and danger and/or triumph to a story character. It is the way story characters act and react during the action that is appealing. Those character-related elements are what students really enjoy.

Continue to probe and take their responses until you either hit a stone wall ("It's exciting just because it is." "But why?" "Just because it is. Period.") or when you arrive at a realization that action, excitement, humor, and scariness all revolve around the characters and the way story characters act and react to each situation in the story.

If the discussion arrives at a dead end too soon, using the abstract term *story,* ask your students to recall specific stories they have liked. Repeat the questions for these example stories.

Don't expect any great breakthroughs in this one discussion period. We're just beginning to explore the power of storytelling. It's okay to simply leave the question on the table for further discussion if your class is stumped about why they enjoy the aspects of a story they list. Your goal is always to lead them toward appreciating the central role of the energy and emotional expression of the teller and of characters in their story (rather than the plotting elements around those characters).

TEACHING POINTS TO EMPHASIZE:

Three important teaching points for student storytellers are made apparent during this exercise. First, the same short list of story elements makes stories fun to read (or listen to), and makes them seem real. (See Exercise 1.4.) That short list is headed by *story details.* Details create reality. They also provide the information readers need to be able to imagine a story in their heads as they read. The better they can imagine a story, the more fun they have with it.

Second, stories are about characters. As listeners, we often forget to give characters the credit for our enjoyment and attribute it to the events or actions those characters perform. But it is character information (goals, problems, flaws, motives, emotional reactions, etc.) that draws us close to a story and makes it seem both more real and more enjoyable.

Third, the reaction of an audience to story elements is controlled by the *way* the story is told, that is, by the energy, commitment, enthusiasm, and emotional expression of the teller. It is always more important for a teller to get the "feel" of a story right than to get the words and content right.

Super Simple Storytelling Exercise 2.1

WHAT IS A STORY?

*Explore what separates a story from other narrative
forms and gives this special form such power and appeal*

⟩ **APPROPRIATE GRADES: Second and up**

⟩ **TIME REQUIRED: 15 to 30 minutes. The final part of this exercise could be extended into overnight homework.**

GOAL:

      Every student has read stories, heard stories, and written stories. Yet few (if any) are able to define and describe the term *story* and separate story from other narrative forms. That is, we all recognize a story, but haven't thought about what uniquely defines a story. Yet this explicit understanding is at the very heart of being able to successfully write a story. This definition is the place to start any story-related program.

DIRECTIONS:

      This exercise flows through a sequence of four steps, all asking the same questions: *How do you define a story? What is a story?* It is, in part, a precursor activity to Exercise 2.2, *Is It a Story Yet?*

Step 1. **Begin with this general question to your class:** "You've all read stories, right? You've all listened to stories, right? And you've all written stories, right? So you all know what a story is, right?" Pause to let them answer "yes" each time you say "right?" Then ask, "So what *is* a story? What makes a story a story? What makes a story different from an article or a textbook? How do you *define* a story?"

      As each student answers, establish whether their answer is a synonym for story ("A story is a tale, a fable, or a fairy tale."), a characteristic of a good story ("A story is fun to listen to." "A story is exciting."), or a possible definition. When I do this exercise with a class and get either a synonym or a characteristic of a story, I say, "Yes, tale is another word for story. But what makes a story a story?" or, "Yes, a good story is fun to listen to. But is 'fun to listen to' a *definition* of a story, or a *characteristic* of a good story?" Then I move on to the next student.

      When someone responds with a definition-like term, explore its limits and applicability. (Example: Student answers, "A story is something written down in a book." You respond, "A story could be written down. But does it have to be? Couldn't it also be oral, told from person to person, like the stories you tell that happened to you? So a story is either written or told. That could be in a definition.")

Avoid including storytelling elements in this definition. An understanding of the process will come later. For now focus exclusively on the story, the thing being told.

Take the time to build as many solid elements as possible. List them on the board as they are mentioned. Avoid digression into lists of types of stories and remember to explore the limits of each answer. Does it define or characterize a story? Does it describe *all* stories? Some stories? Help the students to differentiate between definition and descriptive characteristics.

Step 2.   Now that they are thinking in definition terms, have each student write their own definition of a story. They may use some of the terms presented during the class discussion or others that occur to them. Give them enough time to think through and write down a complete definition.

Step 3.   Each student reads their definition in turn to at least three other students. After this exchange, students should have a moment to revise their definition if they choose.

Step 4.   Let students nominate other's definitions that they particularly liked to be read aloud to the whole class. Have four to six students read. Now create a list of the elements that, as a class, you think should be in your definition of a story. Don't worry about wording or overlap between elements. Make a list your class can agree on of which terms and elements should be included in, and excluded from, a definition of "story."

Typically, this list creates such rambly definitions as: A story is something either written or told that has a plot and characters and setting with a beginning, middle, and an end, that tells about something that really happened or something someone made up.

The students' definition probably has terms and verbiage it doesn't need. It may not be particularly useful. You may not agree with their definition, and this book most likely will not agree with it, either. But let it stand for now. As your class moves through the next few exercises, a clearer picture of a story will emerge.

Options/Variations:

As a final optional step, assign as homework that the students revise their personal definitions and show, explain, or justify how that definition uniquely identifies the elements that make a story work.

TEACHING POINTS TO EMPHASIZE:

This should be *their* definition with little prompting. After they have completed a composite definition, see how many of the story myths I listed earlier are stated or implied by their wording.

The students' definition will probably be plot based. Ask them to recall stories they have liked and what made them like the story. These answers will be predominantly character based. Ask them if that is consistent with their definition.

Super Simple Storytelling Exercise 2.2

IS IT A STORY YET?

Explore the essential elements of a story

❭ **APPROPRIATE GRADES: All**

❭ **TIME REQUIRED: About 15 minutes**

GOAL:

Your class has already struggled through a tentative definition of a story. However, it is likely that they were speaking with their intellect, from what they have been told, rather than listing the characteristics that excite them and draw them into the stories they read.

Exercise 2.1 asked, What is a story? You could have substituted the question, What makes a story fun? (Exercise 1.4 addresses this very question.) "Fun" is a catch-all term for most students that includes humorous, exciting, memorable, energizing, etc. Those are not independent characteristics. Those elements that make a story fun are the same elements that define it as a story and the same elements that make a story so powerful.

This exercise takes a different slant on the same core question. In that way it will help your students cut through to the real heart and soul of the definition of a story.

DIRECTIONS:

This exercise requires that you either read or tell a short story to your class. Included here is one I often use because it is short, it strongly accents all the key story elements, it is versatile and easy to mold to your personal style of story presentation, and it works well.

As you tell this story, you will stop periodically to ask your class if it is a story yet. Students must then defend their answers. Why is it? or Why isn't it? The portions of the story appear in italics.

Read this first part with a neutral, matter-of-fact tone.

> *Little Brian woke one morning after an all-night, hard rain. He headed off to school just as the rain ended. Clouds began to drift apart. Sunbeams filtered down, splashing light on the grass and sidewalk around him.*
>
> *That afternoon, Brian came home from school to find his mother waiting for him on the front porch.*

Stop for discussion. Ask, ***Is it a story yet? Does what I have already said have everything you need it to have to be a story, or is something critical still missing?*** Make your students vote by show of hands. How many think it is? How many think it isn't? Typically at this point 85-90 percent will vote "no."

Ask them why they voted as they did. Start with those who said it *is* a story. Make them show how this fit with their definition of a story.

Have those who voted "no" justify their answer. Why isn't it a story? What critical bits of information are missing? What information do they still need to know? Summarize and repeat the key information they say they still need so it is fresh in everyone's mind.

Interestingly, students will readily and accurately identify the core elements of a story during even the earliest stages of this exercise by articulating what is missing from the story, even though they failed to mention any of these elements while defining a story during Exercise 2.2.

Finally, ask the class what the story is about. Have them explain their answers. You will typically find a wide variety of answers at this point because the information defining what the story is about has not yet been included. We have locked onto a main character, Brian, but know neither his story goal nor the obstacles that keep him from reaching that goal.

Repeat or summarize the first part of the story before continuing. Read this new segment with as stern and furious a voice as you can muster.

> *Her fists were jammed onto her hips. Her foot angrily tapped on the wooden floorboards of the porch. Her eyes glared down the steps Brian would have to climb up if he was ever going to make it into the house for dinner that night.*
> *"Brian! What on earth happened to you today? Your teacher called!"*

Again, stop for discussion. Repeat the questions from the first break. **Is it a story yet? Does what I have already said have everything you need it to have to be a story, or is something critical still missing?** Again, have students vote by show of hands. Typically all students now vote "no."

Ask them why they voted as they did. Start with any who said it is a story. Have those who voted "no" justify their answer. Why isn't it a story? What critical bits of information are still missing? What information do they still need to know? Ask them what important bits of information they learned during this story segment.

Finally, ask the class what the story is about. Have them explain and justify their answers. You'll find that their answers now all revolve around the conflict and struggle the main character must face.

Repeat or summarize the story so far before continuing. Use your "very angry" voice for the mother and an innocent but somewhat whiny voice for Brian. He should sound as if he were groping for an answer, as if he were making up an excuse. It is important to make the mother sound overly angry and to exaggerate Brian's overly innocent reaction.

> *"But mooommm. I already know she called. I was standing right beside her in the office when she did."*
> *"She was furious, Brian. She said you were an hour and a half late for school. Now why were you late?"*

Again, stop for discussion. Repeat the key questions from before. **Is it a story yet?** Etc. Etc. Have the students vote by show of hands. Typically all still vote "no."

Again ask them why they voted as they did. Start with any who said it is a story. Have those who voted "no" justify their answer. Why isn't it a story? What critical bits of information are still missing? What information do they still need to know? Ask them what important bits of information they learned during this story segment.

You will find that all the information your students want revolves around the story characters, their actions, their motives, their plans, their reactions, and what Brian is going to *say*. Point this out to your students. After all, it is characters that drive every story. (Note that, if you make the mother *really* angry, few if any will want to know what actually happened in the morning any more. They will focus on whether or not Brian gets out of being in trouble in the afternoon.)

Repeat or summarize the story so far before continuing. It is important to use your "very angry" voice for the mother and an innocent but somewhat whiny voice for Brian. His final answer should also sound concerned and sincere.

> *"But moooom. It rained last night."*
> *"Brian, the rain ended before you left for school. That's no excuse. Now why were you late?"*
> *"But moooooommm. After all that rain, all the worms crawled out on the side-walk. I was afraid the sun would dry them out and kill 'em, or that some of the mean kids would step on them and squish 'em. I had to put the worms back in the grass where they'd be safe. . . . There were a lot of worms, mom."*

Again, stop here for discussion. Repeat the vote. You'll find that many hesitate and some (typically one-third to one-half) shift their vote to "yes."

Ask them what happened in that segment to change their vote. What did they hear that suddenly made it a story? Discuss these elements that they needed to make it a story.

Ask those who still vote "no" what they still need to know. Virtually all of these comments will revolve around wanting to know what the mother does next and if Brian is going to be punished.

Saying that you'll add that part on, pour all the loving warmth and sweetness into this last line that you can.

> *And Brian's mother said, "Brian, I love you."*
> *That's the story of Brian.*

Your dramatic—more correctly, melodramatic—presentation of the story is critical to its success. Brian should act overly innocent. Mother must act overly mad (except on her last line). The more extreme each is, the better.

TEACHING POINTS TO EMPHASIZE:

There are three critical bits of information listeners need to call this a story: identity of the main character, the problem or struggle that character faces, and what the character is going to do about that problem, the resolution. The first two define what the story is about and how it must end. The third lays out the essential plotting elements. Stories are defined by the problems and struggles of characters.

To better illustrate this point, say, "The truth is, Brian's mother wasn't mad at him. She was *worried* about Brian and what might have happened to him. But if I told you that, and *then* asked you what you want to know, almost all of you would want to know what happened in the morning. Why? You'd be looking for a problem. But when I made the mother angry, you didn't worry so much about the morning. You had a dandy problem on the front porch in the afternoon. The madder I make her in the afternoon, the less you care about the morning."

It is also true that the angrier you make the mother, the better the class will like the story. That is, they will become more engrossed in, and involved with, the story as the mother grows angrier. Brian's mother is the problem he faces in the story. The bigger the problem, the better the story.

It's true. Readers and listeners search for a problem to use as the central focus of the story they are receiving. I have tested it with hundreds of student audiences.

There are two more discussion items that come out of this exercise. First is humor. If they laughed while you told this story, it was probably when you whined, "But mooooommmmm." Why laugh there? Ask them. They will attribute it to the *way* you said it. They will be partially right.

More important, that line is a ***character reaction***. A stressful situation arises, and our character reacts. Those reactions are always an audiences' favorite part of a story. Those reactions are what students will remember best and longest about the story.

Finally, compare the key elements uncovered in this exercise: character, problem, and character reaction, to the elements included in their Exercise 2.1 definition for a story. Are they the same? similar? Discuss this with your class.

Super Simple Storytelling Exercise 2.3

THE BIG THREE

Explore how core character elements create the story

> **APPROPRIATE GRADES: All**

> **TIME REQUIRED: 10 minutes**

GOAL:

If students begin the process of learning a story by understanding the core character information, they greatly increase the probability that they will produce a successful story-telling. However, this isn't a "natural" place for students to start. They want to start by learning plot, the surest way to undermine their own story. This exercise helps them establish a new and better habit.

DIRECTIONS:

Bring three students to the front of the class and announce that these three students are going to create a story for the class.

Each student will create one of the three core character elements: identify the main character, define that character's goal, and create obstacles and problems. However, the specific wording you use in soliciting these bits of information is important.

The goal of this exercise is to demonstrate that core character information always creates and defines a story. Reinforce that concept regularly.

The wording I have found to work best is as follows:

To the first student: "The other two students are going to make up a story. All you have to do is make up that first, most important, bit of information they need, which is . . . " Here I pause to let student and class mull over what information should come first. "Which is . . . the character. Every story needs to start with *who* the story is going to be about. This character you're going to make up can be, but doesn't have to be, a human being. It does have to be a fictional, never-before-made-up character. It could be an animal—a dog, a frog, an elephant, a snake, a snail, or a mosquito. It could be a bush or a tree. It doesn't even have to be alive. It could be a cloud, a chair, or your shoelace. You can have them make up a story about anything. But it does have to be a brand-new fictional character. What do you want them to make up a story about?"

Let student number 1 now create a character first impression: the species identity, name, age, and just enough physical information so everyone envisions the same character. You can veto any character you don't like. I always veto aliens because it takes too much background information for everyone to understand the species, their world, and their basic life patterns and needs.

You repeat and summarize whatever they pick. "Once, there was a young, floppy-eared rabbit named Seymore."

To the second student: "Now the second bit of core character information. *In this story* what did Seymore want to either do or get? It doesn't have to be anything that would make sense for a rabbit to want to do or get. He could *want* to do *anything*. What do you want Seymore to want to either do or get in this story?"

Your wording here is important. If you ask for the character's goal, (what you really want) you'll get nothing but blank stares. Ask for what the character wants to either do or get and you'll get great answers.

Again, summarize the created information thus far. "Once, there was an old, floppy-eared rabbit named Seymore who wanted to eat some chocolate chip ice cream. He was tired of carrots and lettuce. He was tired of always going to the salad bar. He wanted dessert. He wanted some ice cream!"

To the third student: "Now the third bit of core character information. Why hasn't Seymore gotten any ice cream? What's keeping Seymore from getting his ice cream? Something must, or he'd already have it. So what's keeping Seymore from getting any ice cream?"

You are asking for obstacles, either problems or flaws. The wording shown above will spark their creation. Asking for a problem or obstacle typically won't.

Allow them to make up three or four potential obstacles. Stop the student anytime they drift into a plotting sequence (a series of events that could happen in the story). You want only the potential obstacles, not how they will fit into the story.

Again, summarize for the class. "Once, there was an old, floppy-eared rabbit named Seymore who wanted to eat some chocolate chip ice cream. He was tired of carrots and lettuce. He wanted dessert. He wanted some ice cream! BUT, Seymore had no money to buy ice cream. And his mother said he couldn't have any because it was bad for him and would rot his teeth. Besides, the ice cream store owner hated rabbits and would shoot any rabbit that came near his store. But Seymore *really* wanted some ice cream."

Now turn to the class and ask, "How is this story going to end? What's the last thing that will happen at the end of this story?"

They will answer, "It ends when Seymore gets some ice cream." Most likely, they will try to include the plotting sequence that explains *how* Seymore will get his ice cream. Cut such discussion short. You want only what happens at the very end.

Now say, "Getting ice cream is one of two possible endings for this story. Does anyone know the other?" The other, of course, is that Seymore *never* gets any ice cream. It usually takes a while for students to come up with this option. If any suggest that the story ends when Seymore dies (and fourth-, fifth-, and sixth-grade boys surely will) ask if, after he dies, Seymore still wants some ice cream. That will fit their answer back into one of the two plausible endings for the story.

The main character's goal defines the story's end and creates structure for the story.

Open up the discussion for other possible obstacles and problems, both internal and external. Stop anyone who begins to present a plotting scenario. They should only be allowed to suggest other obstacles that could keep the character from reaching their goal.

As a class, discuss which obstacles will make for a better story. Consistently it will be those obstacles that create the greatest risk and danger for the character. Risk and danger create the suspense and tension every story needs to propel a reader through to the exciting climax.

Ask if any students think they know how the story will go. Many will say yes. Don't allow them to launch into their version of the story. Rather, ask them *why* they think they know how the story goes. The discussion will lead back to the chosen obstacles.

Obstacles create plot.

During the exercise your job is to keep the story moving and to prevent students from interjecting plot. No plot is mentioned or discussed during this exercise. However, once these basic character elements have been created, every student intuitively "knows" what has to happen in the story.

Options/Variations:

For third grade and up, add a fourth person. After the above discussions, this student has to define the personality profile for the main character. This is the hardest of the four basic pieces of character information for most students to make up.

To simplify this task, ask the student simply to make up how the main character reacts in two general situations. Have them make up what the character does (physically) when something goes right and when something (anything) goes wrong.

They must be specific in their description of the physical reactions of the character. Typically, they answer with an emotional state. "Seymore feels sad." That's no good. Readers need sensory information. Different characters do different things when they are sad. What does Seymore the rabbit do and say when he's sad? Often they will still need prompting and suggested options to clearly define a character's physical response to good or bad situations. As they invent the way the character reacts, exaggerate and demonstrate it for the class.

TEACHING POINTS TO EMPHASIZE:

This exercise powerfully demonstrates the true heart of every story: core character information. The character goal creates story structure and direction. It defines the ending point. It gives purpose and significance to all events and interactions in the story. Either they help the character toward a goal, or they hinder that process.

Problems and obstacles define conflict and story plot. Plot is the sequence of events a character undertakes in an attempt to overcome obstacles and achieve a goal. Create character, goal, and obstacles, and you have created the basic plot.

Finally, character reactions provide interpretation of the story events. They create energy and humor. They draw readers and listeners into the story.

Review Exercise 2.2 (*Is It a Story Yet?*) with your class. These elements are the exact ones they needed to call it a story.

Once your students get used to starting stories with core character information, they'll find that it's easier and far more effective than more traditional approaches. In truth, it's a simple, four-step habit: character, goal, obstacles (which define conflict), and reaction (which leads to personality). The more often they practice it, the more automatic it becomes.

Super Simple Storytelling Exercise 3.1

THE MEMORIZATION BLUES

Explore the problems created by memorizing a story

> **APPROPRIATE GRADES: Second and up**
> **TIME REQUIRED: 10 minutes**

GOAL:

Most beginning tellers want to memorize the words of their story. This exercise is designed to demonstrate several of the major drawbacks to that approach to storytelling.

DIRECTIONS:

Select six students. You may either have them stand in a line in front of the class or remain in their seats. Tell the class that you want to show them something about memorizing a story. Say that you will make up a short scene one sentence at a time and that the selected students must hear each new sentence, memorize it, and repeat it using exactly the same words you used.

You will say the first sentence. Then the first student will repeat the first sentence. You will repeat the first sentence and add a second sentence. The second student will repeat both the first and second sentences. You will repeat those two sentences and add a third. The third student will repeat all three sentences. And so on.

Reinforce the idea that the primary job of these students will be to hear each new sentence, memorize it, and repeat *exactly* the same words you used.

Tell the rest of the class that their job is to listen and watch carefully the *way* each student says their lines.

While you can improvise these scenes, I recommend that you create and memorize a six-sentence scene to use for this exercise. I also recommend that you create strong, easy gestures to associate with each major action in the scene. These gestures will make it easier for you to remember the scene and will help students remember the sentences.

Two scenes I have often used are printed below. Each is divided into six segments for use with a six-student demo team. As you learn these or other scenes, concentrate on the characterizations and the expressiveness that you will use to make the scenes sound exciting and dynamic. Try to make each scene sound "bigger than life" when you tell it.

During the exercise, help students who are struggling to remember their lines by repeating the gestures that accompanied those lines. Usually those visual cues will get them going again. Students typically will not accurately repeat all the lines of this story scene. That's fine. As long as they struggle and *try* to recreate the sentences you spoke, it doesn't matter how successful they are. It is far more valuable to keep the exercise moving.

After you and your chosen students have completed the scene, discuss the quality of their telling—the energy and expression they used while telling—rather than how accurate they were in memorizing a fixed set of words. Use the teaching points below as focal points for this discussion.

Scene 1. The Witch.

1. The witch turned and entered the room.

2. With her red, beady eyes she searched for Natasha.

3. "I feel your presence, my pretty," she hissed.

4. Natasha bolted from behind the old, overstuffed couch and dashed toward the brick wall next to the fireplace.

5. As Natasha uttered the secret, forbidden words, "Hubba, hubba," the bricks dissolved.

6. Natasha dove through the shimmering hole and fell into the endless void beyond, calling, "I'm falling!" as the witch cursed and hissed from above.

Scene 2. Little Willie's Bubble Gum.

1. Mrs. Johnson rose from her chair and marched to the blackboard.

2. "Pay attention class," she said.

3. Little Willie sat at his desk in the far back corner of the room.

4. His bubble gum was well chewed and ready.

5. Little Willie slithered out of his seat and crawled silently inch by inch up the aisle,

6. And placed his wad of bubble gum right in the middle of Mrs. Johnson's chair!

TEACHING POINTS TO EMPHASIZE:

Problems arise for a teller when they focus on the words themselves rather than on the scene and its meaning, energy, and emotion. When a teller's focus is on remembering a stream of words, their focus is *not* on the way they say those words. Expression and emotion tend to drop away from their telling. Their voice becomes a monotone, their volume low, their pace stops relating to the scene and relates only to the rate at which they can remember and mouth the words.

The last three tellers in this exercise typically fall prey to this memorization syndrome. They sound like boring robots as they struggle to remember the correct words. They tend to speak haltingly and to continually backtrack and correct themselves as they remember more of your wording.

The truth is, there is no one correct wording. Many different wordings will effectively convey a scene *as long as the teller has gotten the emotional expression of the scene right*. It is a myth to think that you can memorize the words of a story and thereby effectively communicate it to an audience. It is not the specific wording audiences listen most closely to. The emotion, tone, pacing, and energy (expression) of a teller lead the audience to understand the words. Rather than helping, memorizing the words of a story actually impedes a teller's ability to effectively tell the story.

Super Simple Storytelling Exercise 3.2

STAND AND WATCH

Explore what creates teller physical comfort

> **APPROPRIATE GRADES: Third and up**

> **TIME REQUIRED: 10 minutes**

GOAL:

Our natural tendency is to concentrate on the words we plan to say and ignore how the words will be said. Through a lifetime of informal telling experience, tellers get away with ignoring how they say something so long as the event being told happened to them and so long as they feel comfortable during the telling. When either or both of those conditions is violated, tellers ignore *how* they will say something at their own peril. The result is a feeling of nervous anxiety, the fidgets, a sure indicator that no one planned for *how* a story was going to be told. This exercise allows students to experience and understand that feeling and discuss ways to prevent it.

DIRECTIONS:

Have half the class stand, feet together, hands at their sides, in a single curving arc around the classroom walls. Tell them that their job is simply to stand. Tell the other half of the class that their job is to sit and watch the half who are standing. You stand patiently, nodding on occasion as if everything were going exactly according to plan, and let a full 90 seconds (or more—I often go a full two minutes with adult groups) tick past before saying anything other than to remind the standers not to talk or move.

Now tell the standing half to remain standing but also to count the ceiling tiles (or some other simple counting activity they can complete without having to walk around the room). The half who are sitting should continue to sit and watch.

Give the standers another 90 seconds to count. Then have them sit and, without discussion or chit-chat, have the other half stand and form a single arc around the classroom walls. Have this half stand, hands at sides, feet together, for 90 seconds (or more) while the first half sits and quietly watches.

Give the standers a simple task that they can accomplish without walking around the room. Counting all of the legs in the room is one I often use. Let them work at this task for 90 seconds while the first half watches before asking this second half to return to their seats.

Now discuss their experience. How did they feel while just standing? Did they feel differently while standing and doing something? What was the difference? Could sitters observe physical differences between the time standers were just standing and when they had some task to perform?

Typically, each student feels more comfortable and relaxed while they have something to do. Shoulders relax. Nervous habits cease. Bodies look less stiff. People appear more natural and comfortable—all characteristics of The Golden List of audience wants and needs.

TEACHING POINTS TO EMPHASIZE:

If an audience is to believe in a story, they must believe that the teller is enthusiastic about, and believes in, their own story. Tellers who look relaxed, comfortable, and natural appear to like their own stories better than do those who appears stiff, tight, and nervous. When hands, arms, feet, and bodies know their part in a story, they will feel more comfortable and relaxed. The teller will appear more natural and confident. The audience will become more deeply involved in the story.

What arms, hands, feet, face, and body do is determined by *how* a teller will tell a story, not by the story itself. The teller who adequately plans how they will tell a story sets the stage for easy success.

Super Simple Storytelling Exercise 3.3

DESCRIBE THE SCENE

*Explore what makes a teller look and
sound real and natural when telling*

> **APPROPRIATE GRADES: Third and up**

> **TIME REQUIRED: 10 minutes**

GOAL:

We describe best what we see most clearly in our mind's eye. But what does effective description look like and sound like? This exercise is designed to demonstrate this element of storytelling and to introduce its importance and origins for a storyteller.

DIRECTIONS:

Bring three students to the front of the room. Ask one to describe their own livingroom. Tell this student that they have decided to cooperate with a house robber and must describe their livingroom well enough so that the robber can easily negotiate that room during darkest night without making a sound or needing a light and still collect all the valuables.

Task other students to carefully watch how these descriptions are delivered, paying particular attention to details and gestures.

Following this first student's description, select a room for the second student to describe about which they have only a vague or general sense—maybe one they have seen only once or have only heard about. The faculty lounge, principal's office, mayor's office, the Senate chamber, the oval office, or another such room will do. Tell the second student to describe this room in equal detail.

Following the second student's description, select a room for the third student to describe about which they know nothing. You might chose your parents' livingroom, the county recorder's office in some distant city, or a mythical or fictional room. Have this third student describe this room as best they can.

Now compare descriptions. Compare the number and type of details offered; the number and crispness of the gestures used; the tonal quality of the voice; the sense of confidence, or believability, created; the vividness, sharpness, and completeness of the images listening students formed in their minds; and how interesting each description was.

Probe behind student answers by asking why they reacted as they did and what the tellers did to make them form the images and impressions they formed.

TEACHING POINTS TO EMPHASIZE:

We describe best what we see most clearly and in the most detail in our minds. It is easy to make a description of something a teller knows well sound interesting and convincing. The problem is that a teller has rarely seen the scenes and events they try to describe while telling a story. To make a story sound real and interesting, the presented detail (description) must sound and look real and interesting. One major task of learning a story is to create sensory images of each scene, character, and action that are as vivid and detailed as if the teller had actually seen them. For that is the way to make the detail, gestures, wording, and tone used during description sound real and believable.

Super Simple Storytelling Exercise 3.4

SAY IT HOW?

Explore how orchestra players convey mood, feeling, and attitude

> **APPROPRIATE GRADES: Third and up**
> **TIME REQUIRED: 20 minutes**

GOAL:

We each expertly use body, face, voice, and gesture to routinely convey every nuance of every attitude and emotion possible. We each portray them differently. But we each have learned exactly how to portray them all. The problem is, we do it subconsciously. We do it all the time, but do not, consciously, have the slightest idea of how we do it. If a storyteller were consciously aware of, and held conscious control over, exactly what they did with each of their personal orchestra elements to convey emotional and attitudinal information, effective storytelling would be an easy task. This exercise helps students become consciousof what it feels like to manipulate their personal orchestra to convey meaning.

DIRECTIONS:

Divide the class into groups of four to six. Use Figure 7.1 (or a similar sheet of your own creation) for this exercise. On the left of this figure is a column of six random, simple words. On the right are three columns of emotional states, or *ways to say something*.

Figure 7.1. Say It How?

WORDS	GROUP #1	GROUP #2	GROUP #3
YES	ANGER	RAGE	INDIFFERENCE
MY	FEAR	TERROR	DEPRESSION
WHY	SORROW	HATRED	BOREDOM
NOW	HAPPINESS	ECSTASY	DOUBT
NO	CONFUSION	CONTEMPT	THOUGHTFULNESS
OVER	HOPE	BLISS	CAUTION

Start this exercise with the emotions in column 1. One student in each group picks and announces to the group one of the words in the right-hand column and an emotion from column 1. For example, say the word 'now' with 'anger'.

Each member of the group then says that one word, trying to best express the designated emotion. It is instantly obvious to everyone that there is no real information in the content (*what* will be said) and that all information must be carried by the *way* it is said. Because students don't feel the chosen emotion at the moment and can't use content to suggest how to effectively say it, they must consciously think about what they do to effectively express that emotion.

The group should compare how each student chose to express the designated emotion, noting the variety of ways to denote an emotional state and also how effective each is.

Then have another student pick another word from the list on the right and a different emotion from column 1 to launch the group into a new round. Stay with the emotions in column 1 until each group has tried at least four different combinations of word and emotion before having them shift to the emotions in column 2.

This is usually a raucous, fun exercise. A whistle or other attention-gathering devise will be useful in getting the groups to shift when you want them to.

You will note that there is greater hesitancy in, and resistance to, portraying the column 2 emotions. The groups degenerate into talk and banter. The room is actually quieter.

After allowing each group to struggle with the column 2 emotions for a few minutes, lead a class discussion about the difference between column 1 and 2 emotions. Use the teaching points listed below as a guide.

Finally, shift to the emotions in column 3. However, change the format for this round. A student silently, secretly selects a word and a group 3 emotion and says their chosen word to the group expressing their chosen column 3 emotion as best as they can. The group then has to guess which emotion was being expressed. After the group has figured it out and had a moment for discussion, a second student picks a word and a column 3 emotion to express.

Lead a final class discussion, first about the difficulty they experienced in differentiating column 3 emotions and second about the general difficulty of making their emotional expressions look real and natural. They are struggling with trying to consciously direct a process they routinely control subconsciously. The more conscious this controlling information becomes, the more effective their storytelling will be.

TEACHING POINTS TO EMPHASIZE:

We all know exactly how to effectively express every shade of every emotion. We do it every day. But we don't consciously control the process of expressing these emotions. We control the way we express an emotion subconsciously, automatically.

When the speaker doesn't feel the emotion they are to express (and usually storytellers do not feel the way their characters do during a story), and when the speaker can't rely on content to communicate an emotional state, the job must be done consciously. Because we aren't used to consciously controlling the way we say something, the job feels awkward and unnatural. We aren't sure of exactly what to do.

The emotions in column 1 of Figure 7.1 are normal, comfortable, garden-variety emotions. They are easier to portray because we see then regularly and have a better image of what they should look like.

The emotions in column 2 are extreme versions of the column 1 emotions. It is likely that none of your students have ever actually seen another human being portray any of these emotions. They seem embarrassing to act out. They are also uncomfortable and embarrassing to watch. Watching a ranting, raving, enraged teller would pull any rational human out of the story to focus on the stage performance.

While accurate portrayal of the standard emotions we all experience every day carries a story and makes it seem real, *portrayal* of extreme emotions is both difficult and counterproductive to the story. It disrupts both teller and audience. If a character is terrified, a wise teller portrays (expresses) simple fear while telling about the terrified character (unless the emotional exaggeration is used for humorous effect). The audience will understand and the story flows smoothly and effectively.

Conversely, the column 3 emotions are all subtle emotional states whose interpretation usually depends on context. Indifference, boredom, and depression all look pretty much the same. We have to know what's going on to differentiate them. Column 1 emotions are easy to visualize and accurately convey. Column 2 emotions are disruptive and uncomfortable. Column 3 emotions are extremely difficult to envision and portray—unless they are carried to an extreme version (usually for humor).

When creating an emotional state to learn for each scene of a story, the ordinary types of emotions—like those in column 1—will serve the teller better than either extreme, as demonstrated in columns 2 and 3.

This exercise demonstrates how inexperienced we are at consciously manipulating voice, face, hands, and body to express an emotional state. When a teller uses practice and exercise to bring subconscious information (how we express emotional states) into consciousness, expressing the emotions and attitudes of story characters will be far easier and more effective during the telling of a story.

Super Simple Storytelling Exercise 3.5

I FORGOT MY HOMEWORK

Explore the elements of effective oral communication

> **APPROPRIATE GRADES: Second and up**

> **TIME REQUIRED: 10 minutes**

GOAL:

It is difficult to make an expressed emotion seem real when the content doesn't relate at all to that emotion (as students were asked to do during Exercise 3.4). It is easier when the speaker says a whole sentence instead of just a word and when they can imagine saying that sentence within some greater context.

DIRECTIONS:

Bring four student volunteers to the front of the room. Invent a simple four- or five-word sentence and have each student repeat the sentence to show that they have learned their "script." Three sentences I often use are: "I forgot my homework.", "There is no school today.", and "We have a math test."

One by one have the volunteers repeat the sentence, BUT give each an emotion or attitude to project and portray when they do. They may not change any of the words or improvise add-ons. They must repeat that one, same sentence, and still convince the class that they really feel the emotional attitude you assigned to them.

Good emotional states to use include (but are certainly not limited to): proud, angry, happy, excited, shocked, sarcastic, resentful, flirtatious, and confused. Tell the students that their job is to "convince everyone that, because of (what they are to say), this is the most (emotion they are to express) moment in their lives." (For example, "*Because* they forgot their homework, this is the proudest moment of their life.")

Note that the first four emotions listed have ready opposites:

Emotion	Opposite
Proud	Ashamed
Angry	Joyful
Happy	Sad
Excited	Bored

Make sure that at least two of the four volunteers are assigned emotions with readily available opposites.

After all four have taken their turn with the sentence, open a class discussion on what each student might have done to seem *more* proud, angry, etc., and to seem *more convincing* in their portrayal of that emotion. Require each student to describe their suggestions for improvement in detailed physical terms. Not "She should look really disgusted and angry," but "She should cross her arms, hunch her shoulders, stick out her lower lip, tighten her eyebrows, and talk in a low, whispery voice."

Allow the class to debate what best communicates the essence of the emotion in question. Then give the volunteer a second chance at the sentence. Tell them that they can incorporate any of the class suggestions they like, but that this is their one, final chance to earn an Academy Award™ for overacting. Tell them to pour all of their energy and conviction into this one sentence and into the emotion they are to adopt.

Options/Variations:

Two continuations of this exercise are both beneficial and popular. First, dismiss only those volunteer students who were not assigned emotions with ready opposites. Select a volunteer partner for each of the remaining original group. Have one of the original students repeat the sentence, pouring all of their energy into an over-exaggerated emotional presentation. Then have their partner say the sentence portraying the *opposite* emotion. Have the class compare and contrast the physical and vocal performances between these opposites.

Second, dismiss all the original volunteers and ask for new volunteers who think they can do a better job of convincingly portraying the assigned emotions. Give this second group one turn at saying the sentence with their assigned emotion. Then have the class compare and evaluate the various performances they have seen.

TEACHING POINTS TO EMPHASIZE:

Everyone recognizes every gradation of each emotional state and incorporates them into normal communication. However, we do neither consciously. We control both our presentation of emotional states and our interpretation of other's emotional states subconsciously.

It therefore feels awkward and silly to convey a strong emotion you don't feel. It's not the way we are used to acting. But storytellers do it all the time. Becoming aware of what different emotions look like—that is, what they physically and vocally involve—and of any possible variations in that presentation arm a teller with a conscious understanding of the primary tool for *how* they will tell a story.

Finally, have students note the difference in the class's response between lackluster, energyless presentation of an emotional state and a high-energy, exaggerated presentation. When one of the volunteers poured energy, effort, and originality into how they said the sentence, the class paid attention, liked it, and laughed. The energy and conviction of *the way* a story is said is what engages an audience.

Super Simple Storytelling Exercise 3.6

YOU WANT ME TO GO THERE.?

Explore the conscious control of vocal communication

> **APPROPRIATE GRADES: Third and up**
> **TIME REQUIRED: 15 minutes**

GOAL:

Every human employs their own system for expressing emphasis and emotion in every sentence they ever say. But we humans control the way we say things subconsciously. This exercise allows students to experience the feel of consciously manipulating their vocal orchestra elements.

DIRECTIONS:

Divide the class into groups of five or six. Print the following six-words on the board in large letters: "You want me to go there.?" Add both period and question marks at the end. Tell the class that there are twelve ways to say this group of words. The emphasis may be placed on any of the six words and still make sense, and they may be said as either a statement or a question.

In each group one student goes first. They say the words ("You want me to go there.") as a statement, placing the emphasis on the first word, *you*. The second student says the words as a statement, placing the emphasis on the second word, *want*. The third student says the words as a statement, placing the emphasis on the third word, *me*, and so forth around the group.

The group does not passively listen to each rendition of these words. Rather, it is the job of the group to ensure that each student actually places the emphasis on the correct word and that they make the sentence sound real and natural the way they say it. The group should not move on to the next speaker until all are satisfied that the current speaker said the sentence as they were assigned to say it.

After most of the students in each group have tried the sentence, ask the class what a person does to place emphasis on a specific word in a sentence. They will still struggle to articulate the available techniques, even though they have just been listening for and employing them. There are five possible ways to emphasize a specific word:

1. Raise the pitch (by far the most common)

2. Increase volume

3. Prolong the word, saying it more slowly

4.   Pause before the word

5.   Use gestures to draw attention to that one word.

Let the students return to their group work. After completing all six versions as a statement, have them try each version again, making the wrods a question. Tell them that one of the 12 ways to say the words is significantly harder than the other 11. Ask them to identify which it is. Give them several minutes to search for this most difficult version.

The most difficult version is to place the emphasis on the final word, *there*, and say the words as a statement. The reason has to do with how we form questions and statements. To signal a question we raise the pitch on the final word. To signal a statement we lower the pitch on the final word. However, the most common way to place emphasis on one word is to raise the pitch on that word. If that word is the final word in a sentence, it sounds like a question.

To place emphasis on the word *there* and make it a statement, the most common means of creating emphasis must be abandoned and one or more of the alternate emphasis schemes must be employed. However, this always feels more awkward and sounds less real.

Now that students have limbered up their minds, ears, and tongues for the conscious control of sentence emphasis, tell them that we never simply say a sentence. We always have some attitude, or emotional meaning, we want to convey in addition to the basic sentence content. Your students do this automatically every time they speak.

Write four emotional attitudes on the board below the six words (e.g., disgust, relief, shock, joy, sadness, anger, sarcasm). Have the students repeat the exercise. However, this time one student picks one of the six words to emphasize, decides whether it will be a statement or question, and picks one of the listed emotional attitudes to adopt and portray. The student on their left must say the words, successfully meeting those three parameters.

If students feel that this is impossible (or nearly impossible) to do, remind them that they actually do all of this and more in every sentence they say—all without any effort or struggle on their part at all.

TEACHING POINTS TO EMPHASIZE:

We each use a complex system of vocal controls to signal meaning to a listener. We have each mastered and perfected this system through years of practice and effort. However, it is extremely difficult to control each of these vocal traits consciously. If a teller tried to consciously focus on the emphasis and emotion of each individual sentence, they would surely forget the story they were trying to tell. It is better to employ that natural, subconscious system we have each developed and allow it to automatically create tone, pace, emotion, and emphasis as a story is being told. The trick is to find out exactly what information each brain needs to successfully engage that natural, powerful, effective system. That is the Super Simple system for storytelling.

Super Simple Storytelling Exercise 3.7

HITCH HIKER

Explore the conscious control of orchestra elements

❭ **APPROPRIATE GRADES: Third and up**

❭ **TIME REQUIRED: 10-15 minutes**

GOAL:

Previous exercises have focused on becoming aware of the complex vocal system. *Hitch Hiker* helps students become aware of body postures, gestures and other movements, and speech patterns.

DIRECTIONS:

Bring five volunteer students to the front of the room to play this raucous and very popular orchestra game. Place two chairs side-by-side facing the rest of the class, as the "car." One student sits in the driver's seat; the other four line up near the passenger's side.

The rest of the class is tasked to observe and prepare to critique and discuss both the performance of each volunteer student and of the concept of physical movement to portray an emotional state.

On your direction, one student steps forward and thumbs for a ride. The driver stops and invites the hitch hiker into the car's passenger seat. As the hitch hiker settles into the car, they must adopt a definitive emotional state and a set of physical and vocal mannerisms to project that emotional state while they begin a conversation with the driver. The driver must immediately adopt the same emotional state and set of physical and vocal mannerisms while continuing to "drive."

Allow the students to develop their physical portrayal of this emotional state for 15 to 20 seconds while they converse. Then signal the next hitch hiker to step forward. Immediately the driver slides out of the car while the old hitch hiker slides into the driver's seat so this new hitch hiker can slide into the passenger's seat. The new hitch hiker adopts a different definitive emotional state and a set of physical and vocal mannerisms to project that emotional state while beginning a new conversation with this new driver. The new driver must immediately adopt the same emotional state and set of physical and vocal mannerisms while they converse and drive.

Allow all five students plus the original driver to experience the hitch hiker and driver roles before ending the exercise with a class discussion focusing on how clear, demonstrative, and interesting each hitch hiker's emotional portrayal was and how quickly and accurately each driver was able to pick up and mimic that emotional state.

TEACHING POINTS TO EMPHASIZE:

It is extremely valuable for each storyteller to understand how physical movement (gesture, facial expression, eye movement, and body posture) translates into emotional states in a listener's mind. To a large extent, this is the emotional expression every listener values and clamors for. Exercises like *Hitch Hiker,* which force students to become more aware of what it feels like to manipulate their storytelling orchestra and what effect that conscious manipulation has, are valuable steps along the road toward mastering *how* a story is going to be told.

Super Simple Storytelling Exercise 3.8

MUM'S THE WORD

Explore the use of nonverbal orchestra elements to convey a story

> **APPROPRIATE GRADES: Fourth and up**

> **TIME REQUIRED: 15 minutes**

GOAL:

Natural conversation relies on an intermingled concert of verbal and nonverbal information. Nonverbal communication (gesture, facial expression, and body posture) plays a more important role than most beginning tellers realize both in conveying the characters, events, and details of a story and in creating the listener's belief in the teller's belief in and enthusiasm for their own story. This demonstration allows students to explore the power of nonverbal communication.

DIRECTIONS:

This is a fun, powerful, and graphic demonstration of the allure and potential of gesture. It does, however, require you to learn and energetically present a short mime story. No, you do not have to be a mime or even know any mime moves or routines to successfully perform a mime story. Yes, you do have to be comfortable with exaggerated physical movement. As is true for all storytelling, the trick is to find a mime story with the kinds of events and character actions that are comfortable for you to perform.

Such stories are called "mime" stories only because there are no spoken words. Such stories rely exclusively on gesture and facial expression and on the two kinds of information that are the easiest to physically depict (or mime): character actions and character reactions. Any such story will do. However, they are hard to find in printed texts so I have included one here that is easy to learn and is always successful. Admittedly, this one story isn't right for every teller. No one story is. But many teachers have had both fun and success with it.

Have three volunteers come to the front of the class. Tell them that they will demonstrate how easy it is to learn a story. Tell them that you are going to present a story. They will hear the story once and be able to repeat it without missing even one word.

After the snickers of disbelief die down make them a bet that they will be able to retell the story without missing any words. Have the three volunteers sit in front while you present the story. First tell the class that you are sure you won't lose the bet because there are no words in the story. Tell them that you want to demonstrate the energy, power, and allure of gestures, a natural part of everyday communication that tellers tend to forget when they get a story as printed text from a book.

I will provide a description of this story in second person, as if I were directing you through each scene. It relies on large, easy physical gestures and movements and on exaggerated facial expressions to show the character's reaction to the various situations in the story. Picture yourself acting out each element of the story. If this particular story doesn't appeal to you, search the library for ones that fit better with your natural style.

The story is called "The Swimmer."

You're ambling, shuffling through the desert. It's 130° and you haven't had a drop of water in five days. You're hot. Wipe your brow; fan yourself; stretch open your collar to let the heat out; pant.

In the distance you see something and squint, shade your eyes, and strain to make out what it is. Point and smile to indicate that you like whatever it is you see.

Run (jog) to get there. Jog leisurely for four or five seconds as you let your eyes trail down the back wall and across the floor as if they were locked on this object that gets closer and closer as you run.

Stop. Point down just in front of yourself, nod, and smile again to indicate that whatever you saw earlier is now just in front of you.

You know there is a waist-high wall between you and what you want with a sign on it that says all trespassers will be instantly shot. How do you convey this situation to an audience? Act sneaky. Crouch slightly and hunch in your shoulders. Cast quick, furtive glances over both shoulders.

Satisfied that no one is watching, place both hands firmly on the wall, wiggle your bottom as if in preparation to climb (a great humor-grabbing movement), and climb over one leg at a time.

Again crouch and glance over both shoulders. Satisfied no one saw, bend down and scoop up great handfuls of water to drink. Splash some water on your face and under your arms (another guaranteed laugh). Slurp a final handful of water and beam a satisfied smile at the audience.

As you wipe your hands on your pants, you are struck with a great idea. Raise one index finger next to your face and cover your mouth with your other hand as you snicker derisively at the grandeur of your idea.

Again crouch, hunch, and check over both shoulders. Slide both hands up to pretend to unbutton the buttons of your shirt (or blouse). Pretend to peal off your shirt and toss it aside. Again check to make sure you are alone. Pretend to tuck your thumb into the waistband of your pants. The more you wiggle as you pretend to slide your pants down to your ankles the better it looks.

Step out of your pants, toss them aside, and, with a smile of delight, place your hands together for a big, slow dive into the water. Arch up onto your toes as you pretend to dive, bending low as you enter the water. Straighten up and swim the breast stroke with a satisfied smile. Bend your knees on each leisurly stroke as if this were the most pleasurable moment of your life.

Stop on the third stroke, just as if you heard something splashing in the water behind you, and turn to look over one shoulder. As you turn, bring your hands up in front of your face to become the Jaws of Death. Holding the heal of your hands together, curve your fingers into killer fangs or razor shark's teeth. The jaws open vertically three times. I find it is easier to frown while being the jaws.

> *Return to being the swimmer. Start with your head back over your shoulder. Then snap back to the front and react. Use spread arms and face to show desperate, panicked terror. Now swim—faster—but not as fast as you can because you have to do this two more times.*
>
> *After three horizontal breast strokes, return to being the jaws. As they get closer they seem to get bigger. So open up from the elbow instead of the wrist this time. Again, open the jaws and killer teeth vertically three times.*
>
> *Return to being the swimmer. Repeat, and over-exaggerate, the terrified reaction before swimming three faster, horizontal breast strokes. Again become the jaws and open, stiff-armed, from the shoulder, three times vertically.*
>
> *Return to being the swimmer for a final time. React. Swim three speedy breast strokes. To now exit the water and reach safety, don' wade (or walk) out. It looks better to pretend you are in a little kiddy pool with four inches of water and a six-inch high lip. Bend way over, pretend to place both hands on the lip of that pool, and take an over-exaggerated step forward, stomping hard on both feet as you make that step. Everyone will now understand that you are back on land.*
>
> *Tap your chest to show that your heart is pounding. Wipe the nervous sweat off your brow. Turn your shoulder and laugh tauntingly at the jaws—you won't be eaten today!*
>
> *As you turn back around, you realize 200 people are sitting on this side of that body of water, staring at you standing, dripping water like a fool, with your clothes back over on the other side.*
>
> *To finish the story you do a standard double-take—literally, two separate reactions to the same situation. The first is slow. Move nothing but your head, which slowly pans around the room, mouth dropped open in an "Oh, I stepped in it this time" look. Now the second reaction, which is fast. Cover up.*

As everyone laughs and applauds, straighten, bow, and call the three volunteers back up. Walk them through each step of the story, encouraging them to act, overact, and improvise as they go. Every innovative, exaggerated movement they make will be met with howls of laughter and applause.

Finish the exercise with a big round of applause for the volunteers and by reminding the class that gestures and facial expressions are powerful because they are visual. Because they have seen this story twice, every student could successfully, accurately perform it. They have all learned a story just by watching it and by forming all of the story imagery into pictures.

TEACHING POINTS TO EMPHASIZE:

Character emotions and reactions are easily and effectively portrayed through facial expression. Character actions and movement are easily and effectively portrayed through gesture and body movement. Gestures also provide valuable detail about the location, size, and shape of objects in a scene. These nonverbal elements are natural, effective, and efficient parts of oral communication and of storytelling.

Further, have students note how positive their reaction was to the performance of this story and to their fellow students' actions during their performance of it. Actions (gestures, movements, facial expressions—literally information through any nonverbal orchestra element) project great amounts of energy into a storytelling. *Comfortable*, steady incorporation of nonverbal orchestra elements into the telling of a story makes the teller appear more confident and more interested and involved in their own story. They make the audience believe that the teller believes in their own story. If those orchestra actions are exaggerated it is a reliable and steady source of humor.

The key word, though, is "comfortable." Gestures are a powerful and effective storytelling tool, but certainly not an essential one. No one element is. Gestures should be used to the extent that a teller's natural style affords the opportunity to comfortably incorporate them into the telling. Stories can be effectively told without gestures and by those who don't feel comfortable with reliance on gestures. However, exercises and activities that develop more comfortable use of gestures might be a good way for such tellers to gain better, more comfortable access to this storytelling powerhouse element.

Super Simple Storytelling Exercise 3.9

GESTURE A WORD

Explore the use and limits of gestures as storytelling tools

> **APPROPRIATE GRADES: Fourth and up**
> **TIME REQUIRED: 40 minutes**

GOAL:

Gestures are a natural and powerful part of everyday communications. It is important for storytellers to know how to effectively integrate gestures into their story performance. One step toward that end is to understand the limits of gestures, that is, to understand which types of information can be effectively and easily communicated through gestures and which cannot. Developing that understanding is the purpose of this exercise.

DIRECTIONS:

Divide the class into four-person teams for this raucous and powerful demonstration of the limits and effectiveness of gesture. A three-person team will do, but five is too many for each person to participate actively. Instruct each team to create a simple three-sentence story. If you see groups creating rambling compound and complex sentences, you can repeat the basic instructions, placing more emphasis on the word *simple*.

After all groups have completed their stories, instruct the groups to create a specific gesture for every word in their story. One word, one gesture. One gesture, one word. Groups may not rewrite their stories. They must struggle with what they have. Some words—articles and prepositions, for example—do not lend themselves to clear gestures. The group must still create a gesture they will use for each and every word in their story. "Gestures," of course, are not limited to hand movement only and could include body movement and facial expression.

Have all the members of each group practice saying the story while performing each of the gestures the group has created. After it is clear to you that most members of each group have memorized the story and their set of gestures, have two groups combine.

One person from each group will perform their story for the other group. However, this teller will use the group's set of gestures *only*. They will not speak any words when they present the story. The group may choose their representative storyteller for this telling.

This is not a game of charades where a gesture is repeated until understood. The group that is watching may not blurt out what they do, or do not, understand. The teller presents the story at normal storytelling cadence, just as if they were actually telling the story with words. The audience watches in silence until the story is over.

After the teller has completed the story, the audience group must walk back through the story saying what they think the story was about and what each gesture meant. Allow a minute or two of general discussion about the effectiveness and success of the group's gestures before having the other group's chosen storyteller perform their story.

After completing this first round of story presentation, have the groups separate and allow the groups four or five minutes to revamp any gestures that didn't communicate as accurately and effectively as they had hoped.

Each group now combines with a different group and repeats the telling process, using a different group member as the chosen storyteller.

TEACHING POINTS TO EMPHASIZE:

Gestures are effective and efficient at conveying some kinds of information, but certainly not all. What do gestures effectively communicate? Movement (action verbs), most emotions and feelings, location, size and shape, some nouns, most pronouns, and some modifiers. However, gestures often are better at portraying phrases or concepts than individual words.

Also notice the energy and delight gestures carry. These stories are fun to watch even when you haven't a clue what the story is about. It wasn't the stories that were so attractive. It was the gestures through which they were told. Gestures are a powerful and alluring instrument in a storyteller's orchestra.

Super Simple Storytelling Exercise 3.10

EXAGGERATION

Explore the conscious use of orchestra elements

> **APPROPRIATE GRADES: Third and up**

> **TIME REQUIRED: 15 minutes**

GOAL:

The function and effect of various orchestra elements can best be demonstrated and developed by isolating those elements one at a time and exaggerating their use and action.

DIRECTIONS:

This exercise requires you to know at least one scene of a familiar story and to have planned several performance bad habits to demonstrate while telling it.

Bring four volunteers to the front of the room. (Use more or fewer depending on how many demonstrations you plan to present.) Tell the volunteers and the class that you are going to tell one scene from a well-known story. After you have finished, the first volunteer in line will retell the scene. BUT they must first figure out what one prominent, obvious error you made in the way you told the story (that is, in the use of one of your orchestra elements) and over-exaggerate the use of that same orchestra element in the opposite way.

You will now tell 20 to 30 seconds of the scene, intentionally misusing one particular orchestra element (grossly under- or overusing that specific aspect of the way you tell the story). The best orchestra elements to feature for this exercise will be those with which your class struggles most, those which they are most prone to misuse, and those you want most to discuss with the class.

Six I often use (partly because there is a clear and definite opposite for each) are:

➤ Vocal tone—Speak in a monotone, varying pace and volume, but never tone.

➤ Vocal pace—Speak at a steady and very rapid pace, never slowing or varying the pace.

➤ Vocal volume—Shout (or whisper) the whole scene.

➤ Eye contact—Make no eye contact with the audience, but stare at walls and ceiling while telling.

➤ Gestures—Use no gestures. You may simply leave your hands at your sides. To emphasize what I am doing, I usually stuff both hands into my pockets.

➤ Nervous habits—Continually rock from foot to foot (a nervous move-ment) or fidget with your hands.

You may focus on any orchestra element (vocal or nonvocal) for one of these demonstrations. Simply under- or overuse that element so that the student who follows will have to exaggerate its use in the opposite way.

After you have told the chosen story segment, ask the first volunteer in line to identify both the orchestra element you misused and what you did wrong with it. The class can help if the student is stumped. After they have correctly identified your telling error, give them a few seconds to envision how they will tell that same story segment exaggerating the use of that same orchestra element in the opposite direction.

Follow their telling with a brief class discussion about the appropriate use of that aspect of telling a story and, if you so choose, with a second student trying to out-exaggerate the first student.

Move to the second volunteer in line and a new orchestra problem to focus on. Use the same scene for all of the demonstrations and follow the above pattern for each.

TEACHING POINTS TO EMPHASIZE:

The inappropriate or exaggerated use of any aspect of telling a story will distract listeners and pull them out of the story. Each orchestra element is individually important, but all must play in balance and harmony with the other elements to create an effective whole.

Super Simple Storytelling Exercise 3.11

A BETTER EXCUSE

Explore the conscious, coordinated use of all orchestra elements

> **APPROPRIATE GRADES: Third and up.**

> **TIME REQUIRED: 10 to 15 minutes**

GOAL:

Having focused on individual instruments in each teller's personal orchestra, and having concentrated on individual performance techniques, it is appropriate to step back and try to meld them all together, still without muddying the water by adding concern for story content.

DIRECTIONS:

This exercise is delightful for the class and a good close to the previous tightly focused orchestra exercises. The exercise requires one volunteer, who should be picked for their brash and flamboyant style and for a lack of self-consciousness when performing in front of the class.

You will create a stressful situation, the class will create an excuse a student might use to get out of the situation, and the volunteer will try to deliver that excuse convincingly. Almost any stressful situation will do because the stress is not important to the exercise and exists more for humor.

I use two situations most often The first is accidentally arriving late to school the day after the principal, superintendent, and governor all told the student they would not tolerate any more tardiness and that if the student were late again they would be expelled forever and thrown in jail. The other is a student forgetting to do their homework under the same kind of extreme threat.

Now ask the class what excuse the student might use to explain their failure and avoid the extreme consequences you outlined. Let eight to ten students offer suggestions, the wilder the better. Your job will be to combine the best elements of the suggested excuses into one gigantic whopper of a story. Again, the wilder the better. Plausibility and practicality should not be considered in inventing this outrageous excuse.

Offer instructions to the volunteer storyteller along these lines: "You know the general excuse we just created for you to give in your defense. You are going to walk to the door, turn around, and pretend to enter the classroom. When I (ask for your homework or ask why you are late) you give me the general excuse the class just invented. Don't worry if you don't say exactly what the class invented. You'll get the general idea right. But before you enter the classroom, take a moment to think of how you would feel if everything in your excuse had really happened to you and tell the story to me that way. Pretend it all really happened. Think of what you would say and how you would say it, and tell it that way."

Give the following instructions to the class: "Don't listen to the excuse (to *what* they say). We all know it's phony. You just made it up. Listen instead to the *way* they say it and decide what they do to make it sound real and what they do to make it seem phony."

Have the student enter and allow them to complete their excuse without interruption. Now ask the class what they did to make it seem real and what they did to make it seem phony. Do not accept comments on any aspect of the story, only on the volunteer's performance, on their use of their orchestra.

After building a list of the pluses and minuses for this telling either allow the same student to take another shot at making it seem more real or allow a second student to try.

TEACHING POINTS TO EMPHASIZE:

How a story is said has a greater impact on an audience than what is said. Energy, conviction, and a sense of reality are all carried in *how* the story is said, not in its content. The class was riveted to these tellings not because they were good stories but because (and when) the teller poured energy and expression (even if it was melodramatic overacting) into the way they said the story. That's what draws listeners into a story. That's what will draw listeners into *your* story. You don't have to act goofy. You don't have to act at all. But you do have to use your orchestra to make the story seem real and to make listeners believe that you care about and believe in your own story.

Super Simple Storytelling Exercise 3.12

ROLE PLAY

*Explore the instinctive use of orchestra elements
to convey character attitudes and roles*

› **APPROPRIATE GRADES: Fourth and up.**

› **TIME REQUIRED: 10-15 minutes**

GOAL:

The way we use our personal orchestra seems to come as a whole package based on our feelings and attitudes. This exercise allows students to consciously explore what those packages look like and consist of.

DIRECTIONS:

Assign roles (characters) to pairs of students, a stressful situation which forces them to interact, and goals for each in that interaction. Then allow the students to improvise their interaction so long as they stay in character and pursue their assigned goal. Assign the class the tasks of watching *how* these students interpret their assigned roles, determining what each student does (and does not do) to make their character seem real, and evaluating the strength and interest of each created character. They will discuss their findings and must support their assertions with comments on the use of specific orchestra elements by the volunteer students.

I usually allow the students to go for 30 to 45 seconds or until it is clear that they are stuck and out of ideas for what to say. Success in this exercise is measured by the students' willingness to try to physically and vocally personify their assigned roles. The key to their ability to do that is in the assignments you give them.

Arm each student with five bits of character information:

➤ The identity of their character

➤ The character's general personality

➤ The situation for this interaction

➤ Their attitude in this interaction and the reason(s) for it

➤ Their goal in this interaction.

What do examples look like?

A gruff, ex-Army drill sergeant principal (identity and personality) confronts a shy, nervous, scattered, new teacher (identity and personality) when the teacher is two days late reporting to school (situation). The principal wants to set an example for other teachers of how strict he is (attitude and goal). The new teacher wants to make the principal admit that it was his fault the new teacher was late (attitude and goal).

A kind-hearted and solicitous father (identity and personality) confronts his spoiled, greedy daughter, who has him wrapped around her little finger (identity and personality), because she stole and used his credit card (situation). He wants to be fair but firm and get her to admit she did wrong (attitude and goal). She wants him to give her the credit card permanently (attitude and goal).

I have also created confrontations between a nervous, unsure, rookie bank robber and a clever, fast-talking bank teller; between a bully and a smart but not athletic kid; and between an exasperated teacher and a student who can't ever seem to follow the rules.

After assigning the roles, allow each pair to improvise their encounter. Then have the same pair repeat the confrontation, reversing their personalities. Situation, goals, and identity remain the same. Personalities reverse and attitudes adjust if absolutely necessary to be plausible with the new personalities.

After several pairs have completed their scenes, hold a class discussion about how orchestra elements depict character personality, feeling, and attitude. How does a story-teller create a believable character? What makes a character interesting? What was most fun to watch in each portrayal? What worked well? What would you do differently? Focus student talk and answers not on the content of what each student said but on their use of various orchestra elements to accomplish their performance goals.

TEACHING POINTS TO EMPHASIZE:

This exercise is really an improvisational acting exercise and is always challenging and difficult to complete successfully. It is, however, much easier to do when the students are given clear mental images of character, attitude, and feeling. These emotional and physical images serve to direct the storyteller's orchestra to project the same images to the listener.

One of the central keys to successful storytelling is to create strong, specific images of the characters and the way they feel at every moment of the story. Personality creates general attitude; situation creates feeling. A storyteller needs to know both to understand how a character acts and responds—even if the teller must create (or infer) this information when it is not provided in the printed story.

Because this exercise requires students to act, emphasize that storytelling doesn't require acting. However, it does require that the teller *understand* how the characters feel and act. Understanding how orchestra elements (body posture, facial expressions, gestures, eye movement, and vocal patterns) serve to define and communicate attitude and feeling helps the teller project the feelings and attitudes of each character to an audience in whatever way is comfortable and effective for the teller.

Super Simple Storytelling Exercise 3.13

INTERRUPTER

Explore how both sides of the brain contribute to story learning and telling

❭ **APPROPRIATE GRADES: Fourth and up**

❭ **TIME REQUIRED: 15-20 minutes**

GOAL:

Kindergartners create rambling stories that go nowhere but are filled with infectious, enticing energy and passion. Middle-schoolers write with plot-conscious precision, but tend toward emotionless tedium. We need both elements in our stories: logical plot flow and infectious energy. But they come from different parts of the brain. Here's a fun exercise to demonstrate that distinction and to help spur students' creative juices.

DIRECTIONS:

Every student in the class needs a partner. Partners must sit as close as possible because it will get raucously noisy and they need to hear each other. Partners agree on who is number 1 and who is number 2. Student number 1 is designated as the **Storyteller**. Their job is to improvise and tell a one-minute, fictional story.

Student number 2 is designated not as the listener, but as the **Interrupter**. The interrupter's job is to regularly interrupt the Storyteller by blurting out any random word that crosses their mind. It's better if the word has absolutely no connection to the story being told.

The Storyteller must incorporate each blurted word into the next sentence of their story. The storyteller may not refuse a word or pretend not to hear. They must listen for, accept, and use every word the Interrupter blurts out.

The Interrupter must interrupt at regular, frequent intervals in a loud, clear voice. As a general guide, as soon as the Storyteller has completed the sentence incorporating one interrupted word into the story, the Interrupter should blurt out another.

What does it sound like? Here is a quick, typical sample of this joint creative process. ST designates lines by the Storyteller. I is the Interrupter.

ST:	A cat leapt onto the alley fence.
I:	Pajamas
ST:	A man wearing pajamas yelled at the cat from an upstairs window . . .
I:	Peanut butter.
ST:	To go eat some peanut butter instead of howling.
I:	Shark.
ST:	But the cat couldn't because a shark was guarding the grocery store.

Time these stories for one minute. There will be lots of noise and laughter. These stories are outrageous fun. Stopping them will require an attention-getting noisemaker. A coach's whistle has always been my favorite.

Have partners reverse rolls and start a completely new story so that everyone gets to experience both sides of this exercise. Again, time this new story for one minute.

Lead a brief discussion about the students' reactions to this experience. Which was harder, telling or interrupting? Which was more fun? (Typically a class will split pretty evenly on their answers to these questions.) Were the stories fun? (Universally they'll answer, "yes.") Did they create any good stories they want to share with the class? (Typically, "no.") Did their stories have strong characters and goals? Powerful obstacles and antagonists? (Always the answer is "no.") But they were fun? ("Yes!")

Announce that you want to repeat the exercise but feel you need to adjust one little rule. The Storyteller's job will remain exactly the same. The Interrupter will interrupt at the same rate as before. But, instead of interrupting with some fiendishly random word, they *must*, at every interruption, feed the Storyteller the "*perfect* word for them to use to keep the story going where it's going and make it better."

After all, the Storyteller has to create all the words. The Interrupter only has to create one word for every sentence or two. So that one word should be the perfect word to make this a truly great story.

Again, the Storyteller may not reject any word the Interrupter provides. The Interrupter may not pass, saying either that they couldn't think of a word or that the teller was doing just fine without them. Interrupters must do their part and interrupt at the same rate as before. All that has changed is the Interrupter's goal in selecting words with which to interrupt the story.

Do two one-minute stories so that both students experience both roles. Now repeat the discussion and compare this experience to the first story. You will notice right away that the room is quieter during this second set of stories.

Was it easier or harder to be the teller this time? Was it easier or harder to be the Interrupter? (Often the Interrupter's words are no easier for the teller to work with and no closer to the teller's plans for the story than they were during the first story.) Were the stories more or less fun? (Most will answer, "Less.") Did they have a more understandable plot structure? (Typically, "yes.") Were the characters better defined? (Typically, "yes.")

TEACHING POINTS TO EMPHASIZE:

Now the point of the exercise. What you and your students have just demonstrated is the difference between left-brained and right-brained thinking. The first story was pure right-brained fun. Everyone intuitively understands that the story will be a nonsense story. Their job is to pour as much fun, farce, and enthusiasm into it as possible.

Because of the rule change, everyone feels responsible for creating a "real story" during the second round. Often the interrupted words are no better and no more helpful than on the first round. But now everyone treats them differently. This feeling of responsibility shifts participant thinking to logical, structural, left-brain thinking. Everyone thinks in terms of plot flow, cause-effect sequencing, rational plausibility, and logical structure. Energy, enthusiasm, and fun are forgotten.

For a story to work, it needs both sides. Every storyteller is more comfortable working on one side of their brain or the other. The trick is to incorporate that side that is less comfortable for you.

The left side remembers order, logic, plot, structure. The right side provides energy, passion, humor, fancy, exaggeration. The left side analyzes core character information. The right side creates characterization. The left side tells us WHAT. The right side tells us HOW.

Storytellers need to successfully involve both sides in their stories if an audience is to believe in and enjoy the telling.

Super Simple Storytelling Exercise 4.1

THE TELL-ABOUT GAME

Explore the structural side of a story or character

> **APPROPRIATE GRADES: Third and up**

> **TIME REQUIRED: 25-30 minutes**

GOAL:

Most tellers need the reassuring anchor of knowing that they know the basic facts and sequences of a story and that they can actually orally communicate these structural elements to another human being before they venture into the murky waters of characterization and "putting energy and enthusiasm into a story." This exercise is designed to provide that reassurance.

DIRECTIONS:

This is an exercise to use as students begin to learn a story to perform. It should be one of the first steps in learning a story. Before using this exercise students should be familiar with the story and have learned the general plot flow, characters, and significant events and turns in the story.

Divide the class into groups of five. A six-person group will do, but more is unwieldy. A four-person group is workable, but fewer won't generate the needed barrage of ideas. Each group needs a timer to ensure that no student runs significantly under or over the set time limits.

One student in the group is "it" and gets two minutes to tell the group about some predesignated aspect of their story. (For some grades and aspects of a story, 60 seconds is sufficient.)

The group then has two minutes to ask related questions of the teller. No question is too obscure, too small, or too detailed. The group may ask for more information about any aspect of what the storyteller has presented. They may also ask for background and motivation information that would explain some of the presented information.

The teller *must* answer every question (even if they have to make up an answer as they go). They may not say that the question is not relevant to their story. They may not say that they don't know or that the requested information was not included in their source book for the story. They must create an answer for every question.

The group's goal is either to catch this student in a contradiction in the information they provide or to ask questions that momentarily stump the storyteller and that cause that student to think of aspects of the story they had never thought of before.

Following this two-minute question period, a new student is chosen to be "it" and the process begins again.

Four topics can be productively used in this exercise format to constructively speed up the story-learning process. The exercise may be repeated, featuring different topics, or may be used only once, focusing on the topic you feel is most important for your students to concentrate on. These four topics are:

➤ The general plot line, or sequence of events in the story

➤ The main character, the five layers of character information about this character, and why they are worthy of being the central character in a story

➤ The antagonist (the embodiment of the greatest and most important problem and obstacle). This topic focuses on what makes this character interesting enough and dangerous enough to drive the story.

➤ The set of problems and flaws (and associated risk and danger) that block the protagonist from their goal and why they will ensure an exciting, powerful, engrossing story.

This exercise may be followed by a brief class discussion. Use this time to reinforce the concept that everyone successfully communicated the basic facts of their story. The more confident they are in their ability to remember this basic story structure, the more energy they will be able to pour into the telling of that story.

Have each student spend a moment deciding whether their description sounded as interesting and exciting as they had wanted it to sound. Also have them review the questions asked of them by the group. Did those questions point out holes in their image of the story? Were new aspects of the story, its characters, or individual scenes uncovered?

TEACHING POINTS TO EMPHASIZE:

Most tellers are more successful when they learn the left-brain facts of a story first and then work on how to bring the story to life through story characters, through their natural enthusiasm, and through the energy and emotion of their presentation. It is critical to move on to the right-brained questions that define how a story will be told. But it is equally important to first feel secure in the left-brained story structure and events.

Super Simple Storytelling Exercise 4.2

ONE-ON-ONE-ON-ONE-ON-ONE

*Explore effective story structure and any assigned
aspect or element of a story in progress*

> **APPROPRIATE GRADES: Third and up**
> **TIME REQUIRED: 15 minutes**

GOAL:

We refine story elements best with feedback. Most storytellers, however, develop a story in isolation, devoid of outside help. What could be more constructive, then, than trying some story structure and presentation; receiving instant, detailed feedback; and, after a moment of reflection, getting to revise the material and try it again? That is the idea of *One-on-One-on-One-on-One*.

DIRECTIONS:

This is the most powerful and effective story-related exercise I have ever seen. It's easy to use and never fails to improve both the story at hand and the student's understanding of the form and structure of a story and of storytelling. It is an oral exercise.

First assign a story topic for this exercise. If this exercise and topic are being used as part of the development of an existing story no lead time is necessary. Announce the topic and launch into the exercise. Normally, these topics relate to specific aspects of a story you want your students to further develop (e.g., tell about the main character, about the character's struggles and problems, about the antagonist, or about the story line itself).

If this exercise is being used to develop student awareness of how to shape, organize, and deliver effective stories, announce the topic several days ahead of time. You *can* use fictional topics, but it is better to start with factual events students recall from their own lives. Keep the topics simple and personal so that the stories will be easy to recall and hold in their minds while they tell and then revise their story.

Any readily available topic will do: Something that happened on a summer vacation trip, some time when you got in trouble, something that happened on a bike, something that happened on the school playground, someone who gave you something very special, or someone who has been especially important to you will work well for a *One-on-One-on-One-on-One*. Tell the class that they will tell a one-minute story on that topic.

One day before the session, you improvisationally tell a story on the same topic. Don't make this a rehearsed and polished telling. It's fine if they see you struggle a bit to get your thoughts in order and the words right. This is, after all, exactly what will happen to them tomorrow.

Have students pair off for the exercise itself. All telling will be done one-on-one. These pairs sit facing each other, knee-to-knee and eye-to-eye with no desks or tables between them. They quickly agree on who is number 1 and who is number 2. As soon as they are settled, you call, "Person number 1 begin your story." Person number 1 tells their story to person number 2. Person number 2 listens. There should be no interruptions, questions, or comments from listeners. Their feedback will all be nonverbal.

You time the story, shouting, "Stop!" after one minute. Immediately you direct person number 2 to begin their story. Person number 2 tells *their* story while person number 1 listens. To avoid having to yell, some teachers use coach's whistles for start and stop signals. Don't allow any discussion time between stories. Make these transitions as rapid as possible.

As person number 2 finishes their minute of telling, have everyone switch partners. Again, allow for no discussion or comment time. As soon as they are settled with their new partner, they repeat the exercise. Finally, they switch partners again and each tells their story for a third and final time.

Many teachers vary the times for each telling in two ways. First, there is nothing magic about 60 seconds for the duration of each telling. Some teachers for lower grades shorten the time to 30 or 40 seconds, slowly increasing that time toward one minute over the course of the school year.

Second, many teachers trim a few seconds off the first telling and add a few onto the third round of tellings without announcing it to the class. Tell students each round will be a one-minute telling. Then actually stop them at 50 or 55 seconds the first time and at 70 seconds the third. Stories grow with practice. They'll need more time to tell the same story during the third round.

In less than 15 minutes a vast amount of telling, assessment, and critical listening will have taken place. Each student has told a short story; seen in the face of their listener if it worked effectively; restructured, reworded, and revised that story twice based on the feedback they received and their own impressions of the story; and tested the effectiveness of each of these revised versions through their second and third tellings. While listening, students provide real-time, nonverbal feedback through facial and body reactions for the teller to use. They are also mentally revising their own story and are sifting through the structure and wording of the story they are listening to for any ideas and phraseology they want to borrow and incorporate into their own story.

Every student can do a *One-on-One-on-One-on-One*. No one is embarrassed or forced to struggle in front of the class. *One-on-One-on-One-on-One* greatly enhances confidence and enthusiasm. It builds a solid sense of effective story structure, pacing, and delivery. It gives students a chance to explore variations and options in the way they structure story material.

Options/Variations:

Assigning a clear, manageable, specific topic is critical to *One-on-One-on-One-on-One* success. Four topics are most successful if *One-on-One-on-One-on-One* is used as part of the story development process:

1. **The main character:** Who is this character and what makes them so fascinating and worthy of a story? This allows students to employ all layers of character description and all facets of core character information for their story to present an intriguing, compelling character.

2. **Struggles and conflicts:** What are they and what makes the obstacles, conflicts, struggles, problems, and associated risk and danger in this story big enough and formidable enough to carry a story and engross a reader?

3. **Story line:** How are they going to order and pace the events of their story to successfully lead the listener or reader?

4. **The antagonist.** The antagonist is the embodiment of the problems and obstacles faced by the main character. The bigger, the more dangerous, the riskier the antagonist is, the better readers will like both the main character and the story.

After using *One-on-One-on-One-on-One* several times, many teachers follow the exercise with an evaluation period. Quick written critiques work better than class discussions. Have students make journal entries answering two groups of questions:

First:

➤ How did my story and my telling of it change between the three tellings, and why?

➤ Did my story or storytelling improve over the three tellings? Why or why not?

➤ How would I reorganize this material if I were to tell it again?

Second, of the three stories I heard:

➤ Which did I enjoy the most, and why?

➤ Which scene can I most vividly remember, and why?

➤ What did the teller do to make me remember it?

➤ When did I laugh? What did the teller say to make me laugh?

➤ When was I most bored, and why?

➤ What did the teller say to make me so bored?

These evaluations help students fix what they have learned about their story, and stories in general, in their minds. They also become a good reference list of how to make a story work. What worked *on* a student, will work *for* that student. What bored them will bore others. You might keep these critiques on file as a check on each student's progress.

TEACHING POINTS TO EMPHASIZE:

During a *One-on-One-on-One-on-One* every student both works continuously on their story, and assists others in their work. While a student isn't actually telling their story, they accomplish three important tasks. First, they provide instant, explicit, nonverbal feedback for the teller. Because it is in the teller's face, the teller can't avoid recording and interpreting it. Second, they review and restructure their own story for the next telling. Third, they sift through the structure, phraseology, performance technique, and wording of the teller's story for anything they want to borrow and incorporate into their own work.

This exercise is also an excellent opportunity to review what makes a story work—characters, goals, conflicts, struggles, risk and danger, jeopardy, character reactions, and detail. There are infinite variations in the ways to organize and present this material. Yet every successful story has those elements tightly woven into it.

Super Simple Storytelling Exercise 4.3

WHERE'S THE CAMERA?

Explore available story perspectives and their implications

> **APPROPRIATE GRADES: Fourth and up**

> **TIME REQUIRED: 25 minutes**

GOAL:

Most students never consciously consider the perspective or viewpoint from which they tell. They certainly haven't considered the impact their choice will have on a listener. But they will after they play a game where perspective and viewpoint determine everything and which focuses on the advantages and disadvantages of each.

DIRECTIONS:

This exercise is a demonstration of what perspective and viewpoint really mean. Pick a well-known children's story. Any one will do. I'll use "Little Red Riding Hood" for this example. Assign students to play the parts of each major character: Granny, the wolf, the woodsman, and Little Red.

Now assign two additional key roles: the *camera* and the *narrator*. These two students will do the real work of the exercise. Finally, assign a first and second assistant director. They will act to stir up the pot and help dramatize the difference between perspectives. You will be the story director. That gives you control of starting ("Action!") and stopping ("Cut!") the exercise and also the power to pick which scenes are used for the exercise.

Review the possible perspectives and the difference between perspective and viewpoint. (See "The Super Simple System for Learning a Story," step 4, in Part III, pp. 50–52.)

Pick and discuss a scene from the story: the scene where Little Red and the wolf meet in the forest, for example. Place the four characters in appropriate places around the classroom to act out this scene. (Little Red and the wolf are together in the forest. Granny is alone in her cottage. The woodsman is alone chopping down trees in another part of the forest.)

The first assistant director now specifies the *perspective* to be used while telling this story. The second assistant director, if appropriate, specifies the *viewpoint* character. (Any of the story characters may be designated as viewpoint whether or not they are directly involved in the action of this scene.)

Before starting to play the scene, the student who is the camera must physically place himself or herself where the camera would have to be to tell this story through the assigned perspective and viewpoint.

Also give the narrator a moment to gather their thoughts. When you yell, "Action!" the characters begin to *slowly*—very slowly—move through their parts of the story under your continual direction, doing what they are supposed to do, miming their actions and inter-actions (or at least saying them very softly to each other). You must ensure that the actors go slowly enough to keep pace with the narrator's telling of the story.

The narrator tells the story to the class as if they were a solo storyteller, ***using only concepts, information, language, and phraseology appropriate to the assigned perspective and viewpoint***. That is, the narrator tells exactly what the camera sees. The camera will have to move as necessary to stay in perspective.

Whenever the first assistant director wants to, they call out a new perspective. The second assistant director then calls out a new appropriate viewpoint character. You call, "Cut!" to freeze the action while the camera scurries to the new appropriate camera position.

You yell, "Action!" and the narrator continues telling the story with language, information, and phraseology appropriate for this new perspective and viewpoint as the camera hovers where they should be to video the story from the assigned perspective.

It will be possible to have a perspective and/or viewpoint that momentarily loses track of the main action of the story. That's fine. It shows the limitations of the various view-points. (The directors could assign a third-person perspective with the woodsman as view-point during the scene when Little Red meets the wolf. The narrator can't talk about the meeting at all because the viewpoint character isn't there and will have to talk about the trees, how much wood has been chopped this day, and so forth.)

You should make sure that the first assistant director doesn't shift perspective more often than once every 20 or 30 seconds, but that they do shift it frequently enough so that the class gets a vivid demonstration of the effectiveness of different perspectives and the effect of perspective shifts. Let the story roll forward for three or four minutes while per-spectives are shifted.

Stop the story if the camera and/or narrator get off either perspective or viewpoint. It is better to yell "Cut!" and pause to discuss the situation than to continue with incorrect por-trayal for the class. The purpose of this exercise is for the class to visually and audibly ex-perience the effect and power of different perspectives.

The class must keep track of the camera and narrator and be prepared to discuss both their performance and the pluses and minuses of the various assigned viewpoints and perspectives at the end of the exercise.

After a discussion of camera position and narrator language, switch to a new crew and another story and repeat the exercise. As a final discussion, compare and contrast the success of the two crews and the various perspectives used.

Options/Variations:

Some teachers periodically change narrator and camera during a story, both to spread the experience across more students and to relieve the burden on these two key students.

TEACHING POINTS TO EMPHASIZE:

The perspective a storyteller chooses dictates three major story parameters: (1) where the listener will place themselves within the story space and action, (2) what informa-tion a teller is allowed to provide to the listener, and (3) how the listener will regard each character. These are very important factors in determining the success of a student's story.

As discussed in Chapter 4, omniscient perspective is easy for the teller but pushes the listener farther away from the action and characters. First person is most limiting for the teller but most exciting for listener. Remind students to think carefully about which perspective and viewpoint will most effectively and successfully tell their story in the early planning stages. Finally, they should try to see the world of the story from that perspective and viewpoint, just as if they were a camera hovering in that spot in space.

Super Simple Storytelling Exercise 4.4

THE SCENE GAME

Explore the multi-sensory details in each scene

> **APPROPRIATE GRADES: Third and up**

> **TIME REQUIRED: 20-25 minutes**

GOAL:

We rarely take the time to visualize more than a general image of each scene of a story. Until students get into the habit of creating expansive, detailed mental images of each scene and character, it's nice to get some help in the process from other students.

DIRECTIONS:

This is an exercise to use while learning a story to tell and serves best after several rounds of Exercise 4.1, *The Tell-About Game.* Students should already know the story's characters, the ending point, and the general plot sequencing.

Divide the class into groups of five. A six-person group will do, but more is unwieldy. A four-person group is workable, but fewer won't generate the needed barrage of ideas.

Rules for *The Scene Game* are simple. One student in each group is "it." That student gets 30 seconds to describe to the group an important scene in the story they are going to write. This description should mention who is present and generally what happens, but should concentrate on a description of the setting, the physical scene itself.

The group now has two minutes to ask any question they can think of about that physical setting. The group acts like suspicious police officers grilling a suspect. No question is too detailed or trivial. Their goal is to either catch this student in a contradiction in the information they provide or to ask questions that momentarily stump the storyteller, that cause that student to think of aspects of the scene they had never thought of before.

The student who is "it" *must* answer every question. They may not answer, "I don't know," or "It doesn't matter." They must answer the question even if it means they have to make up an answer on the spot. They, of course, aren't committed to that answer and may change it later. But having to answer will expand their image of each story scene.

Groups should be encouraged to explore all five senses during this questioning and to search for possible inconsistencies or gaps in the teller's story.

After two minutes of being peppered by the group's questions, that student shifts off the hot seat and a second student moves on.

You should drift among the groups as you time each questioning period. Look for groups that are struggling to invent tough, probing questions, or where the group has floundered, unable to think of what to ask. Help them by interjecting one or two obscure questions about background sounds and smells, where the shadows fall, what color the curtains are and whether there is any dust on them, how humid it is, etc. That modeling will encourage them to follow suit with more effective and beneficial questions of their own.

TEACHING POINTS TO EMPHASIZE:

Storytellers rarely think of all the aspects of a scene, even though they visualize the story in as much detail as they can. It is valuable to have others help widen the teller's horizon and make them think about aspects of a scene and a story they hadn't considered. Every storyteller needs this help. The tougher the questions the group asks, the more help it is for the teller.

During this exercise, all group members benefit from every question—even if they aren't on the hot seat. They still consider the answers to every question as if it had been asked about their own story.

After this exercise, do your students see the scenes of their stories better? Do they see them in more detail? Do they see them more clearly? More detail means the story will be easier to tell and will seem more real to the listener.

Super Simple Storytelling Exercise 4.5

THE CHARACTER GAME

Explore story characters with suggestions from a small group

> **APPROPRIATE GRADES: Third and up**

> **TIME REQUIRED: 20 minutes for Step 1; 15 minutes for Step 2**

GOAL:

Formally presenting a character to a group of peers and receiving feedback and suggestions from that group greatly improves a storyteller's image of that character. Using a group to help the teller consider apparently nonessential (even apparently irrelevant) aspects of a character often reveals rich character details and mannerisms that become valuable to the storytelling. In addition, watching one student struggle with a character encourages all other students in the group to similarly develop theirs.

DIRECTIONS:

This exercise is a character development exercise designed to assist storytellers in forming a more detailed mental image of a main character and is best completed in two steps. Step 1 is left-brained, analytical, and intellectual. Step 2 is a right-brained physical exercise. Doing both steps better ensures a consistent, complete character image in the mind of each student writer.

Step 1. Divide the class into groups of four or five. The groups sit in chairs in a circle. One student at a time is chosen to be "it." When it is their turn the student tells the group about their main character for one minute. Their goal is to paint as interesting and complete an image of this character as possible in the allotted time. Have students include answers to the following six questions in their one-minute introduction. These questions both help students decide what to say about their character and stimulate better questions from the group.

1. What are the goals, flaws, problems, and risks and dangers this character faces in this story?

2. What are the unique and interesting aspects of this character's physical being and personality? What are their hopes and fears?

3. How does this character want the story to end, and why?

4. How does this character feel about the story's antagonist, and why?

5. Why does the storyteller like this character?

6. Why does the teller think listeners should care about this character? What will make them interesting and unique to a listener?

The group now has two minutes to ask questions about this character, about any aspect of the five layers of their character information, or about any of the statements the teller made during the introduction. The group's goal in asking these questions is two-fold. First, they should clear up anything that isn't clear to them about this character. If it isn't clear to them, it probably isn't clear to the storyteller, and won't be clear to a listener. Second, they should probe for any undefined or ambiguous aspects of this character in the teller's mind.

Questions about any aspect of the character are legitimate and valuable:

Where was this character born?

What are this character's favorite and least favorite foods?

What color are their eyes?

What was this character's favorite thing to do when they were half their present age?

Name three things this character is afraid of.

What sports is this character good at and bad at.?

Do they like to comb their hair? Do they *have* hair?

How many friends does this character have, and why?

And so on, and so on. All character questions are fair game.

The student who is "it" must answer all questions, even if they have to make up an answer on the spot. But they should be encouraged to ask the group for ideas and opinions on any aspect of the character they are uncertain about. This is an opportunity for the storyteller to seek peer ideas and help in developing and defining their character.

After a two-minute question and discussion period, the group selects the next student to be "it."

Step 2.   Students stay in these same groups for step 2. One student at a time is again chosen to be "it." This student steps outside the circle, *becomes* their main character (adopts full physical and vocal characterization), and re-enters the group as their character. They walk as the character would walk, sit as the character would sit, introduce themselves (the character) as that character would, and tell about themselves and their story for 30 to 45 seconds. Emphasis should be placed on first presenting the character's personality, attitudes, and manner through their characterization and, second, on revealing this character's goals, fears, problems, and desires and personalities through what they choose to say. To do this, let students use the following six questions as a guide to the kinds of information to create for their introductions:

1. What do you want, why do you want it, and why don't you already have it?

2. What are your favorite things to do? Your least favorite?

3. Which of the other characters in this story do you like? Which do you respect? Are there any you loathe or disdain?

4.   Why should this story be about you?

5.   What do you want to happen to the antagonist in the end of the story?

6.   Name one thing you have done you are proud of and one you are ashamed of.

The group now has 90 seconds to pepper this character with questions. All questions must be directed to the character in second person as if it were the character and not the student sitting in front of them. The questions may be about this character, their history, their attitudes, their fears, desires, likes and dislikes or seeking clarification of any statements made by the character, the story, or other story characters. The goal of the group is to probe for inconsistencies in the character presentation and for undefined aspects of the character. In other words, their goal is to stump the character with their questions. The "it" person *must stay in character* during this entire time they are "it" and must answer all questions as their character would answer.

After the question period is over, the character leaves the circle still in character. Once outside the circle, they drop the characterization and return as the next person leaves to become their character.

Options/Variations:

Three common options exist for this exercise. First, apply this exercise to the antagonist instead of to each student's main character. Students must answer the same list of questions for their antagonist that they would have answered for their main character. Interesting, well-developed antagonists have wants, goals, and obstacles. When those are made clear, the story gains power and appeal.

Second, have students *over-exaggerate* their vocal and physical characterizations in Step 2. They will tend to underplay and "under-exaggerate" the character and their mannerisms and quirks. Directing students to over-exaggerate both encourages them to be silly and goofy during the exercise and to more fully explore the physical presentation of their character. They will "get into" their characters more and learn more about these characters they are inventing.

Third, it is important that the audience see a clear distinction between the main character and the antagonist. This means that the storyteller must also clearly see the differences between these two. Have students act out a conversation between the main character and the antagonist. They will act out both sides of the conversation, jumping back and forth between these two characters.

Have students use some interaction between these two characters that will occur in their story but improvise the actual dialog they say during the exercise. It will appear frantic and unnatural as the student jumps back and forth between two complete physical and vocal characterizations.

When each student is "it," they briefly introduce the scene and significance of this moment in their story, pause to gather their thoughts and their mental images of these two characters, and then launch into their production of protagonist versus antagonist. It usually helps them get into character for you to instruct them to over-act for the sake of the group.

The group's job is to ensure that these two characters appear, sound, and act differently, and that the student stays consistent in their two characterizations. Once a student has completed a 30- to 45-second interaction, the group can comment on the two characters and "it" can ask the group any questions they have or can ask for suggestions or ideas that might help develop these two characters.

TEACHING POINTS TO EMPHASIZE:

Successful storytelling depends on creating more complete and more detailed images of each major story character. Strong images include not only the present physical look and circumstances of a character but also their history, their memories, their attitudes, their beliefs, and their mannerisms. Groups help us expand our creative processes and produce stronger, richer, more interesting characters.

Another valuable aspect of group work is that every student will create answers for their own characters to every question asked of any student. Thus, the entire 30 minutes is devoted to non-stop character development for every student.

The goal of this exercise is not to act well, but rather to use character acting as a vehicle to help the storyteller develop a stronger image of their character and to develop those characters in more detail.

It should also be emphasized that the focus is not on anatomical correctness of the characterizations. Students don't have to *be* a duck, a tree, or a bear. Rather, they should personify non-human characters and represent the personality, attitude, and manner (the essence) of that duck, tree, or bear.

Super Simple Storytelling Exercise 4.6

BE YOUR CHARACTER

Explore the characters that inhabit a story

> **APPROPRIATE GRADES: All**
> **TIME REQUIRED: Varies depending on exercise structure selected.**

GOAL:

We rarely spend enough time dreaming up the level and complexity of detail to give our characters the power they could and should have. It is especially hard for students to mentally create a rich and vivid character. It is easier for them if they incorporate physical movement and action into the process of creating a detailed image of the physical and vocal look, habits, patterns, and traits of the major story characters whether or not they plan to incorporate physical characterization into their story.

DIRECTIONS:

This exercise is an extension of Exercise 4.5, *The Character Game.* For this exercise every student must be in the process of developing a story to tell and have the main characters well in mind.

This general exercise has been successfully used in three different formats.

1. **The informal process.** Everyone is given one minute to concentrate on their main character. They should try to imagine the character's look, attitude, expressions, mannerisms, posture, walk, voice (sound and vocal pattern), and way of talking. They may jot down notes if they wish. This work should be done individually.

   The students each now stand and, in full physical and vocal characterization as their character, introduce themselves (as their character) and tell two sentences about this character and their story.

   Two important notes. First, the emphasis is not on anatomical correctness, but on correctness and completeness of personality and attitude. If the character is a dog, they do not have to drop to all fours and bark. But they do have to decide how that dog would act if it were there and personify that character's personality, actions, and reactions. Is this dog friendly, gruff, suspicious, hungry, afraid, alert, lazy, feisty, or arrogant? Would it bite other students, snarl at them, ignore them, tremble in a corner, or yap for attention?

   Second, this is not an acting exercise. It is a character development exercise. How well they physically imitate this character is not important. That they think through all the physical, vocal, personality, and motivational aspects of the character and try to bring them to life in their presentation *is* important. The goal is to develop more complete mental images of the characters.

No one considers how their character scratches an itch or what they do with their elbows until called upon to physically do it. While actually being the character, a storyteller is forced to consider these unexplored aspects of the character and quite often finds (creates) something interesting and valuable that will make the character more vivid and interesting to an audience.

After everyone has stood and introduced themselves, hold a three- or four-minute free-for-all during which the students must circulate through the room *in full characterization* and interact with other characters as their character would. Adding physical movement, improvisational reactions, and a chance to see how other students present their characters adds much to the mental character image each student is developing.

Finally, allow students a chance to take notes on whatever ideas they have gotten or seen during the exercise.

2. **The formal process.** Play *The Character Game*, Exercise 4.5, with full vocal and physical characterizations.

3. **Homework format.** This exercise may be assigned as individual homework. Here the exercise is usually completed in two steps. First, the student practices their characterization on their own. Second, the student adopts a complete characterization and interacts with family or in public. This exercise will only work if it is carried out with, and in front of, other people.

Based on the feedback I have received from teachers and parents, the grocery store is an ideal place for practicing characterizations. Have students go grocery shopping with a parent and start at one end of the store and become one story character as they walk the first aisle. Change aisles, change characters, back and forth between story characters from one end of the store to the other.

Options/Variations:

There are two common variations to the rules stated above. First, you may use characters other than the main one (protagonist). It is often more valuable to work on the antagonist than on the protagonist. Have students do both protagonist and antagonist to ensure that they are both developed and are unique and separate from each other.

Second, you may direct that students *over-exaggerate* all vocal, physical, and attitudinal aspects of their characterizations. We tend to under-exaggerate. Yet we learn more about a character's eccentricities and quirks when we over-exaggerate.

TEACHING POINTS TO EMPHASIZE:

Good characters are a composite of many types of information, including direct sensory data (what they look like, sound like, how they move, how they talk, etc.); their habits and quirks; their likes and dislikes; their attitudes and personality; their thoughts, fears, and hopes; their goals and problems; and their history.

The goal of this exercise is not to act effectively but rather to use character acting as a vehicle to help the teller develop a stronger image of their character and to develop those characters in more detail.

It should also be emphasized that the focus is not on anatomical correctness of the characterizations. Students don't have to *be* a duck, a tree, or a bear. Rather, they should represent the personality, attitude, and manner (the essence) of that duck, tree, or bear.

Super Simple Storytelling Exercise 4.7

THE RETELL GAME

Explore how stories naturally evolve with each telling

> **APPROPRIATE GRADES: Second and up**
> **TIME REQUIRED: 30 minutes**

GOAL:

Many tellers feel that it is improper, even wrong, for them to reword and remold a story to fit their telling style and their audience. This exercise demonstrates that it is not only natural but inevitable, and helps students identify the story elements that most readily and naturally change.

DIRECTIONS:

Divide the class into groups of six to eight. Have each group identify four volunteers (numbers 2 through 5) who step into the hallway until called. One of the remaining group members is designated as number 1.

You will now tell a short story (best is a two- to three-minute story) to all of the class members who remain in the room. As you finish call each group's student number 2 back into the room and have them rejoin their group.

Student number 1 in each group now retells your story to their own group. They may not ask for or receive help from you or other students. They must tell the story as best they can and trust that they will do a fine job of telling it their way.

As all number 1s finish, call student number 3 back into the room to rejoin their groups. Student number 2, who has only heard the version told by number 1, now retells the story to their group. They may not ask for or receive help of any kind from any other student in the group, but must tell it as best they can trusting that they will do a fine job of telling it their way.

Next, student number 4 for each group rejoins their group and listens to number 3 retell the story for the group. Finally, number 5 re-enters and number 4 tells their version of the story.

Now have each number 5 stand and compare the versions that were last told in each group—that is, the story as it made its way to the ends of these different telling chains. What aspects of the story are the same in each group? What have changed? Plot line? Setting? Characters? Character goals, obstacles, and motives? The antagonist? Character reactions and emotions?

Have those students in each group who listened to every version discuss how, when, and why the story shifted. Was it a slow evolution of details? Did one teller emphasize or de-emphasize a character or characterizations? Did one teller's style or energy affect the next teller's version?

TEACHING POINTS TO EMPHASIZE:

All stories change when told by a new teller or when told to a new age or type of audience. The wording of a story also changes over time even though the same person tells it. The wording is far less important than are the images created in the listener's mind by the chosen words and the energy and emotion with which those words are said.

The images that register most vividly in a listener's mind become the basis for their later retelling of a story. The *way* one teller tells different parts of the story, and the amount of detail they include, affects the images a listener holds, and thus that listener's later version of the story.

Even through a string of retellings, however, some elements of a story typically remain unchanged. These include the basic plot line, the core sequence of events, the identity of major story characters, and any strong, repeated quotes (tag lines) by major characters. The elements that typically change from teller to teller include scene details and locations, character reactions and emotions, character motives, character goals (often goals are implied and so can be interpreted differently by different tellers and listeners), and obstacles the main character faces (some will be de-emphasized or over-emphasized as compared to the original version).

Emphasize two aspects for students. First, all stories change. Don't worry about specific wording. Focus instead on an understanding of the story by each audience member and on the images they form in their minds. Second, the emphasis, emotion, enthusiasm, and details of one teller greatly influence the images a listener holds, which then dictate the version of the story that listener will tell. *How* you say it shapes the images listeners hold of your story.

Super Simple Storytelling Exercise 4.8

WHERE IMAGES COME FROM

Explore the role of different word types in forming the images of a story

❭ **APPROPRIATE GRADES: Third and up**

❭ **TIME REQUIRED: 15 minutes**

GOAL:

Students rarely consider which words really produce the images of their story or what contribution different types of words make to a listener's understanding of the story events. However, that knowledge can be critical to a storyteller. It's worthwhile to take a moment to consider the contribution of nouns, verbs, and modifiers to creating and controlling a listener's images of a scene.

DIRECTIONS:

You will read three versions of a paragraph to your class, one without any modifiers, one without any verbs, and one without any nouns. I believe this exercise is most effective if you read each version to different groups, who can then compare their images of the scene. However, it is most often used with a whole class, who then discuss images of this scene between readings.

Almost any exposition paragraph will do. This one works well because it relies on an even mix of nouns, verbs, and modifiers to create the overall scene.

The Paragraph Without NOUNS:

A scraggly old shuffled down the twisty. Looked for a comfortable to sit. Found on the of a fallen, and sat, gazing at the pastoral around. In the heard a deep, resonant. Slowly stood, rubbed aching, and continued to.

The common reaction to this version is that it is comical and nonsensical. Nouns create the basic images in a listener's mind.

The Paragraph Without VERBS:

A scraggly old man down the twisty, black-top road. He for a comfortable place. He one on the stump of a fallen tree, and, at the pastoral scene around him. In the distance he a deep, resonant church bell. He slowly, his aching back, and his walk to town.

The common reaction to this version is that it is a disconnected string of individual images. Verbs create motion and action and connect and complete a listener's images.

The Paragraph Without MODIFIERS:

> *A man shuffled down the road. He looked for a place to sit. He found one on the stump of a tree, and sat, gazing at the scene around him. In the distance he heard a bell. He stood, rubbed his back, and continued his walk to town.*

The common reaction to this version is that it is clear but flat and colorless. Modifiers paint the rich pallet of story colors in a listener's mind.

The Whole Paragraph:

> *A scraggly old man shuffled down the twisty, black-top road. He looked for a comfortable place to sit. He found one on the stump of a fallen tree and sat, gazing at the pastoral scene around him. In the distance he heard a deep, resonant church bell. He slowly stood, rubbed his aching back, and continued his walk to town.*

In all discussions, focus the class on what contribution each type of word (noun, verb, modifier) makes to our understanding of even this simple scene. As they practice and prepare their own stories, their understanding of the role of each type of word can lead them to identify easily corrected weaknesses in their storytelling.

TEACHING POINTS TO EMPHASIZE:

Basic images come from nouns. Without nouns the paragraph is nonsensical, meaningless. Listeners don't know what to picture.

Action and movement come from verbs. Without verbs listeners don't know how to interpret the scene. They are left with disconnected images and are hungry for information about what happens.

Modifiers provide details. Without details, the paragraph is lifeless and boring. Gestures, facial expressions, and shifts in tone or pace can act as details as well as the words of a story.

Successful communication of a story requires strong images from all three types of words. As students rehearse stories, it is valuable to have others specifically listen to the word choices the teller makes to ensure that the teller actively uses all three types of image-making words.

Super Simple Storytelling Exercise 4.9

SHE ENTERED THE ROOM

Explore the visual power of verb choices

❯ **APPROPRIATE GRADES: Second and up**

❯ **TIME REQUIRED: 15 minutes**

GOAL:

Students typically see an image of a scene, or a specific action, in their head, and then tell about it. Whatever words they say will recreate an accurate and vivid image in their own mind. That's the problem. They can afford to be sloppy with word choices because *any* words will work for them. They forget that only carefully chosen words will recreate the vivid images in a listener's mind. This problem is particularly apparent with verb choices. The idea of this exercise is to demonstrate the implications of the verb choices they make—and those choices come up in every sentence of every story.

DIRECTIONS:

Write the words "She _____-ed the room," on the board and then fill in the blank with the word *enter.* Ask the class to describe in detail their image of this person entering the room. Their images will all be vague and general. Why? The verb "enter" is vague and general.

Tell the class that you want to show them how she *really* entered the room. Step out of the room and then re-enter. You may enter any way you choose—saunter in, burst in, crawl in, dash in, creep in, trip in, leap in, back in, skip in, storm in, etc., etc.

Having re-entered the room, ask, "What's a better verb than 'enter' to describe how I came in?" They may not substitute a whole phrase for the blank space. They may not use similes and metaphors. They may only insert a better verb.

Make a list on the board of the good ones that are offered. Let the students argue about which verb is most descriptive, most precise, and therefore, most appropriate for this sentence.

Again tell the class that you want to show them how she *really* entered the room. Step back into the hall and re-enter. You may enter any way you choose—saunter in, burst in, crawl in, dash in, creep in, trip in, back in, leap in, skip in, storm in, etc., etc.—as long as it is different from how you entered the first time.

Repeat this process several times. Let one or more of the students enter the room if you want to. Your goal is to encourage debate among the students as to which is the most accurate, most precise verb to use to describe each entry.

TEACHING POINTS TO EMPHASIZE:

Verbs define the action, the motion, and much of the emotional tone of a story. Strong verbs come from detailed mental images of the action and events of a story. Careful choice of verbs during story learning and telling creates a much stronger sense of power, energy, enjoyment, and vivid imagery in the story.

What are better verbs to choose? Verbs that provide more accurate, vivid information about the action and event being described. The excessive use of adverbs is one sign of weak verb choices. Strong, descriptive, action verbs don't need the assistance of as many adverbs. That allows the teller to cut needless words from the story.

Super Simple Storytelling Exercise 5.1

THE 30-SECOND STORY

Explore every facet of the process of creating, structuring, and telling a story

> **APPROPRIATE GRADES: Third and up**

> **TIME REQUIRED: 20 minutes**

GOAL:

Having students actually write or tell whole stories is very time consuming and stressful. It is a slow, labor-intensive way to develop story skills. It is often far more productive to use an exercise where the class as a whole can focus on a specific problem area (e.g., description, character development, word choice, using multiple senses, etc.) still within the context of a story. *The 30-Second Story* is one of the two most powerful story-writing or storytelling exercises I have ever seen, and one which allows your whole class to quickly and efficiently focus on any specific story concept or technique.

DIRECTIONS:

Bring four students to the front of the room and tell them that they are going to make up a four-minute story, 30 seconds at a time. While this is an oral exercise, it also can focus on any aspect of story creation, structure, and development.

One student starts the story and tells for 30 seconds. Then the second, third, and fourth tellers each tell for 30 seconds. Now the first teller invents and tells the story for a second 30 seconds, and so forth to the fourth teller's second turn, during which time the story must be ended. You time each segment, calling, "Switch!" at the 30-second break points. There are no pauses for thought between tellers. In the split-second that one ends, the next begins, even if the story is in the middle of a sentence.

The *General Rules* keep this story from degenerating into a mindless, boring story, as are most circle stories. The *Special Requirements* focus the class on that aspect of story you want them to work on.

General Rules:

These six rules apply every time your class uses the *30-Second Story* exercise. They should be considered a mandatory part of this exercise because they force the four students to create a single, unified story.

1. The first student starts the story by providing three key story elements during their first 30-second telling: identity of the main character, that character's goal during the story (what they want to do or get), and an initial setting for the story.

2. The second teller, during their first 30-second telling, must create at least one suitable obstacle that blocks the main character from their goal. If the first teller provided one obstacle, the second provides a second obstacle.

3. Every teller must accept the first teller's main character and goal and use them as the focus and purpose for each story segment.

4. Every teller must pick up the story *exactly* where the previous teller stopped, with no temporal or spatial jumps. They may not shift to other characters, other settings, or other events at the beginning of their 30-second period.

5. Any teller may resolve an obstacle but must immediately pose another one to take its place, so that there is always at least one obstacle on the table for the character to struggle against.

6. The final teller must bring the story (goal of the main character) to some resolution during their final 30-second telling.

The class should track and evaluate each of the four students' success with the *General Rules*. This task helps every student learn to recognize and appreciate the role of goal, conflict, and struggles in basic story structure.

Special Requirements:

In addition to the *General Rules*, you will create *Special Requirements* for each telling. *Special Requirements* apply only to the current round of the *30-Second Story*. After meeting these requirements under the pressure of a timed, improvised story in front of the class, students will find it easy to consider that facet of story-writing or -telling in the future. You select the *Special Requirements* to emphasize and focus on any aspect of story you want the class to study.

Some commonly used *Special Requirements* are:

➤ *Character development.* Require that each teller reveal two new bits of significant information about the main character's history, likes, fears, physical presence, personality, activity, etc., during each of their two 30-second telling periods.

➤ *Senses.* We often describe only what we see. Richer stories come from engaging more of the listener's senses. Require that each teller include detailed information about three, four, or all five senses during each 30-second telling.

➤ *Action verbs.* Verbs of state do little to fire a listener's imagination and create vivid, detailed mental images. Require that each teller use no more than two, or even one, verb of state in each telling. Have the class keep track.

➤ *Descriptive detail.* We all drop modifiers and write (or speak) in simple subject-verb sentences when we're not sure of what we're writing about. Hand each teller a slip of paper on which you have written the name of an object with several appropriate modifiers (e.g., a long red string or an empty brown bottle). Each teller will thus have their own object. During each of their two 30-second telling periods each teller must include that object with its modifiers in their story. The class's job is to detect what was written on each teller's paper. Each teller's job is to keep the class from successfully identifying their object. Tellers can succeed only by peppering their 30-second telling with other modifiers, thus disguising the ones assigned to them. Soon searching for descriptive modifiers will be automatic.

➤ *Eye contact.* Require that each teller maintain eye contact with the class when one signal (such as a green flag) is up and avoid eye contact when some other signal (say, a red flag) is up. Soon everyone will know exactly what maintaining and not maintaining eye contact feels like and how to hold any audience with riveting eye contact.

➤ *Scene description.* Young story writers often forget that, just because they can see each scene in their heads, readers cannot also see those scenes. Require that each teller spend half of their 30-second periods describing details of the scenes of the story.

Similarly, characterization, simile and metaphor, word choices, tension, gestures, developing story risk and danger, foreshadowing, voice projection, irony, pacing (written or verbal), or any other facet of story writing and storytelling can become the *Special Requirements* focus of a *30-Second Story.* As your students become more adept at the form of this exercise, you can give them two or three *Special Requirements* to accomplish during each telling session in addition to the *General Rules.*

Discuss with the class as a whole the four tellers' success with both *General Rules* and *Special Requirements.* Then discuss the effective use of, and importance of, the *Special Requirements* aspect of story construction. Finally, have a second group of four create a second story with the same *Special Requirements.* Have the class compare and contrast these two groups, looking for improvement in the *Special Requirements* area.

In 20 minutes, two groups can create different stories while focusing on the *Special Requirement* of the day, and the whole class will have watched and discussed that aspect of storytelling in some detail. Even if used only once a week, this technique will greatly expand your class's mastery of successful story structure and delivery.

Remember that making up a story under pressure, in front of peers, is much scarier than *One-on-One-on-One-on-One* exercises or most other story-development exercises. Introduce the *30-Second Story* without *Special Requirements.* Then gradually build up to more complex requirements, always keeping the tone that of a light-hearted game.

Options/Variations:

Many teachers have found that their class responds more enthusiastically when a system of award points is created for the game. Tellers get points for successfully meeting *General Rules* and *Special Requirements.* Class members get points for noting discrepancies, or for accurately tracking certain aspects of the *Special Requirements.* The race for points is on, and the class is hooked. They all want to be selected to the four-person story creating team because tellers build more points. The audience studies every word, looking for points.

TEACHING POINTS TO EMPHASIZE:

Remember to emphasize both the importance of the *Special Requirement* of the day and the central role of the *General Rules* in creating effective, successful stories. The *General Rules* represent the core layer of character information and the core of a story's structure.

Super Simple Storytelling Exercise 5.2

INTERROGATE THE CHARACTER

Explore story characters beyond the scope of a story's text

> **APPROPRIATE GRADES: Fourth and up**
> **TIME REQUIRED: 10–25 minutes**

GOAL:

Story listeners are often left with questions at the end of a story. These are rarely about what happened in the story. Rather, they tend to focus on character motive (why they did what they did), character feelings (what were you thinking and feeling when you did what you did) and character history (what happened before the beginning of this story). The only way to obtain this information is to bring one of the story characters into the room and interrogate them for the desired information.

DIRECTIONS:

There are two parts to this exercise:

1. Decide on one story character to invite into the room to be questions, decide who will act as the character, and who should question that character.

2. Let the questions fly and watch the development of a character's history make the character more interesting and compelling.

Part 1. After completing a story with the class, discuss the characters. Particularly, decide who the main character is, who the class thinks is the most important character, and who everyone's favorite character is. (There may be disagreement on the last two.) Ask the class to identify the one character who could best answer their remaining questions about this story. Have each student support their answers by explaining why it is important to have these story-related questions answered and why this character is the one to do it.

After the class has agreed on one character they would like to bring into the class for questioning, assign two important roles:

1. **The character.** Have one student volunteer to be the story character who will be questioned. They must stay in character and their answers must be consistent with their understanding of that character.

2. **Story judge.** Appoint a story judge to ensure that neither questions nor answers violate any overtly stated information in the story. This judge must have a solid understanding of the story and must be willing to interrupt either question or answer to correct factual errors.

Finally, decide on who should ask the questions. The class could decide to ask the questions themselves or could have some other story character ask them. In the latter case, questioners should also stay in character and ask only what that character would likely ask.

Part 2.   Now let the questions and answers fly. Questions will obviously focus on information not directly reported in the story. The character will have to make up, or infer, their answers by extrapolating their impressions of the character as reported within the story text. A few questions will act to *extend the story*. (What did you do next?) But the majority will focus on *character motive and history*. (Why did you do what you did? What did you do before? What did you want? What were you feeling? etc.)

Your students will attempt to build a history (called a *back story*) for the questioned character, a valuable tool for student storytellers to use before they begin to learn a story.

Your job will be two-fold: help keep assigned characters and their answers in character and keep track of what kinds of information were requested (which of the five layers of character information—see Part II). You will also have to decide when to stop the exercise and allow that character to step down from the hot seat.

TEACHING POINTS TO EMPHASIZE:

The questions students choose to ask are as important as the answers. Questions identify the kinds of additional information listeners want. Most will have asked for goals and motive (core information); feelings (personality elements), and explanations of character fears, motives, and attitudes (history information).

Help students compare how they view the questioned character before and after the questioning period. Most students will find that the additional character information will make the character more important and interesting. When storytellers provide more character information, they create a more interesting and real character.

Super Simple Storytelling Exercise 5.3

JUDGE THE CHARACTERS

Explore student evaluations of story characters' actions

> **APPROPRIATE GRADES: Fourth and up**

> **TIME REQUIRED: One hour to one-half day**

GOAL:

There is no better way to decide if a character's actions were right or wrong, justified or unjustified, than to hold a courtroom trial where students can present the arguments pro and con and debate the issue. Students love the courtroom drama and get a valuable opportunity to evaluate complex character behavior and its relationship to the students' own world.

DIRECTIONS:

First decide on the most appropriate character to "arrest" and charge with **morally unjustifiable actions**. With only rare exception this will be either the main character or the antagonist. The class must agree on the specifics of the charge (which exact actions were unjustifiable) and will then hold a formal courtroom trial to judge the actions of this character. Remember that the charge is not guilt or innocence (that's a factual question that was answered by story information), but whether the character was *justified* in doing it (a moral and ethical question for students to debate).

Pre-appoint the following positions:

1. **Judge.** The judge is responsible for procedural matters (allowing questions to be asked, handling objections, allowing witnesses to be called, etc.) and ensuring that no direct story information is contradicted by any witness.

2. **Prosecutor(s).** Prosecutors must identify all information in the story that tends to incriminate the defendant (show that their actions are not justifiable) and to identify the story witnesses who could best report that information. Witnesses need not have appeared in the actual story but must have a strong reason to know first-hand the information they will report. Additional background and character witnesses may also be created and called.

3. **Defense counsel(s).** Defense counsel must prepare *for* the defendant what the prosecutor is trying to prepare *against* them.

4. **Defendant.** The defendant must be thoroughly familiar with the story and prepare, with defense counsel, explanations to rationalize and justify their reported story actions.

Other witnesses will be selected from the class membership as needed by either team of lawyers. The rest of the class will act as jury.

Allow a day or so for each team of lawyers to build their case and decide on a list of witnesses. (Many will not have appeared in the original story but will either be outside character witnesses or unreported witnesses to story events.) Witness lists must then be submitted to the judge and approved by both the judge and you. You will probably want to limit the number of witnesses each side may call.

Assign the role of all approved witnesses to different students, who should be given enough time to review the story and decide what they would and wouldn't logically know and how they feel about story events, as well as to infer any history they need to explain their position and their interpretation of story events.

TEACHING POINTS TO EMPHASIZE:

Good stories place characters in serious jeopardy that requires them to make shaky moral and ethical decisions. This is the perfect fodder for a character trial.

There is no factual issue at stake in the trial. Story information establishes the guilt of the defendant. Being justified in a technically illegal act, however, is a moral and ethical question. These questions require us to know the defendant better, to understand their motives and feelings.

At the end of the trial, regardless of the outcome, the story and story characters will be more interesting and more important to your students. Character information creates a sense of closeness. The more often students experience that concept, the more likely they are to fully develop the characters they tell or write about.

Super Simple Storytelling Exercise 5.4

SHADOW VOICES

Explore how inner voices influence character behavior

> **APPROPRIATE GRADES: Sixth grade and up**

> **TIME REQUIRED: 15 minutes**

GOAL:

All characters have a multitude of voices yelling advice and directions at them from inside their own heads: the voices of parents, friends, peers, children, leaders, their conscience, their adventurous self, etc. Often students ignore the influence of—and even the existence of—these voices when they develop their story characters. It is valuable to use an exercise to externally see the influence of these voices.

DIRECTIONS:

This exercise works best for story characters who have struggled with internal decisions during a story, waffling back and forth, listening first to one internal voice and then to another. Hamlet is a classic example. He spends two-plus acts in frozen agony, unable to decide which advice to follow.

After your class has heard such a story, it is valuable to study that noisy indecision and the screaming voices inside the character's head that created it. One way to make the character come alive is to make the voices come alive.

Pick one student to portray the haggard character. As a class, identify the dominant three or four voices that try to influence the character's actions. Pick one student to act as each voice and give them a few minutes to decide what behavior or decision they want to force on the character and what are their most powerful arguments to convince the character.

First, pick a major decision point from the story and have the character, in impro-vised monologue, lead up to that decision. As the character speaks, the shadow voices hover around, pleading, demanding, threatening, cajoling, and otherwise trying to verbally force the character to make the decision they want. Shadow voices may say or threaten anything that is consistent with their position and perspective. They may play on any emotional chord they can find to convince the character to side with them.

Once the character concludes their monologue and makes a decision, let the class review the power and effectiveness of each voice. In particular, focus on overlooked arguments a voice could have effectively used.

Now create a new, but emotionally similar, situation for the character that is not directly linked to the story. Again, allow the shadow voices to try to sway the character's decision.

Finally, discuss as a class the influence of internal voices on personal decision making and how knowledge of them makes the character and decision more powerful, interesting, and meaningful.

As an alternate, pick two story characters who have some important and stressful interaction during the story. Create shadow voices for each character and follow the characters' interaction while the shadow voices try to influence the outcome.

TEACHING POINTS TO EMPHASIZE:

Many of our decisions and actions reflect the influence of various internal voices: our conscience, our anger, the voice of temptation, of parents, friends, and authority figures. Often storytellers focus on the actions (or external struggles) of characters and ignore the internal struggles. Becoming aware of the shadow voices that yell from inside a character's head will improve a teller's ability to make that struggle clear and important to listeners.

Super Simple Storytelling Exercise 5.5

THE HISTORY GAME

Explore what draws listeners to historical figures

> **APPROPRIATE GRADES: Third Grade and up**
> **TIME REQUIRED: 20 minutes**

GOAL:

We learn history as a string of events. But events alone, like the plot of a story, seem lifeless and bereft of interest—until we associate characters with events and view the actions through the eyes of struggling characters. That shift in thinking is behind *The History Game*.

Demonstrate that standard story character information draws us to historical figures.

DIRECTIONS:

As a class, create a list of names of historical figures on small slips of paper. Include at least twice as many names as there are students in the class. Place all the names in a hat and have each student draw out two names.

Students write each name they drew at the top of a piece of paper and divide the page below into two columns. Tell students to label the left-hand column of each page "Things I Know." In this column each student is to number and write four things they know about this historical figure.

When that writing has been completed, have them label the right-hand column "What I Would Like to Know." In this column each student should number and write three things they would like to know about this historical figure (but don't already know).

Have each student pass their papers to another student. This student should first add two additional items to each "Things I Know" list. Then they should add two new items to the "What I Would Like to Know" list.

Again students pass the pages to someone else. This third student adds one new item to each column of each page, as do a fourth, fifth, and sixth student.

You should now collect all of the pages, each of which contains a historical name, ten things students claim to know, and nine things they would like to know.

Review the *kinds* of information listed in each column. The "What I Know" column will be dominated by specific facts and major events. In story terms, *what* we know is *plot* information. The "What I Want to Know" column will be dominated by requests for character information: character history, personality, and core information (motives, goals, fears, etc.).

Read the list of "What I Want to Know" for each historical name to your class and see if these lists of character-based questions make them feel more curious about, and interested in, these historical figures. Curious enough to do some research to find out? Discuss the importance of character information to making historical characters and events come alive for listeners and for making history more interesting.

Second, within the "What I Know" column try to separate what students learned from stories from what they learned as isolated historical facts. If Paul Revere was mentioned, for example, all information was almost certainly learned through a famous poem about, and from stories that include, Mr. Revere. The same is true for much of what we know of George Washington. The cherry tree is a story. Images of Washington as a dashing leader on a prancing white horse are a story and far from the truth of a desperate military leader trying to keep his army from disintegration and defeat. Betsy Ross, Pocahontas, and many other historical figures have been made memorable through stories. Historical stories create context and relevance for factual information, and stories begin and end with characters.

The History Game can be played with events as well as with historical figures. The results will be the same. Students will report known facts and will want to know character information for the leading participants of the events.

Options/Variations:

The History Game can be used for virtually any subject area. Teachers have adapted it as *The Art Game, The Music, Science, or Sports Game,* even as *The Math Game.* All curriculum subjects can benefit from sparking student interest through *The History Game.*

TEACHING POINTS TO EMPHASIZE:

Historical reports can be accurate and still be stories. Historically true stories require the same character-based information that fictional stories need. A story is a story. However, we are used to thinking of just the factual events of history rather than the characters and struggles that lead up to those culminating moments of historical significance. Students can search for character information for every historical figure they research. Listeners will greatly appreciate the effort because it is this character information that provides meaning to historical facts.

Super Simple Storytelling Exercise 6.1

SNEAK THEM IN

Explore students' ability to direct and control stories

> **APPROPRIATE GRADES: Kindergarten to fourth**
> **TIME REQUIRED: 5-15 minutes per story**

GOAL:

Young students aren't ready to structure and present complete stories. Better to start by progressively turning over control of stories to the class. This gradual control teaches them story structure and cause-and-effect plotting without having to turn the process into a formal exercise.

DIRECTIONS:

Over the course of a number of partially improvised stories, this exercise progresses through three successive levels of student control over the stories you tell. Because your telling of these stories will regularly be disrupted by "yes-no" decisions, and because the focus of this exercise will be on student discussions and decisions, this storytelling can be very relaxed and informal. You can afford to refer to notes or source material during the story and to pause to reform your thoughts—just as you would if telling an unrehearsed, personal, day-to-day story.

You can either improvise these stories from an invented character core or base them on stories you know. It is, however, best if the students are not already familiar with the story.

Level 1:

Tell a story to your class. After you have established the core character information and story tone, stop at regular intervals to have the class make "yes" or "no" decisions about the story. It is best if these decisions are about discrete actions ("She walked up to the door of the gingerbread house. . . . Class, did she go in, or not?") or about character reactions ("When she turned around, she was alone. Everyone else in the troupe was gone! Class, was she frightened, or not?").

The class will now have to predict the more logical answer based on what they know of the story so far. Have students who propose an answer *justify* their answer in terms of the events of the story. It is best not to use stories they know. Their justification will always be, "That's the way the story goes." For unfamiliar stories, they will have to forecast what they want to have happen at the decision point based on early story information. You can prompt the class with questions or considerations concerning their justification for their answer. Then you must decide which group of students—those wanting a "yes" or those wanting a "no"—provided the most convincing arguments. You must accept that argument and proceed with the story using that verdict (yes or no) to dictate the story's next event.

This means you may have to improvise portions of the story to include essential information. You can use a "magician's choice," where you only give the illusion of a decision to the students. This allows you to keep the story going where you need it to go. If the class votes that "yes" a character should go inside and you don't want the character to do that, say, "Yes, they decided to enter, BUT the door was locked and they couldn't get in." If you want them to enter and the class votes "no," say, "No. They didn't enter the door. They snuck around the gingerbread house and climbed in a window."

You have still allowed them to debate the story structure and see the effect of their decisions without relinquishing real story control. After completing the story, discuss student decisions and their effect on the story. Use this opportunity to introduce cause-and-effect sequencing in a story as well as relationship between character chore information and the major events of a story.

Level 2:

Stop the stories you tell not with "yes-no" questions for the class but by allowing them to fill in the blank. ("The second Billy Goat Gruff tip-tapped across the bridge and saw a_____. Class, what did he see?") Again, the greatest value is not in students' actual answers but in forming arguments to justify their answer. Each suggestion must make sense within the structure and information already provided in this story.

Allow for some debate before announcing a consensus answer and continuing the story. This debate both gives students a chance to mentally analyze the story's structure and gives you a chance to gather your thoughts before launching back into the story.

Level 3:

As students gain a better understanding of the structure and form of a story, allow them to fill in whole ideas by stopping to ask, "And then what happened?" Asking them plot-related questions allows you to hold control over the all-important characters so that you can more easily improvise the story toward its logical conclusion.

Students must still justify their suggestions. You must still weigh their arguments and accept the one that is best supported by story-based arguments. Follow each story with a review of how their decisions affected the story, its characters, and the flow of events in the story.

TEACHING POINTS TO EMPHASIZE:

Events in stories by young children often seem to just happen. There is no logical flow from scene to scene. Having students debate the story merits of different decisions strengthens their understanding of the form and flow of stories. It teaches cause-and-effect thinking in how they structure their own stories. It will also introduce the merits of character-based stories.

Super Simple Storytelling Exercise 6.2

THE CIRCLE STORY

Explore the form and structure of story

> **APPROPRIATE GRADES: Kindergarten to fourth**
> **TIME REQUIRED: 5–10 minutes**

GOAL:

Younger students gain value from improvising group stories and watching the language and story development other students create. That is the general idea behind circle stories. Optional requirements on the story can be used to impose some standard for the material each student adds.

DIRECTIONS:

The class or group sits in a circle for circle stories. One student (or you) starts the story. After a specified period of time the next student picks up the story. And so on around the circle. Telling times typically range from 30 seconds down to 10 seconds.

The process is fun for students and does give them practice in oral communication. However, there are two glaring problems with this fairly popular story activity. First, students have a tendency not to closely connect their portion of the story with what has come before, so that the overall story is disjointed and pointless. Second (partly because of the first problem) the stories tend to be dismally boring. The only two students actively listening are the current teller and the student who will tell next. Others tend to wander.

Following are two types of solutions that teachers have tried:

1. **Random teller picking.** If anyone could be the next teller, everyone will pay much more attention to the story. You can roll dice, draw cards, or spin the bottle to see who will tell next. (Yes, it is possible to have to tell twice in a row.)

    The "Spider Story" technique allows selection to be random and allows you to keep track of who has told. The first teller holds the end of a ball of yarn or string. After their telling, they toss the ball to some other student, who holds onto the string, tells, and then tosses the ball to another teller. Each student who has told continues to hold onto the string so that the string forms a "spider web" as it is tossed back and forth across the circle. Those students who are not holding onto the string have not yet told.

2. **Enforced structure.** Place some requirements on each teller so that the story takes on some overall structure, order, and shape. Decide on the severity of these structural mandates based on the developmental level of your students and on the aspects of a story on which you want the class to focus.

Commonly used mandates are:

> ➤ Each new teller must repeat the last line by the previous teller to start their segment. This encourages story continuity.

> ➤ Tellers may introduce neither new characters nor settings within the first half of their segment. This prevents premeditated jumps to a new story idea.

> ➤ Before telling, each teller must say the name of the story's main character, correctly identify their story goal, and name the current problem against which they are struggling. This keeps all tellers working on the same story.

> ➤ Each new segment must include some new information about the main character. This keeps all tellers focused on the same character and on possible character development.

You may also require that each teller use some dialog, include new, relevant story details, or perform any other story-related task during their time to control the story. The ultimate controlled circle story is *The 30-Second Story*, Exercise 5.1.

After each story, discuss with students how successful their story was, or wasn't. Was the story engaging? Imaginative? Gripping? Did the students grow bored? Why? When? What could have been done to make the story more captivating? What did individual tellers or the group as a whole do that worked well and contributed to a successful storytelling? The more students analyze their own story, the better they will be during the next circle story.

TEACHING POINTS TO EMPHASIZE:

Stories are difficult to invent as a group. No one has enough control to piece together all of the elements of a successful story. Still, group stories are often creative and full of surprise and energy. Having powerful story elements (a strong main character, a strong story goal, and substantial jeopardy blocking character from goal) will always make it easier for students to invent their story segments.

Super Simple Storytelling Exercise 6.3

PASS THE PICTURE

Explore the links between different character descriptive elements

> **APPROPRIATE GRADES: Second and up**
> **TIME REQUIRED: 10-15 minutes**

GOAL:

The five layers of character information are all linked. The look of a character relates to their personality. Their voice seems to fit with their personality. Etc. This exercise demonstrates that linkage and gives students opportunities to practice creating interesting sets of character information. They will see a face and let it, alone, suggest voice, history, personality, etc.

DIRECTIONS:

To prepare for this exercise you must have cut out head and shoulder pictures from magazines and newspapers. Each picture should be big enough to cover up a student's face. There is no need to trim the pictures. The entire photo, including the head and any background, will work better. An initial stack of a dozen photos will work well for *Pass the Picture.*

A student closes their eyes and randomly picks one of these photos. It doesn't matter if the picture is of the same sex that the student is. Storytellers have to present both male and female characters convincingly to an audience.

The student is allowed 15 seconds to study the face. then they turn it around so that the rest of the class can see and hold the picture in front of their own face. Using a character voice that the student thinks best fits with the person in the picture, the student says:

"Hello. My name is _____. I live in _____ and I am a (Occupation)."

Continuing in first person in this character's voice the student tells the class:

➤ One thing that they want (a goal)

➤ Something about their personality

➤ One important thing that has happened to them in the past

Additional information about character fears, dreams, activity, and history can be added for older grades, who would be capable of improvising a more complete characterization. Often students are more willing to jump into character while holding a character picture (like a mask) in front of their face.

Follow this brief report with a class discussion. Did the voice and character information fit with the picture? How? Why? (or Why not?). Allow a second student to create a second interpretation of the same image. Then move to the next student and a new picture.

TEACHING POINTS TO EMPHASIZE:

Seeing a face makes it far easier to invent the corresponding voice, personality, and history. If students try to similarly create vivid images of the characters in their stories, it will assist them in constructing the other layers of character information.

Remind students of how enjoyable these characterizations were to watch. The energy naturally carried by character dialog is an effective way to hook listeners into a story. Including vocal and physical characterizations as part of a student's storytelling is certainly not essential. But they are powerful, effective tools to use.

Super Simple Storytelling Exercise 6.4

RULER OF THE ISLAND

Explore the use of personal storytelling orchestras

> **APPROPRIATE GRADES: Second and up**

> **TIME REQUIRED: 10-15 minutes**

GOAL:

This is an orchestra exercise. Its goal is to assist students in becoming conscious of how they control their verbal and nonverbal orchestra elements.

DIRECTIONS:

Ruler of the Island is similar to *The Wave Game* (Exercise 1.1) except that *Ruler of the Island* allows far more movement and the incorporation of more nonverbal orchestra control.

Students stand in a circle. The teacher designates one student as "it." This student enters the circle and begins to repeat "I am the Ruler of this Island. . . . I am the Ruler of this Island. . . . " using the exact same vocal pattern every time they say the line.

Each time the student says this line, they must strut in a consistent, unique, and royal way and must also gesture in a consistent, unique, and royal way. This student continues to strut, gesture, and repeat the line around the circle. Every repetition of the line should be an exact carbon copy of every other repetition of the line. Vocal tone, volume, pitch, and variation should be the same. Movement and gestures should be the same.

After the student has said the line four or five times, the teacher taps a second student to enter the circle. This second student must fall into step behind the first and *exactly* mimic the voice, movement, and gesture pattern of the first for three repetitions of the line. This second student then stops the first, says, "Excuse me, but there must be some mistake. *I* and the ruler of this island."

The first student exits the circle and the second student begins to repeat the line, "I am the Ruler of this Island . . . " *except* that the vocal, movement, and gesture pattern this student decides to use must be different than those used by any previous student.

The teacher continues to designate students to enter the circle, who first mimic and then replace the ruler until either everyone has had a chance or the teacher decides it is time to stop.

Hold a brief class discussion. What was hard about mimicking? What was easy? Critique the effectiveness of various students' attempts to mimic another student. Was it hard to remember to be exactly the same on each iteration of the line? What made one student more or less engrossing to watch than another? Which students were best able to control their orchestra to be the same every time they said the line?

TEACHING POINTS TO EMPHASIZE:

Consciously controlling all of the major orchestra players is difficult work that requires diligent concentration. It would have been very hard, indeed, to remember all of the vocal and physical directions *and* remember the changing words of a story. The more aware students become of their personal storytelling orchestra during exercises, the easier it will be for them to ignore their orchestra while they tell a story and turn orchestra control over to their storytelling conductor.

Super Simple Storytelling Exercise 6.5

STAGE COACH

Explore story structure and telling through a high-energy physical game

> **APPROPRIATE GRADES: Fifth and up**
> **TIME REQUIRED: 15–20 minutes**

GOAL:

Stage Coach is a wild, high-energy game run in the form of a story. With the addition of a few requirements on the storyteller, the game can help students recognize and control major story and storytelling elements.

DIRECTIONS:

1. **The set up:** *Stage Coach* is a rowdy game, good for physical exercise and laughter as well as storytelling development. The game works best with groups of a dozen or less. Split larger groups and conduct two games. Every student except the storyteller in each group needs a sturdy, movable chair. These should be spread far enough apart so that two people could walk between. Two rows of chairs is ideal. Three is all right.

   Each chair is now designated as part of a stage coach: the spokes, the driver, the strong box, the shot gun, individual passengers, the suitcases, the springs, the horses, etc. Scenic items such as sage brush or rocks can also be used, as can other people who will interact with the stage: robbers, a rancher, etc. (You can also play this game as a battleship, train, or virtually any other common thing on which people could gather and interact.)

   Each student must repeat their designation several times out loud so that everyone can remember which person represents which part of the stage coach.

2. **The general rules:** One student will begin a story. During their telling they must meet some storytelling requirements you specify. Once they have met those requirements, they will try to steal a seat from one of the other students, forcing that student to become the next story-teller to continue the story.

3. **The requirements:** Any combination of storytelling requirements is appropriate for this game. Some commonly used requirements include the following:

   ➤ Each teller must advance the story for some minimum amount of time (usually 15 seconds).

   ➤ Each teller must use the main character and story goal created by the first teller.

➤ Each teller must provide two new bits of significant information about the main character.

➤ Each teller must include four new, relevant, scenic details.

➤ Each teller must provide some new information about the main character's jeopardy.

➤ Each teller must either resolve or introduce one new story obstacle.

➤ Each teller must include at least three lines of appropriate dialog.

➤ Each teller must include one simile or metaphor.

➤ Each teller must describe one exciting story moment.

Typically, only two, or perhaps three, requirements are included in any one playing of *Stage Coach*. Either a teacher or an observer student must be present to resolve any disputes regarding whether or not a teller has successfully met all requirements.

4.   **The game:** The storyteller, standing in front of the students sitting in their chairs, begins the story. As soon as they have met the storytelling requirements you have created for each teller of this story, they are free to try to exchange places with anyone in any seat. They accomplish this by mentioning that person's specific part of the stage coach. As soon as someone's part is mentioned (and so long as the teller has already met all storytelling requirements) the person in that chair must stand and circle their chair before they can sit back down. If the teller can beat them into their seat, the teller sits and the person who had been sitting becomes the next teller to continue the story. Each new teller must meet all telling requirements before they can attempt to sit down. If the teller mentions a part of the stage before such time, there is no need for the person in that chair to circle their seat.

The wild and raucous part comes during attempted chair exchanges. The learning part comes from having to watch each teller closely enough to know when they are eligible to take your chair.

This exercise has value because every student must analyze every word by the teller, listening for them to meet the storytelling requirements. Students will hear what details, dialog, obstacles, etc., sound like within the context of a story.

TEACHING POINTS TO EMPHASIZE:

Stories are successful blends of many individual elements. While they flow seamlessly through a good story, each individual element had to be intentionally included by the storyteller. The more familiar students are with the sound and placement of these different elements, the easier it will be for them to successfully incorporate them into their own stories.

APPENDIX
The Definition of Storytelling

I was fortunate enough to chair the effort of the National Storytelling Association (NSA) to create the association's definition of storytelling in 1997–1998. It was an intriguing project. What do working storytellers think it is that they do? What terms and concepts could they agree upon? Could we create a meaningful definition that would acknowledge all of the styles, traditions, and uses of storytelling without making it so broad and vague as to be useless?

We interviewed hundreds of tellers and had groups and guilds of full-time and casual storytellers review our work. After a two-year effort we created the following extended statement defining the range and gambit of storytelling as the NSA definition.

STORYTELLING: The art of using language, vocalization, and/or physical movement and gesture to reveal the elements and images of a story to a specific, live audience.

Why Define Storytelling?

We see the title "storyteller" everywhere—writers, directors, ad agencies, composers, producers, painters—all suddenly call themselves storytellers. But is storytelling a universal title, or does the word really refer to a more specific art form?

Storytelling, literally the live, oral, and physical performance of a story for an audience, is the oldest of all human art forms. Certainly before humans painted crude drawings in caves they told stories to each other.

There is a growing and vibrant community of storytelling practitioners in America. We in that storytelling community believe it is important for us to present a clear, concise definition of the word, *storytelling*, to explain what storytelling really is before its increasingly inappropriate and widespread use so dilutes the term that it has no real meaning at all.

Through this definition we hope to increase general awareness of, and appreciation for, storytelling and to promote increased opportunities for storytelling in American institutions and society.

$\mathcal{W}$hat *Is* Storytelling?

Storytelling is both the most basic mode of human communication and a powerful performance art form. At its core, *storytelling is the art of using language, vocalization, and/or physical movement and gesture to reveal the elements and images of a story to a specific, live audience.*

Several key characteristics implied by this general description show how storytelling is unique from other art forms and from other modes of presentation of story material.

1. **Storytelling is an interactive performance art form.** Direct interaction between the teller and audience is an essential element of the storytelling experience. An audience responds to the teller's words and actions. The teller uses this generally nonverbal feedback to immediately, spontaneously, and improvisationally adjust the tones, wording, and pace of the story to better meet the needs of the audience. If formal theater has an invisible "fourth wall" between the actors and the audience, storytelling completely demolishes that wall to directly and tightly connect the teller and audience.

2. **Storytelling is, by design, a co-creative process.** Storytelling audiences do not passively receive a story from the teller, as a viewer receives and records the content of a television program or motion picture. The teller provides no visual images, no stage set, and generally, no costumes related to story characters or historic period. Listeners create these images based on the performer's telling and on their own experiences and beliefs. The interactivity mentioned above is necessary to support this co-creative effort and for the listeners to complete their portion of the story creation process.

3. **Storytelling is, by its nature, personal, interpretive, and uniquely human.** Storytelling passes on the essence of who we are. Stories are a prime vehicle for assessing and interpreting events, experiences, and concepts, from minor moments of daily life to the grand nature of the human condition. It is an intrinsic and basic form of human communication. Many researchers date the emergence of stories to the very emergence of language itself. More than any other form of communication, the telling of stories is an integral and essential part of the human experience.

4. **Storytelling is a process, a medium for sharing, interpreting, offering the content and meaning of a story to an audience.** Because storytelling is spontaneous and experiential and thus a dynamic interaction between teller and listener, it is far more difficult to describe than are the script and camera directions of a movie or the lines and stage direction notes of a play. Storytelling emerges from the interaction and cooperative, coordinated efforts of teller and audience.

*W*hat *Isn't* Storytelling?

The key to understanding the separation between storytelling and other performance art forms or other story-related crafts lies in the word *telling*. By that word we mean the live, person-to-person, oral and physical presentation of a story to an audience. "Telling" involves direct contact between teller and listener. It mandates the direct presentation of the story by the teller.

Thus, for example, story *writers* are not story*tellers* until they stand up and tell the story (orally and physically) to their audience. As long as the medium for offering their story is printed materials read in isolation by the reader, they are not story*tellers*.

Second, storytelling is differentiated from other art forms by the *intent* of the performer, of the performance, and of the audience. If the performer's main *intent* is to tell stories, and, while so doing, they sing or dance, we consider that to be storytelling. If, however, their primary intent is to sing songs, and between songs they tell stories, the performance is singing, not storytelling. Thus, storytelling is separated from the continuum of other performance art forms by the purpose or intent of the performance. Acting, playing instruments, making movies, painting, and writing are not storytelling. Their intent is different.

In describing these bounds on storytelling, it must be noted that storytelling is not the property of any one culture or nationality. There are many cultures on Earth, each with rich traditions and customs for storytelling. While we believe that the general descriptions and criteria mentioned here are universally acceptable, there are other, more specific expectations in many groups and cultures around the world.

*R*oles and Responsibilities in a Storytelling Event

A central, unique aspect of storytelling is its reliance on the audience to develop specific visual imagery and detail to complete and co-create the story. Thus, understanding the essential roles of teller and listener (audience) may help clarify an image of what storytelling really is.

The storyteller need not supply visual sets, costumes, pictures, or actors to play each part. The teller's role is to prepare and present the necessary language, vocalization, and physicality to effectively and efficiently communicate the images of a story. In addition, it is the duty of the teller to ensure that their stories, and the story characters, will be relevant for, accessible to, and appropriate for each specific audience, and that their material is in appropriate story form. Finally, the teller is tasked to recognize feedback provided by the listeners and to incorporate that information, as necessary and appropriate, into their performance of the story.

The listener's role is to actively create the vivid, multi-sensory images, actions, characters, and events—the reality—of the story in their mind, based on the performance by the teller and on their past experiences, beliefs, and understandings. The completed story happens in the mind of the listener, unique and personal for each individual.

$\mathcal{F}$rom the Kitchen Table to Carnegie Hall: The Levels of Storytelling

So far we have talked about storytelling as if all storytelling events were the same. Intuitively, we know this cannot be true. The mandates, expectations, and performance of a polished professional performer telling on a raised stage to a thousand listeners *must* be different from those of friends sharing stories around the kitchen table.

In truth, however, the basic descriptions of these two storytelling events are exactly the same. Storytelling is storytelling, regardless of the polish of the performer or the size and composition of the audience. There are, however, differences in the expectations of the teller's preparation, rehearsal, staging, and selection of language and gesture, as well as about the listener's response and feedback.

It is helpful to describe and differentiate, in general terms, four types of storytelling:

➤ Informal, spontaneous, conversational storytelling (conversational telling with family, friends, and colleagues in an impromptu format). We all burst into story on a regular basis. We neither plan nor organize the text of what we tell, nor practice and consciously control the vocal and physical elements of how we tell it. Still, this is legitimate storytelling, storytelling in which we all know sequential flows will be interrupted, in which forgotten elements will be hastily stuffed in once remembered, in which language will be less precise and more conversational. Listener feedback tends to be more vocal and direct. Listeners to these informal stories feel free to interrupt, to ask questions, to interject comments. Often this level of storytelling is only marginally distinguishable from the normal flow of conversation and does not interrupt, but accompanies, other activity. We all intuitively understand these characteristics. We accept and expect them, and participate in the stories accordingly.

➤ Informal, spontaneous storytelling (campfire, classroom, etc.). This is telling where, once the teller has begun the story, the audience ceases other activity and behaves more like a formal audience. The teller more formally *performs* the story, adopting more vocal dynamics and a less conversational tone. Still, all participants understand that the event of this storytelling was not pre-planned and that this story was not specifically rehearsed and prepared for this telling. Because of the activity and dynamic of the moment, someone says, "Hey, I've got a story about that!" Momentarily other conversation and activity are set aside. But, because of the informality of the setting and the event, our expectations of the teller's performance, and of the story itself, are different than they would be for a formally announced event.

➤ Formal presentations, where the stories are included as part of a larger presentation whose goal is not the telling of stories. Seminars, sales presentations, and sermons are common examples in which a teller has prepared story material and formally delivers it to an audience but where the story is not the central purpose or intent of either teller or listener. Here we expect the teller to perform with precision and polish. We expect them to skillfully incorporate audience feedback into the performance. We realize that a story told in this setting is a tool used to promote some other purpose and so expect the story's true meaning to unfold only when considered in relationship to that purpose.

➤ Formal storytelling performance (planned and rehearsed, edited). At formal storytelling events, our expectations of both the teller's performance and the story presented are high. We expect the teller to be well prepared and to deliver the story with strong and precise language and physical presentation. We expect the story to be significant and meaningful. Our purpose for being there *is* the stories and their performance, so we place much greater demands on their quality.

*W*hat Is a Story?

So far we have discussed the process, the *telling* of a story. A word is in order about *what* is said, the story itself. The storytelling community places few expectations and restrictions on the nature, theme, and structure of the material performed at a storytelling event. Such decisions are generally left to the teller.

Most dictionaries define a *story* as a narrative account of a real or imagined event or events. Within the storytelling community, a story is more generally agreed to be a specific structure of narrative with a specific style and set of characters and which includes a sense of completeness.

Specifically, a story may be viewed as a logically organized body of information presented in some sequential order and that focuses on the experiences and actions of characters. The central emphasis, or theme, of a story is the internal and external goals, problems, and struggles of one or more of the story's characters. The general purpose for their telling is to share those character's experiences with the present audience.

Through this sharing of experience we use stories to pass on accumulated wisdom, beliefs, and values. Through stories we explain how things are, why they are, and our role and purpose. Stories are the building blocks of knowledge, the foundation of memory and learning. Stories connect us with our humanness and link past, present, and future by using past experiences to teach us to anticipate the possible consequences of our actions.

REFERENCES

Libraries and bookstores house shelves full of books of stories and about stories. But few will have references specifically on the process of storytelling. Following are the sources I have found most useful and dependable.

*M*agazines

You should consult your local storytelling guild newsletter in addition to these sources.

Clark, Thomas, ed. *Writers Digest*. Cincinnati, OH: F & W Publications.

Joy, Flora, ed. *Storytelling World*. Johnson City, TN: East Tennessee State University.

Kardaleff, Steven, exec. ed. *Storytelling Magazine*. Jonesborough, TN: National Storytelling Network.

*B*ooks and Articles About Storytelling

Baker, Agusta, and Ellin Greene. "Storytelling: Preparation and Presentation." *School Library Journal* (March 1978): 93-97.

Barton, Bob. *Tell Me Another*. New York: Heinemann, 1986.

Birch, Carol, and Melissa Heckler, eds. *Who Says: Essays on Pivotal Issues in Contemporary Storytelling*. Little Rock, AR: August House Publishers, 1998.

Breneman, Lucille, and Bren Breneman. *Once Upon a Time: A Storytelling Handbook*. Chicago: Nelson-Hall, 1983.

Browne, M. Neil, and Stuart Keeley. *Asking the Right Questions*. Englewood Cliffs, NJ: Prentice-Hall, 1981.

Burrell, Arthur. *A Guide to Story Telling*. London: Sir Isaac Pitman & Sons, 1946.

Clay, Marni. *By Different Paths to Common Outcomes*. York, ME: Stenhouse, 1998.

Cunningham, Patricia. *Phonics They Use*. New York: HarperCollins, 1996.

Cunningham, Patricia, and Richard Alington. *Classrooms That Work*. New York: HarperCollins, 1994.

Davis, Beth. *Elementary Reading Strategies That Work*. Boston: Allyn & Bacon, 1996.

Davis, Donald. *Telling Your Own Stories*. Little Rock, AR: August House, 1997.

DeVos, Gail. *Storytelling for Young Adults*. Englewood, CO: Libraries Unlimited, 1995.

Greene, Ellin. *Storytelling: Art and Technique*. New York, R. R. Bowker, 1996.

Hamilton, Martha, and Mitch Weiss. *Children Tell Stories, a Teaching Guide*. Katonah, NY: Richard Owen, 1990.

Hartesty, Jerome. "Whole Language Applied to the Classroom." *Teaching Point, the Journal of the Whole Language Umbrella* (Fall 1994): 26–32.

Haven, Kendall. *Write Right!* Englewood, CO: Libraries Unlimited, 1999.

Hood, Ann. *Creating Character Emotions*. Cincinnati, OH: Story Press, 1998.

Lapham, Lewis, and Michael Pollan. *The Harper's Index Book*. New York: Henry Holt, 1991.

———. *The New Harper's Index Book*. New York: Henry Holt, 1996.

Livo, Norma, and Sandy Reitz. *Storytelling: Process and Practice*. Englewood, CO: Libraries Unlimited, 1986.

McDonald, Margaret. *The Storyteller's Start-Up Book*. Little Rock, AR: August House, 1993.

Mooney, Bill, and David Holt. *The Storyteller's Guide*. Little Rock, AR: August House, 1997.

Noble, William. *Show, Don't Tell*. Middlebury, VT: Paul Eirksson, 1991.

Peck, Robert. *Fiction Is Folks*. Cincinnati, OH: Writers Digest Books, 1983.

Pellowski, Anne. *The Family Storytelling Handbook*. Little Rock, AK: August House, 1995.

Roney, Craig. "Back to the Basics with Teachers." *The Reading Teacher* 42–43 (1989): 520–523.

———. "Storytelling in the Classroom: Some Theoretical Thoughts." *Storytelling World* 5, no. 1 (1996): 7–9.

Ross, Ramon. *Storyteller*. Little Rock, AK: August House, 1986.

Shedlock, Marie. *The Art of the Story-Teller*. New York: Dover, 1932.

Trousdale, Ann, Sue Woestehoff, and Marni Schwartz. *Give a Listen: Stories of Storytelling in School*. Urbana, IL: NCTE, 1994.

*G*uides to Stories for the Curriculum

Adamson, Lynda. *Literature Connections to American History: Resources to Enhance and Entice*. Englewood, CO: Libraries Unlimited, 1997.

———. *Literature Connections to World History: Resources to Enhance and Entice*. Englewood, CO: Libraries Unlimited, 1997.

Ammon, Bette, and Gale Sherman. *Worth a Thousand Words: An Annotated Guide to Picture Books for Older Readers*. Englewood, CO: Libraries Unlimited, 1996.

Belt, Lynda, and Rebecca Stockley. *Improvisation Through Theater Sports*. Seattle, WA: Thespis Productions, 1991.

Bradon, Kathryn, Nancy Hall, and Dale Taylor. *Math Through Children's Literature: Making the NCTM Standards Come Alive*. Englewood, CO: Libraries Unlimited, 1993.

Butzow, Carol, and John Butzow. *Intermediate Science Through Children's Literature: Over Land and Sea*. Englewood, CO: Libraries Unlimited, 1995.

———. *Science Through Children's Literature*. Englewood, CO: Libraries Unlimited, 1989.

Calvert, Stephen, ed. *Best Books for Young Adult Readers.* New Providence, NJ: R. R. Bowker, 1997.

Denman-West, Margaret. *Children's Literature: A Guide to Information Sources.* Englewood, CO: Libraries Unlimited, 1998.

Doll, Carol. *Nonfiction Books for Children: Activities for Thinking, Learning, and Doing.* Englewood, CO: Libraries Unlimited, 1990.

Donavin, Denise, ed. *American Library Association's Best of the Best for Children.* New York: Random House, 1992.

Eastman, Mary. *Index to Fairy Tales.* Boston: F. W. Faron, 1926. Supplements issued in 1937 and 1952.

Flack, Jerry. *From the Land of Enchantment: Creative Teaching with Fairy Tales.* Englewood, CO: Libraries Unlimited, 1997.

Fredericks, Anthony. *Social Studies Through Children's Literature: An Integrated Approach.* Englewood, CO: Libraries Unlimited, 1991.

Gillepsie, John, ed. *Best Books for Children.* 6th ed. New Providence, NJ: R. R. Bowker, 1998.

Harms, Jeanne, and Lucille Lettow. *Picture Books to Enhance the Curriculum.* New York: H. W. Wilson, 1996.

Homa, Linda, ed. *The Elementary School Library Collection.* Williamsport, PA: Brodart, 1998.

Lima, Carolyn, and John Lima, ed. *A to Zoo.* New Providence, NJ: R. R. Bowker, 1993.

MacDonald, Margaret. *The Storyteller's Sourcebook.* Detroit, MI: Gale Research, 1995.

McElmeel, Sharron. *Educator's Companion to Children's Literature.* Vols. 1 & 2. Englewood, CO: Libraries Unlimited, 1996.

———. *Great New Nonfiction Reads.* Englewood, CO: Libraries Unlimited, 1995.

Miller, Wanda. *U.S. History Through Children's Literature: From the Colonial Period to World War II.* Englewood, CO: Libraries Unlimited, 1997.

Olsen, Mary Lou. *More Creative Connections.* Englewood, CO: Teacher Ideas Press, 1993.

Rogers, Linda. *Geographic Literacy Through Children's Literature.* Englewood, CO: Libraries Unlimited, 1997.

Rosow, La Vergne. *Light 'n Lively Reads for ESL, Adult, and Teen Readers: A Thematic Bibliography.* Englewood, CO: Libraries Unlimited, 1996.

Seaborg, Glen, ed. *Once Upon a GEMS Guide: Connecting Young People's Literature to Great Explorations in Math and Science.* Berkeley, CA: University of California, Berkeley, 1996.

Sprug, Joseph. *Index to Fairy Tales.* Metuchen, NJ: Scarecrow Press, 1994.

Young, Terrence, and Coleen Salley. *The Neglected Genre: An Inquiry-Based Exploration of the Science/Literature Connection.* New Orleans, LA: University of New Orleans, 1998.

INDEX

ABOUT THE AUTHOR

The only West Point graduate to ever become a professional storyteller, Kendall Haven also holds a Master's Degree in Oceanography and spent eight years as a Senior Research Scientist for the Department of Energy before finding his true passion for storytelling and a very different kind of "truth."

He has now performed for more than 2,000,000 children and 800,000 adults in forty states throughout sixteen years of storytelling, and has won numerous awards both for his story-writing and storytelling. Haven has conducted workshops for more than 12,000 teachers from more than 800 schools in more than twenty states on storytelling's practical, in-class teaching power, and has become one of the nation's leading advocates for the educational value of storytelling. He has performed at more than twenty-five national conference and festivals, at more than 100 state-level events, and at more than fifty corporate and professional conferences.

With fifteen books and dozens of articles, he has more than 1,000,000 words in print. Recent releases include two instructional books on the use of story: *Write Right!*, on teaching creative writing, and *Super Simple Storytelling*, on using and teaching storytelling. Other recent releases include one children's fiction novel, two science story-activity resource books, and seven collections of themed historically accurate stories: *Close Encounters with Deadly Dangers*, *New Year's to Kwanzaa*, *Amazing American Women*, *Marvels of Science*, *Marvels of Math*, *Voices of the American Revolution*, and *The Science of Science Mysteries*.

Haven has also published five audio storytelling tapes and created a three-hour, high adventure radio drama–style miniseries for National Public Radio on the effects of watching television, which has won five major national awards.

His recent awards include the 1997, 1996, and 1995 Storytelling World Silver Award for best story anthology, the 1993 International Festival Association Silver Award for best educational program at a major national festival, the 1992 Corporation for Public Broadcasting Silver Award for best children's public radio production, and the 1991 Award for Excellence in California Education. Haven has twice been designated an American Library Association "Notable Recording Artist," and is the only storyteller in America with three entries in the ALA's *Best of the Best for Children*.

Haven has created stories for many nonprofit organizations, including the American Cancer Society, the Institute for Mental Health Initiatives, several crisis centers, the Children's Television Resource and Education Center, a regional hospital, and the Child Abuse Prevention Training Center of California.

A former member of the Board of Directors of the National Storytelling Association, Haven is a member of the Educational Advisory Committee of the National Storytelling Association, and the founder and Chair of the International Whole Language Umbrella Storytelling Interest Group. He is a co-director of the Sonoma Storytelling Festival, past four-year Chair of the Bay Area Storytelling Festival, and founder of storytelling festivals in Las Vegas, Nevada, and Boise, Idaho.

Kendall Haven lives with his wife in the rolling Sonoma County vineyards of rural Northern California.

from **Teacher Ideas Press**

More Tales for the Classroom
by Kendall Haven

CLOSE ENCOUNTERS WITH DEADLY DANGERS
Riveting Reads and Classroom Ideas

Predators and prey of the animal kingdom hunt, fight, and survive in these spine-tingling accounts that will entrall your students. Fifteen action-packed tales are filled with accurate scientific information on many of the world's ecosystems and their inhabitants, including lions, anacondas, and sharks. Suggestions for activities and research follow each story. **Grades 4–8.**
xv, 149p. 6x9 paper ISBN 1-56308-653-0

AMAZING AMERICAN WOMEN
40 Fascinating 5-Minute Reads

These concise, action-packed reads detail the lives of some of the women who helped shape our nation. The stories are so enlightening and inspiring that some students have been known to read more about these heroes *on their own!* A great springboard for study across the curriculum. **All Levels.**
xxii, 305p. 6x9 paper ISBN 1-56308-291-8

MARVELS OF MATH
Fascinating Reads and Awesome Activities

Show students how dynamic mathematics really is with the riveting stories and intriguing facts found here! Haven offers 16 dramatic accounts of the innovations and triumphs of mathematicians throughout history. Accompanying each story are terms to learn, discussion questions, and activities and experiments that amplify the story's theme. **Grades 3–9.**
xii, 172p. 6x9 paper ISBN 1-56308-585-2

MARVELS OF SCIENCE
50 Fascinating 5-Minute Reads

Ideal for both read-alouds and reading assignments, these 50 short stories take just minutes to read but amply illustrate scientific principles and the evolution of science through history. **Grades 3 and up.**
xxii, 238p. 6x9 paper ISBN 1-56308-159-8

STEPPING STONES TO SCIENCE
True Tales and Awesome Activities

Science comes to life for young students in these 13 action-packed stories! Historically accurate accounts combine with extension activities to teach young learners the basic skills and procedures of science. **Grades 2–5.**
xi, 155p. 8½x11 paper ISBN 1-56308-516-X

For a free catalog or to place an order, please contact: Teacher Ideas Press/Libraries Unlimited at 1-800-237-6124 or
• **Fax: 303-220-8843**
• **E-mail: lu-books@lu.com**
• **Web site: www.lu.com**
• **Address: Dept. B007 • P.O. Box 6633**
   Englewood, CO 80155-6633